Writing Back to Modern Art

Writing Back to Modern Art assesses the 'critical modernisms' of the three leading art writers of the second half of the twentieth century: Clement Greenberg, Michael Fried, and T.J. Clark.

Focusing on issues of aesthetic evaluation, subjectivity, and meaning in art and art writing, Jonathan Harris identifies points of significant agreement and sharp intellectual disjunction between these critics in their respective accounts of modernism in the visual arts since the 1860s. Developing the notions of 'good' and 'bad' complexity in modernist criticism, Jonathan Harris proposes an historical and theoretical framework for understanding the development of modern art writing and its relation to the 'postmodern' in art and society since the 1970s. Though centred on an examination of canonical modern artists and their place in modernist-critical historiography, with chapters on Manet, Cézanne, Picasso, Pollock, and Frank Stella, *Writing Back to Modern Art* suggests ways to think outside of these discourses of value and meaning.

Jonathan Harris teaches Art History in the School of Architecture at the University of Liverpool. He has published widely on art and art history, specializing in twentieth-century American art, the rise of the 'new art history', and the relations between art history and social theory. His recent publications include *Critical Perspectives on Contemporary Painting: Hybridity, Hegemony, Historicism* (2003) and *The New Art History: A Critical Introduction* (Routledge, 2001).

Writing Back to Modern Art

After Greenberg, Fried, and Clark

Jonathan Harris

Routledge
Taylor & Francis Group

LONDON AND NEW YORK

First published 2005
by Routledge
2 Park Square, Milton Park, Abingdon, Oxon OX14 4RN

Simultaneously published in the USA and Canada
by Routledge
270 Madison Ave, New York, NY 10016

Routledge is an imprint of the Taylor & Francis Group

© 2005 Jonathan Harris

Typeset in Sabon by
Florence Production, Stoodleigh, Devon
Printed and bound in Great Britain by
Antony Rowe Ltd, Chippenham, Wiltshire

British Library Cataloguing in Publication Data
A catalogue record for this book is available from the British Library

Library of Congress Cataloging in Publication Data
Harris, Jonathan (Jonathan P.)
    Writing back to modern art: after Greenberg, Fried and Clark/
    Jonathan Harris. – 1st. ed.
        p. cm.
    1. Art criticism – United States – History – 20th century.
    2. Greenberg, Clement, 1909–1994. 3. Fried, Michael. 4. Clark,
    T.J. (Timothy J.) 5. Modernism (Art) 6. Art, Abstract. I. Title:
    Critical complexities of Clement Greenberg, Michael Fried, and
    T.J. Clark. II. Greenberg, Clement, 1909–1994. III. Fried, Michael.
    IV. Clark, T.J. (Timothy J.) V. Title.
    N7485.U6H37 2005
    701′.18′097309045–dc22   2004023986

ISBN 0–415–32429–7 (pbk)
ISBN 0–415–32428–9 (hbk)

Contents

Illustrations

Acknowledgements

I presented a schematic version of the argument in this book in a lecture at the University of California, Los Angeles, in November 2001. I would like to thank Al Boime for inviting me, and for helpful comments from staff at the Department of Art History there who heard my talk. Al Boime has been a friend, ally, and supporter for a number of years now and for his comradeship I am very grateful. During 2003–2004 I was in receipt of an Arts and Humanities Research Board leave grant that enabled me to complete this book on time. Along the way I have felt similarly supported and valued by Margery Amdur, Rebecca Barden, Barry Gibbs, David Craven, David Dunster, Eric Fernie, Lucy Forsyth, Lindsey Fryer, Sam Gathercole, Christoph Grunenberg, Ysanne Holt, Amelia Jones, David Oldham, Fred Orton, Simon Pepper, Marcia Pointon, Griselda Pollock, David Roffe, Jerome Satterthwaite (port in many a storm), Paul Smith, Geoff Teasdale, Colin Trodd, Alan Wallach, and Andrew Wilson. I had interesting and productive dialogues about my concerns here with Brandon Taylor, Caroline Jones, and Stephen Eisenman. Tom and Kate Hills, along with Mary Hills, have looked after me as part of their family for many years now. I will always be honoured to count you as my kin! Anne MacPhee, at the University of Liverpool, has been a true friend, and influential beyond your own reckoning in the visual arts discourses you have helped to establish among the cultural institutions in that city.

My debt to Clement Greenberg, Michael Fried, and T.J. Clark will be obvious to anyone who reads this book through to its end. I have learnt more about modern art, art criticism, and art history from them than from anyone else. Tim Clark's wisdom and wit, which I am glad to say I know personally – not just through his printed words – has been a continuing energizing force and source of strength in my intellect.

Jane Linden has always offered true support and a 'loyal opposition' in our on-going arguments over art and how to understand it. I thank you sincerely for this commitment.

Jim and Jules: without you I cannot imagine what would have become of my life. I am still taken aback by the joy you bring me daily! This book is dedicated to you, my lovely sons.

A writer's self-consciousness, for which he is much scorned, is really a mode of interestedness, that inevitably turns outwards.

John Updike, *Self-Consciousness* (London: Andre Deutsch, 1989): 21

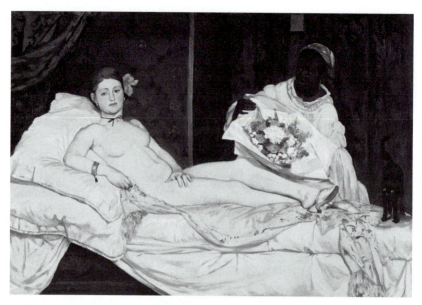

1 Édouard Manet, *Olympia*, 1863 © Photo RMN/© Hervé Lewandowski

2 Vincent Van Gogh, *Pair of Shoes (Een Paar Schoenen)*, 1886 ©
Amsterdam, Van Gogh Museum (Vincent van Gogh Foundation)

3 Paul Cézanne, *Mont Sainte-Victoire*, 1888–1889 © Staatliche Museen zu Berlin, Nationalgalerie, Museum Berggruen, Privatbesitz/photographer: Jens Ziehe/bpk 2004

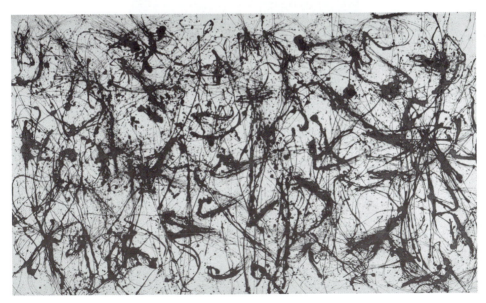

4 Jackson Pollock, *No. 32, 1950*, 1950 © ARS, NY, and DACS, London 2005. Photo by courtesy of Walter Klein/Kunstsammlung Nordrhein-Westfalen

5 Pablo Picasso, *Woman with a Zither ('Ma Jolie')*, 1911–1912 © Photo
SCALA, Florence/Museum of Modern Art (MoMA), 2004

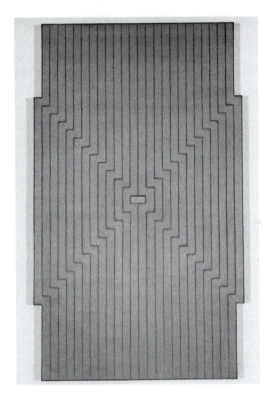

6 Frank Stella, *Six Mile Bottom*, 1960 © ARS, NY, and DACS, London, 2005. Digital Image © Tate, London 2004

7 Tate logo. Tate is the trademark of The Board of Trustees of the Tate Gallery

8 Morris Louis, *Alpha-Phi*, 1961 © 1961 Morris Louis, © Tate, London 2005

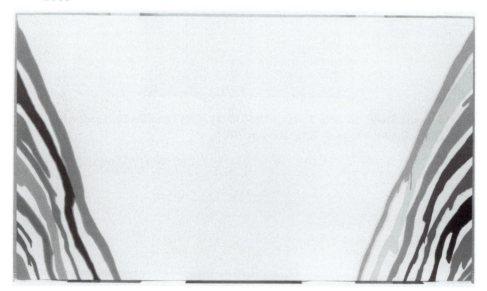

9 Richard Wilson, *20:50*,
2003 © The Saatchi Gallery,
London

10 Cindy Sherman,
Untitled No. 228, 1990.
Courtesy the artist and
Metro Pictures

Introduction

Looking and writing back

This study examines the roots of value and evaluation in writing about modern art. Its focus is on the interwoven criticism, or what I shall call 'critical complexities', of three authors: Clement Greenberg, Michael Fried, and T.J. Clark. Only a little familiarity with some of their now extremely well-known essays and books should indicate that 'criticism' in the sense in which I will use it does not exclude other forms of interest and kinds of writing evident in their works. Two of these forms of interest and kinds of writing have the names theory and history. One of my chief aims here is to show how criticism, theory, and history are inextricably bound up together within Greenberg's, Fried's, and Clark's writings. I shall argue, in the end, that Clark's work (and his interests) differ fundamentally – in critical, theoretical, and political terms – from those of Greenberg and Fried. But what the three share, fundamentally, is a belief that criticism (that is, saying what art is good or bad, and why), theory (that is, mobilizing 'first principles' about the nature of the world, and how it may be understood), and history (that is, accounting for change and development in culture and society) are inter-connected and mutually conditioning things. I will go on to say much more about these conjoined forms of attention, understanding, and judgement. 'Value' and 'evaluation' will emerge as products and processes of discrimination inevitably shaped by the urgency of these writers' interdependent critical, theoretical, and historical perspectives. I chose to use the term 'roots' in my opening sentence. It has two particular meanings that I wish to emphasize. The first, genetic, sense is concerned with 'origins' – a hunt for the 'source' or 'basis' of things. The second, human, sense is concerned with what the *Oxford Paperback Dictionary* calls 'a person's emotional attachment to a place in which the person, or his or her family has lived for a long time'. The critical complexities of Greenberg, Fried, and Clark, whatever their differences and antagonisms (I shall come to stress these, as my own interests become clearer) may be seen as 'places', or 'positions', that also share this at once intellectual *and* emotional drive or pitch. This quality to their writings has been one of the factors that continues to draw me to them: as authors, and as flesh-and-blood people that I believe I have glimpsed through their writing.

I have chosen to focus on these three writers for a variety of reasons explained more fully in this Introduction and throughout the book. One of the most important is that Greenberg, Fried, and Clark have all associated themselves very closely with particular artists central to the history of modern art. These were, in some cases, artists the critics actually knew and befriended – for example, Greenberg's relationship with Jackson Pollock in the 1940s and 1950s, or Fried's with Frank Stella in the 1960s. In other cases one of these writers has produced an essay or book that has become, by now, almost indelibly linked to a certain artist's work – for instance, Clark with Édouard Manet's paintings *Olympia* (1863) [Plate 1] and *A Bar at the Folies Bergère* (1882). One of this book's major themes will be this 'binding together', one way or another, of critic with artist, and a consideration of its implications for the history of modern art and criticism. I touch on other important examples of such particular – and well-known – 'bondings', stretching back to the 'beginnings of modernism' in the 1860s: for example, the critic Charles Baudelaire and Manet (again), the two contemporaries and self-declared friends. Moving into the period at the turn of the nineteenth century and after, I examine two 'text-only' relationships, both also well-known in art history and philosophy of aesthetics: Martin Heidegger's interest in Vincent Van Gogh's painting of shoes [Plate 2] and a portion of Maurice Merleau-Ponty's writings on Paul Cézanne's art [Plate 3]. Heidegger and Merleau-Ponty, two of the most influential philosophers of the twentieth century, became leading representatives of diverging streams of so-called phenomenological thought. This was indebted to Immanuel Kant's philosophy of 'self-criticism', an interpretation of which Greenberg harnesses in his account of modernism in the visual arts. I include Heidegger and Merleau-Ponty in this book because of my focus on the question of value and evaluation: both believed (as do Greenberg, Fried, and Clark)

that great artworks carry a burden of philosophical meaning and significance – that a painting by Van Gogh or Cézanne indeed has a
philosophical status and value *in itself*. I will consider this idea, which
is also a judgement, later in this Introduction and will return to it many
times throughout the chapters that follow.[1]

I am acutely aware, as I hope you are too, that there is no getting
away from the fact that this book is a study of canonical male artists
and (almost entirely) canonical male middle-class white writers on art.
There is much this study *does not* set out to do, and one of those things
is to consider women artists and writers on art. One defence for this –
likely to be condemned by some as weak and self-serving – is that I am
merely following the road already mapped out by Greenberg, Fried, and
Clark. Of course, however, this study begs, and is intended to beg, the
question of the link between judgements of 'greatness' in art and the
identity (however faceted) of those making the art. And, of course, this
study begs, and is intended to beg, the question of the link between
judgements of 'greatness' in art and the identity (however faceted) of
those making the judgements. Of the three, only Clark raises these two
questions explicitly, in relation to Manet and Pollock, and in relation
to himself as a man writing about male artists. I shall come to some
of these remarks. I hope it will become clear, however, that *I* start (and
continue) with a fairly deep scepticism *altogether* about value and
ideas of 'greatness' in art, and in writing about art. The Conclusion,
concerned with art and art-writing after 1970 – a convenient but largely
arbitrary date usually set for the 'end of modernism' and the dawn of
'postmodernism' – will include a discussion of the broader politics
of art-making and criticism since then, a period in which questions of,
for example, gender, ethnicity, and the 'postcolonial' world *in relation
to issues of value* became absolutely inescapable. It is from about
1970 onwards, as one would expect as a corollary of this development,
that the writings of Greenberg and Fried began to attract critiques
centred on questions of gender and race. I provide reference here to
some of this material, within my notes, as part of the 'latent' critical
infrastructure to this study. Let it not be missed or forgotten either,
though, that Clark's 'class-specific' – that is, Marxist – critique of
aspects of Greenberg's and Fried's writings also dates from this period.
Beyond these qualifications, I hope it will be abundantly clear
throughout this book that issues of identity, social relations, and politics of a wide variety of kinds, including those of gender, are deliberately
invoked and provoked in my discussion of these men, their paintings,
and their books.

One of those 'issues of identity' is unavoidably autobiographical and it was also partly for the sake of some self-investigation that I set myself the task of examining a group of canonical modern artists and their artworks. As an undergraduate studying art history at an English university in the early 1980s I quickly realized that I had a mordant antipathy to the 'appreciation' and valuing of canonical modern art – in fact, to the appreciation and valuing of any art at all! This is not meant to sound like a confession. I went into my career as a professional art historian publicly highly sceptical of assumptions of 'quality' and 'greatness' in modern art – understood either in terms of a simple 'intuition' of the kind Clive Bell, for example, claimed to have experienced, or in terms of the 'intuition plus theory' model that Greenberg's essay 'Modernist Painting', first published in 1960, came to represent.[2] Without knowing much about the reasons why, I discovered myself to be ('intuitively', shall I say?) hostile to the idea that these paintings and sculptures contained, or symbolized, some value or meaning that put them above all other items in the culture – particularly above those items then, and now, generalized as components of 'popular' or 'mass' culture, some of which I felt, and continue to feel, strong attachment to.

I think I pursued this scepticism over the value of art in ways that were both conscious and unconscious: for instance, by deciding to research and write a Ph.D. about paintings and sculptures, those produced in the US during the 1930s, that remain derided in art history as some of the most awful ever produced *anywhere* – 'poor art for poor people', as it was dubbed.[3] My attitude superintending this period of work, I now recognize, was very confused: on the one hand I believed that questions of value or quality in art were simply irrelevant to *me* understanding why and how art was mobilized by Roosevelt's New Deal state. Particularly irrelevant were 'modernist' art history judgements from the post-1945 period subsequently *imposed* on 1930s art (I shall come to some key problems of terminological definition and usage soon.) On the other hand, the contemporary (that is, 1930s) critical interrogation of value, I knew from my research, was indispensable to my understanding historically why art was thought *then* to be important, vital indeed, as a means of communication. In a way, I chose simply to bracket out – stall, avoid, deride – examination of the full range of questions to do with value or quality in art. I recognize now that my own 'roots' – intellectual, social, and emotional – would inevitably be bound up with that comprehensive examination, which I wasn't then prepared to undertake. The necessity for this examination, however, was implied at every turn in the book that research eventually produced.

What I did value, love – was 'sent' by (a revealing colloquialism Greenberg uses in an interview about his experience of Jackson Pollock paintings; revealing because it is openly emotional)[4] – was reading historical and theoretical texts. This period for me (1980–1986) was a heady time mixing theoretical Marxism and practical socialist politics, along with an engagement with a much more heterogeneous emergent intellectual discourse now called 'cultural theory', then beginning to enter into a somewhat strained orbit and eventual coupling with elements of traditional art history. This body of Theory, identified with an abstracting capital 'T', whatever its wide range of internal differences, continually emphasized the activity of analysis as a kind of 'control' or 'mastering' of objects – including artworks – a notion which, looking back, once again allowed me routinely to bypass, resist, 'think-out-of-significance' specific and sustained attention to artefacts, such as paintings. Such artefacts could never 'speak for themselves', I decided, and art history, whatever the claims of its practitioners, was really only a war of competing explanatory voices. (Even relatively 'traditional' art historians, such as Michael Baxandall, were apparently suggesting at the time that this was the case.) A book I eventually published on socio-historical change in the discipline since the late 1960s took this theme as central to its methodology and general explanation.[5] My role, if I was to have one at all in art history, I came to believe, was to act as an 'adjudicator' between these voices. I decided to undertake this present study partly in order to re-examine my own priorities and axioms, after more than twenty years of study and teaching, and wondering if my 'place', my 'position' on basic critical and art-historical issues, had actually changed, or could. I will lay my cards on the table now: I have already reached a conclusion, though the conventions of academic writing dictate that it should appear to be revealed only at the 'end' of this study! Let me tell you, however, that my experience in writing this book ('experience' being one of the key modernist critical categories I will begin to consider shortly) simply has *not* led me substantially to revise my views. In short, I still do not believe in the possibility of moving decisively onto the pristine ground of, as Raymond Williams once put it, 'the works of art themselves'.[6] However, this study represents, among other things, my best attempt to engage as doggedly as I can with the materiality, the 'thinglyness' – to use Heidegger's rather ugly neologism – of artworks, as well as, simultaneously, with what I believe are the major critical explanations of these artworks' value.

I have read, taught, reread, and continually reviewed Greenberg's, Fried's, and Clark's essays and books for more than two decades now. My engagement with these writers, however, will occasionally employ some idiosyncratic means – these represent an attempt, though mine is not the first, to find novel devices through which to examine some deeply embedded conventions in art writing. I say more about this below.

The period between my studying and writing a Ph.D. about the 'bad art' of the 1930s in the US (1983–1986) and that of reviewing the social history of art history understood as a changing and interconnected set of discourses (1998–2001) was often taken up with teaching and writing for the British Open University. It was as a teacher at the Open University summer schools and later as a co-author for a course prepared and published in the early 1990s that I first encountered many canonical artworks and essays, some of which I examine in this book.[7] This experience of collaborative teaching and writing was extremely formative, not least because during it I came across people for the first time who held views which were, as far as I could tell then, very close, if not identical, to those of Greenberg's and Fried's. To put it bluntly, my nose was rubbed in the idea, and the claimed experience, of modern art's greatness. I was asked (literally I remember on one or two occasions): 'Why can't you see it? Why can't you feel it? What business do you have writing about modern art if it does not move you?' Now, whatever the difficulties of this kind of 'eye-balling' questioning, in retrospect I do not think it was a bad thing to be pressed in this way and be required to formulate a response, if not as part of what seemed sometimes more like a police interrogation than a collegiate seminar, then in writing, as part of a course. This I duly did.[8] But my objections to the *presumption* of the existence of this value, this quality, this experience of modern art, were never substantively addressed by the course as a whole – instead, the kinds of debate over meanings and values the course *did* engage in were always internal to, limited qualifications of, some basic 'modernist-critical' framework of belief in the value of modern art that remained unquestioned, inviolate.

In this book I shall use the term 'modern art' simply to refer, as if neutrally, to paintings and sculptures produced by artists. The terms 'modernist criticism' or 'modernist-critical', which I shall occasionally contract to 'modernism' or 'modernist', will be used *specifically* to refer to the accounts of modern art produced by Greenberg and Fried, and to others I will associate with their positions. Modernist criticism as a body of writings, it should be stressed, *is not* a unified or homogeneous perspective or single entity. My discussion, for example, of Fried's radical critique of aspects of Greenberg's ideas will make that clear. For that matter, as I have said, Open University course books also developed some quite divergent lines of explanation which sometimes implied logical contradiction with the predominant axioms of what is usually called 'Greenbergian modernism' – a designation centred on representations of the pervasive impact of his essay 'Modernist Painting'. Some treatments of women and/or feminist artists, and the use of certain modes of analysis, such as psychoanalysis, are cases in point.[9] In particular, there are two explanatory features to modernist criticism that I seek to examine and undermine here. The first is the idea that 'Modern art and Modernism' *unrolls* (as the antecedent 1980s Open University course title had it) 'from Manet to Pollock', suggesting some – literally 'straightforward' – development and progression, mapped humbly by the chief critics and attendant art historians. In contra-distinction, I argue here that the history of modern art has been, inevitably, *written* backwards, and that it is crucial to locate some of the roots of the account of the earlier phase (particularly that of the time of Manet and the Impressionists) in the 1950s and 1960s, and even much later. Fried's substantial book on Manet, after all, was published only in 1996. Second, the term 'modernism' will be reserved as my name for this specific *tradition of historical and theoretico-critical explanation* exemplified by the writings of Greenberg and Fried, spanning the period from the very early 1940s, when Greenberg's first essays appeared in print, to almost the end of the twentieth century.

My main title, then – *Writing Back to Modern Art* – is intended to emphasize this necessarily *retrospective* character to modernist-critical explanation, though I do not claim that proponents of this account were, or are, unaware of some of its implications. I pursue my critique, as you will see, by arranging the bulk of my chapters – which also constitute a kind of narrative – in what common sense says is 'reverse order'. History (that is, the account of the past), however, is *always* written 'backwards', after the event – though many of its writers don't always signal this, or even seem to be fully aware of it. Attention to the 'discursive structures' of critical analysis or historical narrative means attention to the kinds of language, the figures of speech and modes of rhetoric, that necessarily order and articulate writing. One of my chief aims here, then, is to demonstrate the presence, activity, and consequences of certain key *discursive critical motifs* through which, for example, notions of time and subjectivity in, and for, modern art and modernism are produced. Writers such as Greenberg, Fried, and Clark all, inevitably, use such motifs consciously, but it is also the case that these motifs may sometimes be said to *use the writers*: the writers, that is, are also 'themselves written' by pre-existing rhetorical forms whose effects and affect can never be entirely controlled by any author.

My main title is also intended to stress another reciprocal axis or relation – that governing the interconnections between artwork and critical text, and between 'artist' and 'critic', insofar as the artwork and critical text stand as indices of the existence and relation of their producers. Art criticism in a form recognizable to those living now, a product really of the mid-nineteenth century, was borne of this emergent type of inter-relation between two novel kinds of social, and later, 'professional' type. Artist and critic come historically to *need* each other, in a number of fundamental but also sometimes rather suffocating ways, as Greenberg, Fried, and Clark all attest in their writings. I examine some of the circumstances and forms of this need, and its attendant strains, in the following chapters. In turn, some of the artists held in what they experienced occasionally as a sweaty and uncomfortable embrace, particularly after 1945, voiced their recognition of the de facto indispensability of criticism as an institution, while finding it choking. 'My contempt for the intelligence of the scribblers I have read is so complete,' notably spat the Abstract Expressionist Clyfford Still, for instance, 'that I can not tolerate their imbecilities, particularly when they attempt to deal with my canvases. Men like . . . Greenberg . . . are to be categorically rejected.'[10] 'Writing' and 'speaking' back to modern art, then, will come to life in this study in a variety of pungent though I hope illuminating literal and metaphoric ways.

Composition and self-composition

If Clark's studies of Manet, Pablo Picasso, and Pollock constitute part of the ground upon which I will develop my arguments against modernist criticism, then another part of that ground is the work, published over five decades, of the literary critic, cultural historian and theorist, Raymond Williams.[11] Though Clark and Williams both produced acclaimed, and avowedly Marxist, historical and cultural studies at the same moment in the mid-1970s, their work has rarely been brought into any explicit relation. What divides them most is a dispute over canonical selection and the relationship between such a canon of modern art and the wider culture. Despite this dispute, there is a basic compatibility between Clark's analyses of particular modern artists and paintings and the neo-Marxist perspective Williams adumbrated as 'cultural materialism' – the framework of principles, concepts, and methods needed for understanding artistic production in modern societies.[12] Clark and Williams share the sense, for example, that two particular 'problematics' (that is, a cluster of interconnected concepts and issues), are indispensable within serious historico-critical analyses of modern culture and society. These problematics, which I begin to consider below, may for the time-being be identified simply as *complexity* and *subjectivism*. My study as a whole is erected on the significance I will give to complexity as a key to understanding modern art *and* its criticism – modernist or otherwise. Complexity in art and criticism, I argue, becomes evermore tightly bound up with the subjectivity of modern artists and their modernist critics. 'Subjectiv*ism*' may be defined as an attitude or judgement that, despite appearances, is really an attitude or judgement *about* ones own attitudes, beliefs, or emotions.[13] Complexity and subjectivism, in one sense, may be understood as different sides to the same coin, or piece of paper, though, to pursue these metaphors, it is usually the case that only one side of the coin or piece of paper is ever visible, or attracts our attention, at a particular moment.

'Writing,' Williams states, 'is always in some sense self-composition and social composition.'[14] Let 'writing' here refer to any mark-making, thus including painting and art criticism – again, following Greenberg's, Fried's, and Clark's preferences, I shall consider few artworks here except paintings. Painting pictures and writing art criticism are formative and self-forming activities: they generate artefacts and 'regenerate' their producers in and through the act of production. This production is rarely, if ever, solely personal: it includes the intention to communicate to others existing in a world that lies beyond both the producer and the product. *Some* senses of 'self' and 'the social world' are thus invoked, signified, and confirmed, if not modified, in this production.[15] Pollock's 'drip-paintings', for example, dramatically convey the intimation that a person is attempting to communicate their presence: notice, for example, the series of hand-prints – marks of an actual person, perhaps the artist? – top right in *Number 1A, 1948* (1948). Pollock sometimes seems to want to show painting as itself very like a form of writing, though no actual words appear, no written meanings (not even a signature in this painting?) are discernable 'there on the canvas' of *Number 32, 1950* (1950) [Plate 4]. This picture, partly through its sheer size – more than 2½ metres wide by 4½ metres long – appears precisely to declare the intention to communicate a scrawling calligraphic message while failing to deliver any specific sense.

Self-composition, through production of paintings or essays, has a 'retrodictive' and usually *self-conscious* element to it. He or she who writes or paints recurrently monitors and reviews their own production, making 'some sense of it', and, at the same time, some sense of themselves. Or, perhaps, fails to. Clark believes that such failure – to communicate, to make sense through making and meaning, even, perhaps *especially*, in the best modern art – is significant enough that he returns to the theme throughout his 1999 study of twentieth-century modern art.[16] Clark and Williams are both preoccupied, in markedly different ways, with questions of modern artistic value – over deciding what art 'succeeds' or 'fails', is 'good' or 'bad', and why. They are also both preoccupied with the possibilities, and historical failures, of radical social change in modern societies, those both capitalist and 'state-socialist', during, and at the close of, the twentieth century and the beginning of the twenty-first. Clark's and Williams's perspectives *are*, I believe, equally authentically Marxist in intellectual orientation but the former's tone is relentlessly sombre and pessimistic, while Williams (dead before the Berlin Wall came down and the USSR abolished itself in 1991) retained an admittedly grim optimism about the future.[17] Both *are* aware, however, that any future socialist society worth the name must not replicate any model linked to the past horrors of totalitarianism. Pessimism and optimism – especially in the latter's purified form as utopianism – run wide and deep as attitudes and judgements, however, and may take on some perhaps surprising guises in areas of cultural and art-critical analyses apparently distant from manifest political discourse. Clark's notion of 'failure', as I show below, becomes a capacious symbolic category in his criticism of modern art.

Williams's 'cultural-materialist' understanding of artistic and critical composition as a process simultaneously productive of artefacts, subjectivities, and society as a whole finds a significant parallel in the work of an earlier generation of art historians examined in Michael Podro's 1982 study *The Critical Historians of Art*. In one sense my book is a kind of rejoinder to Podro's, which intimates that the work of his three key early twentieth-century writers – Heinrich Wölfflin, Aby Warburg, and Erwin Panofsky – stands as a kind of gateway to modern art and modernist-critical writing.[18] The same basic tension exists, both *within* their individual writings and *between* them as writers, as that within and between the work of Greenberg, Fried, and Clark. This is the strain between attention to the artefact ('formalism', as it sometimes came to be known) and attention to the world in which, and through which, the artefact comes into existence and attains its meaningfulness.

But Podro is adamant that Panofsky and Warburg are unmatched, for instance, in holding that art, first and last, *is* a form of social 'visual behaviour' and a form of knowledge. Art never merely 'reflects' or 'represents' the world, as much 'crude' Marxist art history claimed, but also helps *constitute* it.[19] The same is true of criticism, and of any humanly made thing. Williams's 'cultural materialism' is also premised on this decisive recognition. Podro invokes another writer that Fried, and Clark to a lesser extent, also seeks out as an intellectual ally – the philosopher Ludwig Wittgenstein. 'Language', the term a suggestive metaphor for any and all human signing activities, is what Wittgenstein called 'a way of life': effectively a 'form of society' and 'social action'. Pollock's *Untitled (Cut-Out)* (1948–1956) and Barnett Newman's *Adam* (1951–1952), however, are paintings produced almost contemporaneously, yet picture or 'sign' very different worlds; these paintings may be 'language games' in paint but they 'speak' no common language to the people that confront them. Podro concludes the same about the 'critical historians of art' – their studies offer finally a set of further problems (complications), rather than any real solutions, to the tenacious riddle of the conflicted relations between attention to form in art, and attention to the world.[20]

If Podro traces the conception of art as a form of social visual behaviour to Panofsky and Warburg writing in the first decades of the twentieth century, then Fried analogously claims that some of Claude Monet's paintings made in the late nineteenth century similarly produce or 'enact' the artwork as a kind of combined literal/metaphoric bearer of social relationships. Fried states that the artist painted pictures of human figures 'as a response to a particular historical situation' and wished to examine, and, in a way, test the relationship between painter and the beholder. The future of what Fried calls 'ambitious' figure painting hangs on how artists such as Monet and Manet responded to this situation.[21] Manet's *Olympia* [Plate 1] and *A Bar at the Folies Bergère* both feature, for instance, a woman staring intently straight out of the painting, in a way many contemporary critics thought was directly confrontational – a kind of intended 'disruption' of the usual business of looking. Clark claims that Picasso's Cubist paintings, such as *Woman with Pears (Fernande)* (1909) and *Ma Jolie* (1911–1912) [Plate 5], nominally both 'portraits', are equally guilty of disruptive social visual behaviour: that is, cancelling-while-appearing-to-promise recognizable likenesses. The issues of 'woman' as symbol, and the depiction of actual women, will recur in my following discussions of these paintings and the critical accounts they have generated – not least because Fried and Clark both appear to accept that the 'meaning of woman' in modern society is bound up importantly with what the former calls 'the problematic of absorption and theatricality'.[22] Clark prefers a different terminology (though I will suggest the ideas have a significant overlap) – 'the society of the spectacle', a notion of the Marxist Guy Debord. I begin a discussion of the relevance of these concepts towards the end of this introduction.[23]

Fried and Clark also share a belief that modern art can produce a critical *self-knowledge*, a 'form of knowing' that mediates between subject and object, viewer and artefact, and which might begin to blur the distinction between 'fact' and 'value'. But it is precisely the (admittedly shaky) maintenance of this distinction that defines the gulf that continues to separate Fried and Clark as critics, and perhaps as historians. It is the gulf that finally defines Fried's interest in modern art – up to the publication, at least, of *Manet's Modernism*, to which I turn substantively in my final chapter – as modernist and Clark's, well, as something else. Modern art, Clark declares in what became an acrimonious exchange of positions with Fried in the early 1980s, simply cannot *be* its *own* value, a presumption he attributes directly to Greenberg and, indirectly, to Fried.[24] Value in art, as elsewhere, Clark maintains, must be created and imposed on objects by people, and is inevitably the creature of self-interest, and other kinds of worldly interest. I turn now to the relation of these various interests with identifications of artistic value.

Class, glass, and opacity

If issues of gendered subjectivity in society come to infiltrate modern painting as a form and representation of social relations then the same is true of *socio-economic class* – the two, of course, have always been bound up together. Sometimes the presence and depiction of classed gender identity in art and criticism is implicit, surreptitious, or coded; sometimes, of course, it is metaphorically rammed down the throat. Henri Matisse's *Blue Nude. Souvenir of Biskra* (1907) pictures a 'primitive' woman inspired by the artist's visit to what was at the time a North African sex-tourism destination for Europeans. This *Blue Nude* rather plainly offers a commodity, and has 'herself' become one, as the title of the painting suggests. Two years earlier a critic described paintings by Cézanne as nothing more than those of 'a drunken privy cleaner', though the gender of this figured creature was not specified.[25] Listen carefully now, for it becomes evident that deciding what modern art has value means knowing (if not always saying) what type of people are equipped to make reliable judgements. Heidegger, for example, muses on what qualities of a painting certain occupational groups are likely to be able to appreciate. The 'thinglyness' of a painting's material existence, what he calls this 'rather crude and external view', is likely to appeal, he states, to '[s]hippers or charwomen in museums' who 'operate with such conceptions of the work of art'. So, in order to denigrate both a modern painter and some potential beholders – users – of modern paintings (Heidegger is writing about Van Gogh's pictures of shoes), a critic and a philosopher both resort to comparisons with cleaners and other manual labourers.[26] Could a bona fide art historian do any better?

The following is an extract from Ernst Gombrich's lecture to the British Psycho-Analytical Society in 1953. I quote a lengthy passage here because it prefigures, obscurely, several elements of my impending argument:

The child is proverbially fond of sweets and toffees, and so is the primitive, with his Turkish delight and an amount of fat meat that turns a European stomach. We prefer something less obvious, less yielding. My guess is, for instance, that small children and unsophisticated grown-ups will be likely to enjoy a soft milk chocolate, while townified highbrows will find it cloying and seek escape in the more bitter tang or in an admixture of coffee, or, preferably, crunch nuts ... in a way the highbrow, the sophisticate, the critic, is a frustrated artist, and if he cannot satisfy his standards, he wants at least to project ... I should ask your permission to support this contention with ... [a] little experiment *ad hominem*. Again I must beg your forgiveness for inflicting yet another work of *Art Officiel* on you. This atrocity is a painting of the *Three Graces* by Bonnencontre [*c*.1900]. I will spare you an analysis of all that makes it odious. Let us rather see whether we can perhaps improve the sloppy mush by adding a few crunchy breadcrumbs. This is the photograph of the same picture seen through a wobbly glass. You will agree that it looks a little more respectable. We have to become a little more active in reconstituting the image, and we are less disgusted. The second image shows the same painting seen at a greater distance through the same glass. By now, I think, it deserves the epithet 'interesting'. Our own effort to reintegrate what has been wrenched apart makes us project a certain vigour into the image which makes it quite crunchy. I'd like to patent that invention for it has great economic potentialities. In future, when you find a picture in your attic of 'The Monarch of the Glen' or 'Innocence in Danger', you need not throw it away or give it to the charwoman. You can put it behind a wobbly glass and make it respectable.[27]

What a passage itself ripe for psychoanalytic dissection! How might any 'charwomen' possibly present in that audience have responded to Gombrich's claims? Though I must resist pursuing some of his assumptions here (I've always liked any kind of chocolate), it is clear that value and meaning in art for Gombrich too are bound up with forms of life and social class. Not just making art, but writing and speaking about it are equally forms of social behaviour – the half-century gulf between this lecture and the present throws the speaker's ideas and means of expression (and the world of which they were a part) into shocking relief. It should also be evident that Gombrich decides that the Bonnencontre painting becomes more 'interesting' the more its surface is disintegrated and becomes harder to see or 'read'. I shall resist concluding that he believes this 'interesting' image is now 'better' or more 'valuable', as the 'image' isn't actually a material artefact – though admittedly its appearance is conveyed through the printed reproduction of a photograph – but rather a phenomenon visible because of the placement of the painting behind the 'wobbly' glass. And I shall return to Fried's retort, apropos of a famous remark made by Donald Judd in relation to his 'Minimalist' art objects (similar in some ways to some very early 1960s so-called 'Post-Painterly' pictures, such as those by Frank Stella [*Six Mile Bottom*, Plate 6]), that it was not enough for art to be *merely* 'interesting' – it had to be *good* too.[28] Doesn't 'complexity', that enigmatic art-critical term I am edging around to now in an attempt to grasp the significance of value, nearly always imply that its designated object is interesting *and* good? Gombrich, whatever his quirks, has hit upon the idea that a fragmentation of form, such as that found in a Cézanne landscape or Picasso Cubist portrait [Plates 3 and 5] somehow may engage and retain the attention of a sufficiently sophisticated beholder. That which is apparently withheld, disguised, or occluded may become the object of a fascinated looking.[29]

Tate Modern's logo, showing the word 'Tate' fading round its edges, sets out to create this effect [Plate 7]. Its intended connotation is roughly 'there is much more meaning and value here in the gallery than is visible', and we are to be enticed and beguiled by all that promised meaning and value which is absent but nevertheless signified.

The Tate sign tells us that canonical modern art simultaneously *is* and *represents* what I shall call an 'occluded totality'. Complexity in great modern artworks, and in modernist criticism, implies and relies upon the signalling of this occluded totality: the gesture towards a *whole* or *greater meaning* or *ideal* which is absent from the visual representation. This absent-but-signified 'totality' or 'whole' has a very wide metaphoric sweep in modern art; it has, for example, been given the names of 'Body', 'Subjectivity', 'Nature', 'God', or 'The People', among others. This absent-but-signified totality or whole, however, always suggests an imagined 'unity' or 'oneness' – Pollock called four of his drip-paintings 'One'. G.W.F. Hegel called this ideal of realized unity and oneness 'sublation': the term inevitably carries the implication of a meta-physical transcendence.[30] Unity has, as its converse, the *fragment*, sign of that wholeness which is occluded and necessarily alienated from oneness. These difficult and allusive terms will be explained and explored in the chapters to come. Another way to express their interdependency would be to claim that complexity and subjectivity in modern art and modernist criticism are *always* bound up together. At some level or point they *always* come to signal each other, though subjectivity, like complexity, takes on a range of sometimes ghostly or ventriloquizing forms within the triadic relations between 'critic – artwork – artist'. I shall demonstrate and elaborate many examples of what I mean in the pages ahead and will return to discuss additional facets of 'complexity' more fully later in this Introduction.

Greenberg once complained in an interview that art was 'over-rated', and he blames this on developments in German philosophy around the time of the Enlightenment, towards the end of the eigh-teenth century.[31] He has in mind the idea, associated particularly with Kant, that art-making is a specially separate kind of activity and provides an experience requiring a specially separate kind of appreciation, under-standing, and evaluation. I will examine some of the details of this tradition of thought shortly. Greenberg adheres to this view but states that a corollary of it being true is that art 'solves nothing' in life, 'either for the artist . . . or for those who receives his art'. Further, he remarks, the quality of life generally in a society is not necessarily reflected by the quality of its art – a view the charwomen and shippers of art might have cause to agree with.[32] When Clark declares that art simply cannot be its *own* value he is pointing, as I have said, to the existence and influence of interests necessarily implicated in judgement, *contrary* to the claims of modernist critics that some, or all of these interests, are suspended in, or simply irrelevant to the proper experience of modern art. I will come to the slippages between accounts of this experience and the *judgement* and *explanation* of art in a while. Watch out for the mention of complexity here in Clark's response directly to Fried. The appropriate reading, that is, understanding, of an artwork, Clark suggests, consists of two possibilities. Either:

> An exclusive and intensive focusing, a bracketing of knowledge, a giving-over of consciousness to its object, or . . . a mobilization of complex assumptions, commitments, and skills, in which the object is always being seen against (as *part* of) a ground of interest and argument. I certainly think the latter is the case.[33] [Italic in original.]

Clark's view, with which I agree, appears to pose critical consciousness as both separate from ('against'), but also 'as *part* of', the object of its attention. The difficulty here is in the meaning of 'part', which has at least two valences – first, 'part' implying that the object, as it were, 'lies upon' the ground of interest and argument but is distinguishable or separate from it; second, more strongly, that the object *is*, in some sense, the ground of interest and argument. I am sure Clark was aware of, and wanted to indicate this complication in the possible interpretation of the meaning of his sentence. It reflects an acceptance – stated rather tacitly, in the context of his argument against Fried – that subject (critic) and object (painting) are *not* finally completely separable in the world of meanings and values; in a world, that is, within which paintings are able to take on meanings, and are sometimes judged to have great value. This great value, to a high degree synonymous, as I will argue, with the designation complex ('having complexity'), resides *ontologically* in both subject and object: it is the co-product of each in their interrelation. Podro reached a similar view in his conclusion to *The Critical Historians of Art*. Wölfflin, Warburg, and Panofsky developed, he claimed, 'critical viewpoints and concepts' that became intelligible 'through their exercise upon the *complex* objects which form the occasion and purpose of their construction'[34] (my italic). What perhaps troubled Podro, though he chose not to confront the issue too directly in his book, was the question of what limits would, could, or should be put on the *range* of artefacts deemed potentially both to 'contain' and 'generate' this authentic complexity or value. Modern art, of course, over a hundred years or more, has raised this problem perennially and dramatically, as is known from the initial critical reception of Manet's *Le Déjeuner sur l'herbe* (1863), and it carries on being raised throughout the twentieth century, up until the works of Mark Rothko, Morris Louis (*Alpha-Phi* (1961)) [Plate 8], Kenneth Noland, and beyond. When might modern art's history of such 'doubted value' have first arisen, where, and why?[35]

Modernism, the decay of collective style, and the past of art

The beginnings of modern art, if not modernist criticism, are usually sought in the mid-nineteenth century in Paris, and Manet is claimed to be the first 'modernist painter'. As this latter epithet indicates, however, problems, confusions, and complications of definition abound in my study. Although *I* will hold to the neutral-sounding 'modern art' in order continually to distinguish artworks from modernist-critical accounts of them, Greenberg and Fried themselves, for their own reasons, call artworks, and their producers, modern*ist*. Another writer – historian, critic, and philosopher – identified the beginnings of modern art with the death of collective or social style in painting. Arnold Hauser argued in the third and fourth volumes of *The Social History of Art* (1951) that this epoch, from the rise of Manet and the Impressionists in the 1860s through to Picasso in the 1930s, saw the history of art become really the history of the work of disparate individuals, living in an ostensibly common world, but driven by radically incommensurate motivations and methods.[36] Their artworks constitute, as I've suggested, a set of 'language games' which nevertheless do not add up to any common language or shareable meaning [compare, for example, Plates 3 and 5]. A rampant subjectivism of artistic intent, the social conditions of which I shall come to later, led, Hauser thought, to the production of artefacts effectively without meaning. 'Avant-garde' artists come eventually to create their works in near-complete social isolation, in 'exile', or in the bohemian garret, not as the result of commissions; nor are their products necessarily intended for even the anonymous buyers in the emerging 'free market' for art. *No* public at all may have been envisaged – or wanted – by these artists, such was their contempt *especially* for the class they themselves usually hailed from, the bourgeoisie. Such artists produce their works only for themselves, Hauser claimed, and the subject of their art really becomes what it is to live and experience life as an artist. This is, for him, the very definition of aestheticism: within it, art ceases to be a 'social activity' and becomes 'an activity of self-expression creating its own standards; it becomes, in a word, the medium through which the single individual speaks to single individuals'. This doctrine, 'art for art's sake', is both part cause and part consequence of the radical social dislocation of art and artists in modern capitalist society.[37]

The notion of style, for Fried as well as Hauser, attains a highly important but deeply problematic status in understanding the origins of modern art and its significance within what the former is still prepared to call the 'modernist tradition'. Both also see style in art as a kind of pathology or trace of social development. Fried, however, believes modern art includes some of the greatest paintings ever produced, while Hauser is almost unremittingly hostile in his evaluations.[38] Without a discernable social legibility there simply can be no value, Hauser seems to conclude, in modern art's patently fractured and occluded views of the world. Think of Cézanne's *Mont Sainte-Victoire* and Picasso's *Ma Jolie* [Plates 3 and 5]. There is a displaced echo here, perhaps, of Alois Riegl's and Karl Schnaase's contention that the ordering device of perspective in Renaissance painting operated as a sign of 'community' – a regulated and meaningful life – and that the dissolution of perspective within modern art signals, among other things, that community's death.[39] Meyer Schapiro's understanding of style has some resonances with this view though his account implicitly refuses the idealizations that the term 'community' usually implies. Styles in art, for Schapiro, are relatively fixed expressions of social group (including class) outlooks, vehicles of expression communicating, for instance, religious or moral values through, for example, the 'emotional suggestiveness of forms'.[40] Style, moreover, necessarily involves *descriptive and conceptual generalization* – an abstracting identification of 'type', against which individual examples and innovations may be measured. Style, like complexity in art, is indissolubly a co-product of artefact and critical attention, mutually implicated object *and* subject.

Fried mentions Schapiro's definition of style because it pertains to a problem the former identifies as crucial to understanding what *he* calls modernism in the visual arts. Modern art after Manet – I mean the canonical paintings of highest quality that Fried, Greenberg, and Clark all agree upon, and which most of my illustrations exemplify – for Fried *does* demonstrate the erosion in 'style as social indicator' that disturbed Hauser so much. And it *is* the case, Fried remarks, that style, understood in the Hauser-Schapiro sense, becomes grossly inappropriate when considering Manet's and his successors' paintings: style understood as generalized type is inadequate in terms of 'legitimacy or validity', and this is partly because of what Fried calls 'modernist painting's drive to transform and renew itself through radical *criticism* of its own achievements' (my italic). This last statement, I hope it is clear, demonstrates precisely the 'binding together' of modern art and criticism that I wish to stress. Moreover, this declaration, made earlier by Greenberg in different words in 'Modernist Painting', that *modern art itself has become a form of criticism* illustrates another key rhetorical figure – personification – often set to work in their writings.[41] Through it something called 'modernist painting' is given the human ability to have 'drive' (intent, will, power) and is identified as internally unified ('itself', 'its own').

Fried claims that the advent of modernism in the visual arts requires fundamental rethinking of the notion of 'style-as-social indicator', but *not* a jettisoning altogether of the concept.[42] This qualification may throw some light on an often-quoted but tenaciously obscure statement he makes at the beginning of one of his most well-known catalogue essays, *Three American Painters: Kenneth Noland, Jules Olitski, Frank Stella* (1965):

> Roughly speaking, the history of painting from Manet through Synthetic Cubism and Henri Matisse may be characterized in terms of the gradual withdrawal of painting from the task of representing reality – or of reality from the power of painting to represent it – in favour of an increasing preoccupation with problems intrinsic to painting itself.[43]

Great modern artists after Manet have *not* stopped attempting to 'show the world', as this statement has often been interpreted as suggesting. However, they have realized, I take it Fried is claiming, that any such attempt has come to involve *simultaneously showing something of the 'means of showing' that world*. 'Modernist painting' and 'modernist painters', that is, have become self-conscious and self-critical – as well as interested primarily in the art of their immediate ('modernist') predecessors. However, this development is, in itself, a social phenomenon – something which Fried himself accepts. Manet painted, he claims, 'not merely his world but his problematic relationship to it ... Manet ... is the first painter for whom consciousness itself is the great subject of his art'.[44] *Self*-consciousness, then, is implicit in Manet's looking at how people look and in representing how people appear. Hauser may well judge such self-consciousness to be 'aestheticism', but its emergence indicates, highly significantly, something of the modern conditions of avant-garde artistic production – socially dislocated, self-ghettoized, marginal – in capitalist society. Fried's last sub-clause remains confusing, however, as he has himself accepted, in its possible interpretation that what he calls those 'problems intrinsic to painting itself' *do not also* include how 'world' or 'reality' might be pictured.[45] If art is always a form of social visual behaviour, then modern art is a particular kind of such social visual behaviour, conditioned by its historical circumstances, and involving those circumstances of changing human consciousness and self-consciousness.

Baudelaire, for instance – often called the first modern art critic – had recognized by the 1840s, according to Fried, that the social conditions necessary for the great schools of painting in the past had disappeared, leading to an extreme form of individualism and throwing the modern artist on to his [*sic*] own resources. In this situation, Fried claims, only the 'most gifted' and those with 'impassioned natures' could 'hope to create lasting art'.[46] Interestingly enough, given a longstanding consensus that Hauser's social history of art is crude and reductive in its analytic detail, Greenberg, reviewing Hauser's magnum opus for *The New York Times Book Review* in 1951, is complimentary. This is because Hauser, Greenberg claims, manages successfully to be both 'art critic' and 'sociologist'. *The Social History of Art* is, Greenberg states, 'an improved history of art' in which society 'contains and throws light on art, receiving light in return, but this reciprocity does not completely explain either art or society'.[47] Watch Greenberg institute here these putatively autonomous categories of experience and knowledge – the 'art critic' on the one hand, and the 'sociologist' on the other! Fried will go one step further, later inventing the category of the 'formal critic'.[48] These inventions are part of the rhetorical machinery that helps to establish 'modernism' and 'modernist criticism' as fact. Notice also Greenberg's use of the metaphor here of light and dark. It is another figure or motif of speech that Fried and Clark also mobilize – and partly through it the 'occluded totality' of value and complexity in modern painting will find its life.

Criticism, however, has no monopoly on the use of figural conventions or modes of rhetoric that openly and insidiously create or encourage assumptions about modern art's nature or purpose. History writing is equally saturated in both, and is similarly incapable of a once-and-for-all shedding of them in order to attain some kind of finally neutral or objective language.[49] However, a critical awareness of the *presence* and *effects* of such conventions, I've suggested, is desirable – for those both writing and reading. For example, the idea of history as a *straightforward* unfolding narrative, from A to Z, or 'Manet to Pollock', remains one of the most powerful discursive conventions. In this book I attempt to destabilize and disrupt the values that underpin this convention by presenting things, rhetorically, from Z to A, or 'Pollock to Manet', and by this device draw attention to the practices of retrodiction ('writing afterwards' or 'writing back'), examining modernist accounts of modern art's 'historicity', that is, its claimed developmental or evolving character.[50] I distinguish historicity from any actual historical accounts, such as those of Hauser, Fried, and Clark, and also from 'historicism' – the perspective ordering certain histories that begin with an assumption of how things will end, an assumption which conditions and directs, teleologically, the flow of narrative and causal explanation. Modernist histories of art, including some of the accounts offered by Greenberg and Fried, have often been accused of such historicism.[51]

If Hauser argued that the demise of collective social style occurred during the mid-nineteenth century, his belief carrying the implication that authentic value in art could not survive this end, it is salutary to point out that another, much more omnipresent, historian and philosopher of the modern in art and society – Hegel – believed that truly great art had actually died out with the ancient Greeks! Hegel's pervading, if increasingly latent, influence over virtually all kinds of nineteenth-century history writing (and many of those in the twentieth) has several points of important intersection with my concerns. Hegel's despondency over the value of *all* art in the last third of the eighteenth century and the first third of the nineteenth (his own 'modern' period), given his sense that the highest realizations of human culture occurred thousands of years earlier, importantly conditions both Heidegger's and Clark's critical-philosophical and art-historical accounts. Pollock's drip-paintings for instance, Clark claims, in their 'rancour and repetitiveness', have something of Hegel's own pessimism[52] [Plate 4]. Heidegger attributes his own doubts over how to value modern art in the 1930s, partly to a reluctant acceptance of Hegel's reflection that art 'no longer counts for us as the highest manner in which truth obtains existence for itself . . . [art's] form has ceased to be the highest need of the spirit'.[53] Though many new artworks and movements have risen since Hegel's death the open question remains for Heidegger whether or not art can still be 'an essential and necessary way in which that truth happens which is decisive for our historical existence, or is art no longer of this character?'[54]

Fried's belief in great modern art's critical significance – a form mediating consciousness and self-consciousness – arguably is indebted to Hegel in general terms, for his lectures posthumously published in 1835 as *The Philosophy of Fine Art* address this central question of the role of art, past and present, in human mental life. Fried indicates something of this influence, while noting the historicist tendencies associated with Hegel that crept into Greenberg's neo-Kantian account of modernism ('Manet to Pollock'), if not, he suggests, into his own.[55] It is one thing to claim and argue connections between artists, artworks, and periods of art; it is clearly another to suggest that certain putative connections were 'inevitable' or 'necessary' developments. The latter claim would merit the accusation of 'historicism'. Fried's essays and books, he is happy to explain, have 'worked back' from what he calls modernist art of the mid-twentieth century [Plates 4, 6, and 8] into French painting of the eighteenth century, in order to examine developments related to the concepts of 'absorption' and 'theatricality' that re-emerge as problems, he argues, in a radicalized form in Manet's painting in the first half of the 1860s.[56] One of Fried's conclusions, based on this work carried out over many years, is that Manet and later modernist artists (Fried's usage, remember) radically re-conceptualized the value and meaning of past, that is, pre-mid-nineteenth-century great art; indeed, that this radical re-conceptualization produced that art's 'pastness', its 'overness' as far as modern artists were concerned. I turn to this, and related claims, later in Chapter 6.

One of the conditions of this re-conceptualization, an important feature of modern society, was the growth and influence of art museums displaying the great paintings of 'the past'. Fried quotes in support of his argument a paragraph from Michel Foucault's essay 'Fantasia of the Library':

> Le Déjeuner sur l'herbe and Olympia [Plate 1] were perhaps the first 'museum' paintings, the first paintings in European art that were less a response to the achievement of Giorgione, Raphael, and Velásquez than an acknowledgement . . . of the new and substantial relationship of painting to itself, as a manifestation of the existence of museums and the particular reality and interdependence that paintings acquire in museums. In the same period, [Gustave Flaubert's] Temptation [of St. Anthony] was the first literary work to comprehend the greenish institutions where books are accumulated and where the slow and incontrovertible vegetation of learning quietly proliferates. Flaubert is to the library what Manet is to the museum.[57]

The museums represent this 'interdependence' of paintings in their collections in two novel ways: first, they assemble in a single space (a visual 'library') a great diversity of pictures from the various European schools which come to be seen by contemporary artists as equivalent formal 'sources' for their own work – ripe for 'quotation', as it were, as 'art' sources, *not*, for instance, as devotional religious artefacts from Italy or public portraits from Holland.[58] Second, the museums, through their exhibitions and catalogue interpretations, 'produce' the intelligibility of these works as definitively that belonging to a concluded 'past' dissociated from the present of art and society.

Modern paintings, then, rather than defined simply in terms of the introduction of novel kinds of subject matter and modes of representation – for instance, Manet's obscure 'narrative' in *Le Déjeuner sur l'herbe* or Van Gogh's 'expressionistic' *The Potato Eaters* (1885) – are understood to appropriate and assimilate formal elements and visual conventions from this 'art of the past' mobilized now as a stock of motifs for contemporary use. These types of quotation include, for example, a re-presentation of genre scenes – for instance, religious painting, as in Manet's *Christ Mocked* (1865); or the selection and suggestion of formal and thematic elements from a number of paintings, such as Titian's and Velásquez's nudes, deployed together, for example, in Manet's *Olympia* [Plate 1]. Modern paintings also elevate the materials of what were once 'minor', less significant genres – such as still-life compositions of landscape, kitchen utensils and clothing, and flowers – into what eventually became understood, art-historically, as highly symbolically charged vehicles of artistic 'vision' and feeling: for example, Cézanne's *Mont Sainte-Victoire* [Plate 3] and *Still-Life with Water-Jug* (1892–1893), along with Van Gogh's *A Pair of Shoes* [Plate 2] and *Sunflowers* (1888). Wölfflin, Riegl, and Schnaase, incidentally, had concerned themselves with the same basic issue: that is, how art of the past could be made a living part of contemporary mental life and modern art.[59] Their incipient modernity *was* this recognition of the problem of contemporary value in art: of how art from the past was to be used, and so attain new value, in the(ir) present of art and society. Fried claims that, after Manet – the master of this deployment of motifs from past art; the architect, in a sense of its 'pastness' defined in relation to the contemporary, the now, of his art – the overriding issue becomes specifically that of how those artists he calls modernist should deal with the paintings of the very recent past – the 'modernist tradition' – in which a kind of 'dialectic' or 'perpetual revolution' of formal developments apparently undermines virtually all previous notions of style and influence.[60]

'. . . Not just interpreters, collaborators'?[61]

By the late nineteenth century this questioning of the meaning of the 'past in art' for modern painters had been joined, Clark argues, by the novelty of an institutional conception of modern artists' own 'singular, continuous past': the *career*.[62] This development is a particularly significant feature of emergent 'retrodictive' art-historical and art-museological discourse. The 'careers' of contemporary painters from the 1860s onwards become tied into the development of the art market, the dealer-system, catalogue publishing, and the new galleries and museums of modern art in the early twentieth century. Artists' careers become bound up with representations of their personalities as well as with economic and critical evaluation of their paintings and sculptures. Within this process the role of critics becomes increasingly important. Critics are called upon to provide what becomes known as the *retrospective* overview of an artist's career, so that, as Clark notes, it appears natural to think of pictures by Camille Pissarro, for instance, as 'primarily episodes in an individual's career – as opposed to, say, contributions to a public dialogue in the Salon'.[63] Retrospective exhibitions of early modern artists had, by Picasso's time, allowed him to see displayed extended evidence of the careers of Cézanne, Manet, Puvis de Chavannes, Gustave Courbet, and J.A.D. Ingres. The retrospective exhibition compounded and confirmed a verdict that was built into the art market's judgement of the economic value of an artist's paintings. It led artists, as much as anyone else, to think of their own work as part of a singular and continuous past.

By the mid-twentieth century 'retrospectives' and permanent records of these in catalogues with illustrations contributed to the sense that contemporary artists – and critics – had that the distant and recent past of art was, apparently, comprehensively available to them, for purposes of comparison, borrowing of 'sources', and judgements as to relative value. Fried touches on this situation in his early 1980s exchange with Clark, observing that what he calls an 'intensely perspectival and . . . circular a view of the modernist enterprise' is sometimes encouraged in which 'both the meaning and value of the present are conceived as underwritten by a relation to a past that is continually being revised and re-evaluated by the present'.[64] His earlier accounts of paintings by Pollock, Louis, Stella, and Noland (discussed later in Chapter 2) allude to this process, in which identification of compositional elements in their artworks have led to basic revisions to critical understanding of *prior* modernist paintings. Fried's statement that modern art *itself* is a critical enterprise should become more intelligible given his remark that:

> The relation between Pollock and Louis [Plates 4 and 8] goes too deep for the notions of influence and style. Familiarity with Louis's work does not merely color one's experience of Pollock's art; it comes close to determining it ... there is an important sense in which Louis's paintings *create* the aspects in question – in which they give significance to aspects of Pollock's art that otherwise could not be experienced as significant, or as having that particular significance.[65] [Italic in original.]

One might consider, for instance, the significance of the unpainted parts of canvas in Pollock's pictures, which in a way are 'thrown into relief', that is, made visible, by the recognition of the presence of such far larger parts in Louis's work. The point is, though, that claims about such formal relation and development – 'from Manet *to* Pollock' – are made possible *because* of necessarily retrospective, retrodictive understanding. 'To understand Cézanne is to foresee Cubism', declared Jean Metzinger and Albert Gleizes in *Du Cubisme* (1912), but Metzinger, of course, had first to see Cubism before he could make this judgement about Cézanne.[66]

Growth in the institutional significance of critics during the twentieth century might elucidate something of the hubristic and baffling qualities of a remark Greenberg made in the late 1950s when he claimed that it looked to him as if 'you could learn more about Matisse's color from [Hans] Hofmann than from Matisse himself'.[67] Notice here the same retrospective conceit – Hofmann is known primarily as a post-1945 Abstract Expressionist painter – wrapped up with the judgement that somehow his paintings, such as *The Garden* (1956), manage to 'speak' about his predecessor's colouristic sense better than do any examples of Matisse's own work. I think this statement is really designed to tell us more about the importance of Greenberg's notion of colour than about either Hofmann's or Matisse's! As I shall discuss in later chapters, Greenberg's own declared retrospective account of modernism in the visual arts explicitly states that the 'self-criticism' he sees as *its* purpose – mobilizing, in this essay, a variety of such personifying and subjectivizing rhetorical figures – is always carried on in what he calls a 'spontaneous' and 'subliminal' way. 'No artist,' Greenberg claims, 'was, or yet is, aware of it, nor could any artist ever work freely in awareness of it.'[68] This 'self-criticism's' authentic identification, understanding, and articulation will be the province, tautologically, of the 'modernist critic'.

Greenberg, Fried, and Clark all emphasize the influence of critics, but for a variety of purposes, and with a variety of results, as I shall show in the following chapters. The actual social relationships between these three, as well as between them and contemporary artists, are historical phenomena which inevitably form part of my object of study. Fried acknowledges, for instance, his debt to Greenberg, mixing critical and personal details in his account of this debt to the person he calls 'the foremost art critic of the twentieth century'.[69] Though embroiled in an antagonistic exchange of positions in the early 1980s, Fried and Clark became friends and have since noted their intellectual sympathies for each other's work, though the former continues to criticize, for instance, aspects of the latter's account of Manet's paintings.[70] Clark and Greenberg met on a number of occasions, and Clark has written frequently about the value, particularly, of Greenberg's early essays on art and culture, though he also subjected Greenberg's later writings and positions to attack.[71] The rise of this critic as a powerful interlocutor for modern art – whether this role is construed as 'interpreter' or 'collaborator' – has, however, much earlier precedents.

Clyfford Still's testy rejection of critics, particularly Greenberg (see p. 8), also has a range of precursors. A number of these remarks will be examined in the following pages. They come from artists and creative writers, as well as from some critics, including those who were, occasionally, also poets and dramatists. Emile Zola, for instance, mockingly described art critics as 'policemen' in an 1867 review of an exhibition of Manet's paintings.[72] Oscar Wilde's essay 'The Critic as Artist' wittily reverses the usual hierarchy of 'artwork then criticism', in order both to question this assumed order of production, meaning, and value, but also to restate it in the face of the exponential growth of criticism, without which now, he ironically declaims 'there is no artistic creation at all, worthy of the name ... criticism is itself an art ... It is to criticism that the future belongs ... There was never a time when criticism was more needed than it is now.'[73] He might have had in mind Stéphane Mallarmé's extraordinary 1876 essay on Manet, which is also a requiem for the painter's most serious interlocutor, the recently dead Baudelaire ('amateur' critic and 'our last great poet', Mallarmé declares).[74] In this piece, however, Mallarmé effectively *ventriloquizes* Manet, making the artist speak through his – Mallarmé's – use of the rhetorical device of the 'first person'. It is through nature, Mallarmé says (Manet says):

that when rudely thrown at the close of an epoch of dreams in the front of reality, I have taken from it only that which properly belongs to my art, an original and exact perception which distinguishes for itself the things it perceives with the steadfast gaze of a vision restored to its simplest perfection.[75]

But whose vision is this? Who is to say? Hostile reaction towards the liberties a critic may take to explain the meaning of an artwork, and to claim, as Greenberg will do almost a hundred years later that artists simply *cannot* be aware of the ultimate purpose of their work ('modernist self-criticism'), could have led Barnett Newman, like Wilde, to adopt a stance that seems absurd but which, in its absurdity, is intended to raise central issues to do with art's interpretation. If critics like Harold Rosenberg and others could understand my paintings 'properly', Newman said, they would see they would 'mean the end of all state capitalism and totalitarianism'.[76] Greenberg and Rosenberg were, for a time, bitter rivals, but for Newman they appear to be on the same and opposite side to him.

Fried made friendships, as I noted, with some of the artists whose work he came to admire and value extremely highly during the 1960s. Stella and Anthony Caro are cases in point. Fried suggests that the role of the 'formal critic' involves adopting (or, perhaps, being compelled to adopt) a position 'analogous' to that of the artist. This is because the serious critic, like the serious artist, has no choice but to seek 'to elicit the conviction' that certain concepts, or procedures, or experiences, are right, given that 'criticism has no neutral, context-free . . . descriptive categories at its disposal'.[77] Notice here, again, that 'criticism' may refer to modern art practice *and* its appropriate explanation – the two are bound together, as modernist critic and artist are for Fried. Later, he will claim that Manet was only able to acknowledge his debt to the eighteenth-century painter Watteau, and declare a commitment to 'realism' in his painting *The Old Musician* (1862), because of the sanction of the proto-art historian Théophile Thoré, possessor of 'one of the finest pictorial intelligences then at work'.[78] *Together* – in a kind of collaboration? – Fried states, Thoré and Manet brought about this modern appropriation of past art.

Fried had made a similar general claim, much earlier, in *Three American Painters* concerning the role of 'formal critics', including, of course, himself. 'Criticism', he declares, which 'shares the basic premises of modernist painting finds itself *compelled to play a role in its development closely akin to, and potentially only somewhat less important than, that of new paintings themselves'*[79] (my italic). To his credit, Fried admits, this could sound like, and might actually be, 'an intolerably arrogant conception'. It reveals also, he says, how risky 'serious' criticism is – carried out, as modernist art is, as a moral endeavour, 'not because all art is at bottom a criticism of life, but because modernist painting is at least a criticism of itself'. The modernist artist and critic moreover, Fried says, live life 'as few are inclined to live it: in a state of continuous intellectual and moral alertness'.[80] A whiff of elitism is surely unavoidable in this, but I shall resist examining more of Fried's stance here – it will be reconsidered in the following chapters. Fried tacitly acknowledges through it, however, that modernist artist and critic, painting and criticism, are bound up together as mutually implicated object and subject, gaining intelligibility only from their dialectical interplay, and a value that resides not in one or the other, but in their inter-relationship. I consider in the following section how this subtle recognition might be reconciled (or fail to be reconciled) with the primacy usually assigned by modernist critics to a claimed 'intuitive' and 'unmediated' experience of the artwork, through which judgements of value are supposedly directly arrived at.

Greenberg, like Fried, at times considers the nature of critical writing with what appears to be a degree of unusual candour. The inevitable disjunction between the direct *experience* of looking at art and the 'reporting' of that experience in writing, he notes, for instance, is a fact that cannot be wished away – there simply is no way of knowing that critics write truthfully about their experiences.[81] He remarks, much earlier that, indeed, it 'is possible to get away with murder in writing about art'.[82] This possibility, presumably, is related to the situation that modern artists find themselves in, because they too, he says, 'do whatever they can get away with, and what they can get away with is not to be determined beforehand'.[83] In a manner similar to Fried, then, Greenberg draws artist and critic together, like risk-taking 'collaborators', observing that criticism (like the public reaction to avant-garde art itself?), though 'most challenging', is about the 'most ungrateful form of "elevated" writing' he knew of.[84] In one of his most well-known essays Greenberg claims that one of the conditions for the development of avant-garde culture was the development of a new kind of criticism in the nineteenth century: 'an historical criticism' exhibiting a 'superior consciousness of history', this being nothing less than 'the first bold development of scientific revolutionary thought in Europe'.[85] This is Marxism, with its philosophical base of historical materialism, in relation to which the birth of the avant-garde coincides both chronologically and geographically. 'Criticism' in *this* politico-philosophical sense, then, appears to have been made a partner (if not actually a precondition?) of modern art. Fried will later add to this, as I've noted, the significance of 'modernist' criticism, which shares what he calls *the basic premises of modernist painting* which is, he claims *potentially only somewhat less important than . . . that of new paintings themselves.*

Theodor Adorno, Frankfurt School Marxist and protagonist of Arthur Schoenberg's atonal modern music, came to believe that a similar collaboration characterized this art-form and its criticism. For Adorno, the problems posed by Schoenberg's musical material *are* the problems of post-Second World War capitalist society – remember Warburg's art is a 'social behaviour'. The disintegration of tonality enacts/echoes the disintegration of idealistic belief in a socialist society. Shoenberg's atonal compositions are therefore themselves kinds of 'social action' and 'social theory'. In the same way Adorno's politico-philosophical criticism may be identified as 'aesthetic'. Adorno's book, *Aesthetic Theory*, indicates this slippage, or merging, of subject and object.[86] The term 'modernism' when used by Greenberg and Fried performs the same slippage or merging, referring jointly to artwork and criticism, artist and critic, object and subject. Given what might be called art and criticism's *dialectical co-determination of value*, how might the key modernist notions of 'aesthetic experience' and 'aesthetic judgement' be re-evaluated?

The subject object

Greenberg declares in a 1961 essay that the adjudication of what is good or bad art can only be decided 'through experience . . . Quality in art can be neither ascertained nor proved by logic or discourse.' However, although experience 'alone rules in this area', Greenberg notes that this is joined *retrospectively* by what he calls 'reflection upon experience . . . the experience, so to speak, of experience'.[87] I will consider this confusing qualification in a moment. A few years later he made an observation on the nature of aesthetic judgement that became something of a modernist-critical shibboleth. Such judgements, he declares, 'are immediate, intuitive, undeliberate, and involuntary . . . [and] leave no room for the conscious application of standards, criteria, rules, and precepts'.[88] Fried, in his early 1980s exchange with Clark, uses this 'weaponized' definition of aesthetic judgement to soften up his then opponent. Simply lacking the requisite intuition to know what good art really was meant that Clark could not be blamed for his Marxist ramblings: intuition of that 'rightness', Fried states, was the critic's 'first responsibility as well as his immediate reward'. If Clark 'shared more than a fraction of that intuition about this Caro or any Caro, or any [David] Smith, Pollock, [Helen] Frankenthaler, Louis, Noland, Olitski, or [Larry] Poons, not to mention the antecedent masters whose paintings and sculptures, continually reinterpreted, stand behind theirs, his [that is, Clark's] understanding of the politics of modernism', Fried pontificates, 'would be altogether different from what it is'[89] [Plates 4, 6, and 8]. Get out of that!

In this passage Fried is concluding his attack on Clark's claim that great avant-garde painting involves a kind of 'negation' of antecedent artistic and social conventions: that great modern art is, in some fundamental sense, *intrinsically* negative. Shades of Adorno are discernable in this position and Clark's later motif, deployed in *Farewell to an Idea*, of the 'failures' in modern art invites similar comparisons.[90] If Clark had any intuitive capacity to know which modern art simply *was* good, Fried is implying, he would not be sidetracked by political interests into such incoherence. Fried himself, however, in a later, less embattled and rhetorically combative moment, is prepared to recognize that such judgements of value, in any *realized* sense – that is, articulated, explained, communicated to others – are inevitably the product of 'interest-informed' observation. Such an acknowledgement renders highly problematic the ideal, and claimed reality, of a pristine 'aesthetic experience'. Though Fried still concurs with Greenberg that 'all judgements of value begin and end in experience', it is the case, he observes, that he had

> stopped using 'subjective' and 'subjectivity' as pejorative notions . . . The idea of objectification in particular is a red herring, which is to say that the subjective/objective opposition . . . is beside the point . . . the task of the critic is, first, not to flinch from making such judgements, which are nothing less than the lifeblood of his enterprise, and second, to try to come up with the most telling observations and arguments on their behalf.[91]

The real substance, that is, worldly existence, of these 'judgements' here is inseparable from what Fried calls the 'observations and arguments' made 'on their behalf'. These 'observations and arguments', I would argue, actually *constitute* part of what Greenberg calls – ambiguously – the 'experience, so to speak, of experience', or – not at all ambiguously – 'reflection on experience'.

I will assume that Greenberg and Fried *have* stood in front of particular paintings and believed they have judged – immediately, involuntarily, intuitively, and undeliberately – that they were 'good'. Both critics remark particularly upon the apparent 'at-once' character to this positive judgement, a perception to which I shall return later.[92] How these acts of apparently 'immediate' judgement actually occurred mentally, or linguistically, remains somewhat shrouded (could their immediacy really be represented in a non-distorting way?), but I am prepared to accept their claims that such judgements did occur. Making sense of such judgements, however – that is, making some meaning and value out of them – requires, Greenberg and Fried both acknowledge, retrospective and retrodictive activity. Once this activity 'begins' – this term, unfortunately, carries with it the fiction that our critics at some point had not already been thinking – then it inevitably enters into a dialectical relation with the *next*, and all subsequent, acts of 'immediate' judgements performed, as the process of retrospection and retrodiction becomes part of the on-going world of experience that one brings into any encounter with paintings. Greenberg candidly acknowledges this when he declaims, while in the act of berating those without 'sufficient experience', that the 'practiced eye tends always toward the definitively and positively good in art, knows it is there, and will remain dissatisfied with anything else'. Though the term 'eye' here may suggest some ability to see without cognition – a notion some of the origins and implications of which I discuss in following chapters – Greenberg states that the critic likely to be able to discern such true value or quality is required to 'learn how to experience, or appreciate, art *relevantly*'[93] (my italic). That is, the 'right' kind of experience of looking is itself learnt through the right kind of 'experience'! This is actually what I think Greenberg means when he talks of 'the experience, so to speak, of experience'.

Now, clearly, the term 'experience' is being made to perform some quite dazzling rhetorical tricks! It was Clark's identification of the problems the term presents, and his inevitably *ad hominem* remarks apropos Fried's own putative experiences of artworks, that led to their early 1980s exchange getting personal. Aesthetic judgement presented as a decisive and unquestionable 'at-once recognition of value' by a suitably equipped individual qualifies as an example of subjectivism defined in the narrow philosophical sense: a judgement, that is, to reiterate, 'about our own attitudes, beliefs, emotions, etc.'.[94] Clark, drawing a parallel between what he regards as bogus religious epiphanies and claimed experiences of revealed aesthetic value, simply has to go after the man:

> Fried is interested in preserving a certain set of practices and sensi-bilities (let's call them those of 'art' or 'sculpture'); the set is specific; at the heart of it I detect a form of pristine experience had by an individual in front of an object, an 'intuition of right-ness' if you like. The relation of this experience to the normal identities and relations of history is obscure, but the language of Fried's actual descriptions, here and elsewhere, suggests that it somehow abrogates them and opens on to a ground of plenitude of knowledge which is normally closed to us . . . since there is no rational grounds *for* doubt [that is, we cannot ourselves directly know Fried's experiences], let's talk about something else – for instance, about why one person should be interested in preserving this kind of experience and the talk that goes with it and another be interested in its destruction.[95]

Clark's implication here is that Fried is really only having the kind of experiences that Fried *wants* to have and that these experiences there-fore are precisely voluntary, mediated, retrodictively conditioned and deliberated, and based on principles and interests that can be identified and assessed. Fried has developed, that is, his own way of experiencing art *relevantly*, to use Greenberg's give-away blunt formulation. Aesthetic judgements, then, are a set of experiences conditioned, made possible, by certain kinds of values and certain kinds of reflections upon such experiences. This counts for all experience, Perry Anderson observed, in the context of a different debate, for it 'is a concept *tous azimuts* which can point in any direction'.[96] One does have the ability, contrary to what Greenberg once declared, to *choose* to like a work of art, but perhaps also to *believe* (and/or to want to believe) that somehow that judgement has occurred without volition, in an apparent revelatory flash. One of the indispensable missing terms with which to understand this process of intertwined judgement and reflection is *ideology*. Ideological critique is, as Clark defines his own critical practice, to reiterate, 'a mobilization of complex assumptions, commitments, and skills, in which the object is always being seen against (as *part* of) a ground of interest and argument'.[97]

The twin legacies and problems of 'voluntarist' and 'determinist' forms of thought haunt this discussion, as might have become clear by now. What limits have been set, could be set, on how people 'experience' and 'understand their experiences'? How are people's actions and values to be reconciled with pre-existing structures and forces? How are such structures and forces challenged and changed by the actions and values of people? Experience *might* point in any direction, as Anderson claims, but people actually construe particular meanings at particular times, *not all or just any*, and this is as true of aesthetic experiences and judgements, as it is of any other kinds. That is, such experiences and judgements have become meaningful – in fact, possible at all – only within specific historical situations. The modernist critics' claim of an 'at-once recognition of value', associated with Fried and Greenberg, has precedent in the reported aesthetic experiences of the Bloomsbury Group's Roger Fry and Clive Bell, and some earlier writers.[98] Such claimed experiences are bound up with, and are products of, modern society; with their stress on experiential conviction, sensibility, and feeling in the search for artistic value they constitute a cultural facet of that society's *modernity* with roots traceable at least to the first decades of the twentieth century.

This search for defensible values is part of the ongoing crisis in modernity itself, as individuals and groups attempt to define themselves and their world *against* the past (of art and society). Clark defines modernity as the turn away from 'the worship of ancestors and past authorities', without which 'meaning is in short supply – "meaning" here meaning agreed-on and instituted forms of value and understanding'.[99] Statements of faith in the existence of high aesthetic value in writings by Bell, Fry, Greenberg, and Fried constitute attempts to 'find' such new meanings believed to be present in certain art objects. The latter pair of critics, however, acknowledge tacitly that criticism itself – involving retrospective explanation – necessarily constitutes *part* of this value. The subjectivistic riddle to this situation perturbed Heidegger, writing only about three years before Greenberg's essay 'Avant-Garde and Kitsch' was published. We should know what art is, Heidegger says, from looking at the artwork. But we can only know what the work of art is from knowing the nature of art. 'Anyone can easily see we are moving in a circle . . . how are we to be certain that we are indeed basing such an examination on artworks if we do not know beforehand what art is? And the nature of art can no more be arrived at by a derivation from higher concepts than by a collection of characteristics of actual artworks'[100] [Plates 2, 4, 5, and 6].

Now consider a photograph of Richard Wilson's 2003 installation *20:50* [Plate 9]. Imagine a woman looking out from within this channelled walkway, in a room whose image is mirrored a little darkly in the reflective surface that would surround her torso. Momentarily one is not sure which side might really be 'up'. Could the photograph itself be upside down? What kind of a world is this? How might this photograph, this installation artwork, continue or transcend the concerns and problems of modern art and modernism?

Art 'itself', Heidegger appears to conclude, simply *cannot* provide 'its' 'own' definition or 'its' 'own' value. I'm labouring the personifications here. If modern art's value rests, instead, with its 'collaborators', the critics, then the name they often given to this value is 'complexity', bound up as it is with the subjective identities of its nominators. In the final section of the Introduction, I turn to this problematic and briefly to the art and world 'after modernism'.

'Narcissus looking interminably into the unclean mirror . . .'[101]

Complexity, when used in relation to an artwork (ninety-nine times out of a hundred) means 'it is good' – but the judgement carries with it the implication that the artefact in question is, in some important way, unknowable, intransigent, or resistant to understanding. The human mind found the pyramid form resistant to it, observed Hegel, but somehow possessing significance by virtue of that resistance: a kind of meaningful meaninglessness.[102] Greenberg declares in 'Towards a Newer Laocoon' (1940) that poetry offers the possibility of meaning, but only the possibility. If a poem realized a particular meaning too precisely, he says, it would lose 'the greatest part of its efficacy, which is to agitate the consciousness with infinite possibilities by approaching the brink of meaning and yet never falling over it'.[103] Consider, then, the uses of 'complexity' (and some of its many effective synonyms) in the following statements:

1   'The works [Bach] composed . . . were so beautifully and so intelligently worked out and elaborated that they exhausted the resources of tonal sound. In Bach's counterpoint, the listener is aware of a remarkable complexity but never a laborious or academic one. Its authority is absolute.'

2   'Describing [Jasper Johns's] *Flag* you see it but you don't understand it . . . a provocative masterpiece of unresolvable questions

... under the surface of the flag's simple iconic presence are complicated lives, happenings and secrets ...'

3 '[Chris Ofili's room in the British Pavilion at the 2003 Venice Biennale] with its complex suspended canopy of coloured glass (an innovative yet deceptively simple piece of engineering) ... [Olafur Eliasson's Danish Pavilion] ... perceptual tricks and conundrums ... tricksy kaleidoscopic mirrors ... geometric oddities ...'

4 'The eye enjoys overcoming difficulty. One must set it solvable tasks, it is true, but the whole history of art is evidence that the clarity of today is boring tomorrow, and that the visual arts can dispense with the partial obscuring of form or confusing of the eye as little as music can dispense with dissonance and an interrupted cadence.'

5 'The arts ... have been hunted back to their mediums, and there they have been isolated, concentrated and defined. It is by virtue of its medium that each is unique and strictly itself. To restore the identity of an art the opacity of its medium must be emphasized.'

6 'Hegel's vision takes up suggestions from Kant: that in the perception of harmonious order we feel the world adapted to our minds, while in the complex orders too great for the mind to grasp – such complexity as was suitable to subjects like divinities and hell – our mind's frustrated activity gave us an analogue of our situation in relation to those things which lay, unknowable, beyond the material world, like God and Freedom.'[104]

Greenberg's, Fried's, and Clark's accounts of the complexities of modern art constitute, I shall argue, a critical discourse centred on the search for value understood to involve, albeit in a variety of ways and to different extents, *a fracturing of meaning*. All three are aware, also, in related, but different and changing ways, that this art they value makes sense only if it is seen as a part, and as a consequence – and, for Clark, as a refusal too – of modernity. Art wants to address someone, Clark claims, 'it wants something precise and extended to do; it wants *resistance*, it needs criteria; it will take risks in order to find them, including the risk of its own dissolution'.[105] This risk-taking is part of what might be called its 'negative dynamic', its reiterated radical rejection of previous conventions and habits, the 'getting away with anything' that Greenberg muses on [Plates 9, 8, 4, 5, 3, and 1].

But the other side of the coin, or piece of paper, is, of course, *the critic making meanings*: speaking for (as) the artist and the artwork.

The two are bound together, as, in Kantian epistemology, are the mind and the world, subject and object – joint conditions of experience, neither one simply the victim, nor the illusion, of the other. The 'only way in which critical viewpoints', Podro notes, 'can become intelligible is through their exercise upon the *complex* objects which form the occasion and purpose of their construction'[106] (my italic). Many sets of related binary terms inform and give form to this subject-object relation played out in criticism, and find a presence in the following chapters: inside/outside; depth/surface; visible/invisible; condensation/displacement; conscious/unconscious; optical/tangible; feeling/meaning; fact/value; fragment/whole; ideology/reality; absence/presence; style/society; painting/beholder; light/dark. Complexity too has many effective synonyms, among them: indeterminacy; 'unfinishedness'; negation; ambiguity; contingency; lack; enigma; opacity; resistance. These terms constitute criticism's rhetorical armoury, along with the chief figurative devices of personification (awarding human qualities to inanimate entities) and objectification (awarding inanimate entities a unified and 'actional' identity).

I set Clark apart from Greenberg and Fried because he alone, of the three, adheres tenaciously to a form of 'ideology critique' dependent upon Marxist categories and assumptions. This is evident in his accounts of paintings by Manet, Picasso, Pollock, and the Abstract Expressionists [Plates 1, 5, and 4]. I will come to Clark's own admission in *Farewell to an Idea* that his 'Marxist determinism' may appear to be – in comparison, perhaps with his earlier studies of Courbet and Manet – what he calls residual.[107] Greenberg and Fried, both familiar with Marxist historical-materialist precepts – the former, at one time, in manifest sympathy with them – in contrast, saw reasons at particular moments in their lives either to reject them, or to fall mostly silent on what significance they might continue to have as part of their critical perspectives.[108] Clark's pessimism concerning the nature and future of capitalist society forms part of what I shall call his understanding of modern art's 'bad complexity'. This stresses fragmentation, alienation, and a pervading scepticism – despite many of his local judgements – over the *possibility* of positive value and meaning in modern art under capitalism. If something of socialism and modernism had both died by the end of the twentieth century, Clark asks at the outset of *Farewell to an Idea*, did that mean 'that in some sense they lived together, in century-long co-dependency?'[109] Clark sees modern art, if not socialism, from its start as 'itself' sceptical of value and meaning, seeking out the edges of things, of understanding . . . It prefers the unfinished: the syntactically unstable, the semantically malformed. It produces and savours discrepancy in what it shows and how it shows it, since the highest wisdom is in knowing that things and pictures do not add up.[110]

In contrast, Raymond Williams, that other heroic complexifier remained – against the odds he calculated himself – a socialist and literary critic committed to what he believed was a wholeness and de-alienation achievable in society, who saw the best of high *and* popular culture as equally important components of 'a whole way of life'.[111]

Writers on art in eighteenth- and nineteenth-century France gave the name *tableau* to the ideal of 'wholeness' and the 'full presence of meaning' in a painting. The term remained, though, partially unexplained and ineffable – this was its own complexity. It was contrasted with the 'morceau', the fragment, which might be brilliantly painted, but which did not, and could not, add up to a finished, legible, whole. Manet's *Le Déjeuner sur l'herbe* and *A Bar at the Folies Bergère* were seen by some critics as examples of this exquisite but essentially fragmentary, unintelligible, painting. The tableau/morceau distinction and judgement will recur, in many other literal and metaphorical guises, in the following chapters. Modernist criticism, I shall argue, *is* the articulation of this division between part and whole, sign and meaning, the visible and invisible, object and subject. Listen to Ernst Cassirer, for instance, declaring in 1918 that the principle of an artwork's 'coherence', as in any scientific inquiry, was to be found in the resolution of the subjective and objective factors. This was a principle

according to which we have some 'totality' of consciousness, perhaps some general cast of mind, from which all factors should be seen to follow . . . In aesthetic feeling a totality of consciousness and its powers is discovered, which is prior to and is a basis for all analysis of consciousness into individual, reciprocally connected propensities. *In each of these two modes of thought the whole with which it is concerned is so seen as not to appear as if put together of its parts, but as if it is itself the source of its parts and the grounds of its concrete determination.*[112] [My italic.]

Are there shades of neo-Impressionist scientism here, in which the *pointillist* dot is revealed to be the true means of showing reality? Shades, too, perhaps of Heidegger's fears of the groundlessness of modern art?

Merleau-Ponty, puzzling away at Cézanne's attempt to paint the means of seeing, asks doubtfully, like Heidegger, after the proof of knowing the truth of what we know [Plate 3]. Could it really be the 'highest point of reason', he speculates, 'to realize that the soil beneath our feet is shifting, to pompously name "interrogation" what is only a persistent state of stupor, to call "research" or "quest" what is only trudging in a circle, to call "Being" that which never fully *is*?'[113] The Latin concept of the *complexum significabile* – 'significant object' – represents an analogous attempt, carrying strong metaphysical connotations, to 'think' the unity of subject and object. Medieval scholars invented the term to try to give substance – meaning – to certain ideas that, though they lacked physical referents, were still considered to be important in the world. For example, it was held that God had 'thought' the existence of the world before the world came into being: its weighty existence *as an idea* in His mind should therefore be recognized.[114] 'Tableau' is a kind of *complexum significabile*, and its achievement in modern art, though inveterately promised, will remain for Clark – though *not* Greenberg or Fried – unrealized. All three *are* believers in modern art's critical complexities, but the 'good complexity' of Greenberg and Fried posits an occluded totality that is the sign, finally, of the sublime, subject-centred, positive, humanist tradition. Clark's 'bad complexity', in contrast, posits an occluded totality that is the sign of contradiction, even incipient meaninglessness; it is subject-*decentred*, '*anti*-humanist', *negating* and *episodic* or 'conjunctural'. It specifically resists the historicist attractions of a notion of enduring 'tradition' and 'evolution' in modern art. Despite this abyss between them, however, Greenberg's, Fried's, and Clark's critical complexities all inherit an enlightenment model of human emancipation metaphorized in aesthetic (that is, critical) sensibility and in modern art.[115] The following chapters might be said to anatomize moments within this metaphoric model.

Consider again Richard Wilson's *20:50* [Plate 9]. *Disorientation* seems to be one of the artist's goals. Wilson had made earlier versions of this installation, which in some fundamental sense really is an *idea* that can be realized in a variety of spaces without loss to that idea's integrity and significance. From Fried's position (which I set out further in Chapter 2) the qualities of this installation, and the presumed intentions of its originator – 'maker' seems problematic when used about an *idea* – put the artwork *beyond*, *after*, and *against* modernism in a fundamental way. Greenberg, Fried, and Clark all decide, though in different ways and for different reasons, that modernism came to some sort of end in the 1960s. This was a matter of *what* the aims of artists became, and *why*, and *how*, they had changed. It was also a matter of a changed culture of writing about art – the Conclusion will explore these changes through a final case study.

Installation art, or that art which Fried in 1967 called 'literalist', is art of an object in a *situation*, and one which, virtually by definition, includes the beholder. *20:50* requires, for example, the presence of a 'beholder' literally physically *in* the work for its purpose to be realized. The 'minimalist' objects created in the mid- and late 1960s had these qualities. Robert Morris, one of Judd's contemporaries, said that this new work took 'relationships out of the work and makes them a function of space, light, and the viewer's field of vision'.[116] Such work Fried condemns as 'theatrical' – his chief term of critical oppro-brium. 'Theatricality' functions within a sequence of terms he mobilizes in order to set *what he calls* modernist art against 'literalism'. 'Presence' is another term Fried also used negatively, though it is rather con-fusingly close to the positive term 'presentness' which he applies to great modernist painting or sculpture. I come to the detail of these terms and their usage in the next two chapters. Fried's fundamental claim is that literal or theatrical art is both part symptom and part cause of 'the sensibility or mode of being' which is 'corrupted or perverted by theater'.[117] It is hard not to see a whole social order indicted here on ethical, if not political, grounds, though Fried stops short of this.

In his *Absorption and Theatricality: Painting and Beholder in the Age of Diderot* (1982), Fried provides a hint that his notion of theatri-cality shares something with Clark's situationist critique of the 'society of the spectacle'. For the philosopher and proto-art critic Denis Diderot, writing before the French Revolution, Fried asserts, the 'object-beholder' relationship, 'the very condition of spectatordom, stands indicted as theatrical, a medium of dislocation and estrangement rather than of absorption, sympathy, self-transcendence'. The future of painting and drama depended, for Diderot, on whether the painter and dramatist would be able 'to undo that state of affairs, to *detheatricalize beholding* and so make it once again a mode of access to truth and conviction'.[118] A parallel social criticism, I believe, permeated Fried's *own* perspective on culture and society around 1967 when he began to use the term theatricality about developments in contemporary art and the wider culture. Greenberg in his early, manifest, political criticism – just before the US entered the Second World War – had claimed that avant-garde culture constituted *then* some kind of desperate work against the forces of capitalism and fascism. Clark continues to hold to this position, though it is combined with no optimism about the society or art of the future *after modernism*. In Chapter 1, I specify further the critical basis for my subsequent accounts of the great modern artists about which Greenberg, Fried, and Clark write.

Modernism's modern art

Figures of subjectivity and meaning in modern art

Greenberg and Fried make what they claim is their 'immediate', 'intuitive', 'undeliberate', and 'involuntary' experiential encounter with
modern paintings the crucible of aesthetic judgement. Yet both tacitly
acknowledge, as I showed in my Introduction, that what goes into this
experience, and what comes out of it, is not finally separable from a
whole world of *other* experiences, values, and interests bound up with
such judgements. Greenberg signals, too, that the process of aesthetic
evaluation is inevitably partly retrospective when he remarks that critics
don't *just* look and judge, but go on to reflect intellectually upon their
experiences of looking and judging. A parallel self-consciousness,
Fried asserts, had become the object of modern painting: Manet paints
his relationship to the world – including his relationship to painting –
and therefore his paintings, like art writing alert to this development,
are themselves kinds of criticism: pictorial criticisms of looking, painting,
thinking, and the wider world[1] [Plate 1]. 'Ambitious' painting and its
similarly ambitious sympathetic criticism become evermore closely
bound up together in the twentieth century – even forming sometimes
what Clark calls a 'collaboration' – in which the critical writing up to
the job, as Fried suggests, is perhaps only a little less important than
the paintings themselves.

The function of this chapter is briefly to elaborate upon the
canon of artists and paintings that Greenberg, Fried, and Clark have
written about, and in relation to which have formulated their accounts
of modern art practice and modernist criticism. This task involves a

preliminary examination of some important interwoven ideas, and an outline of related matters of dispute between these critics. These concern: (1) their use of figurative language; (2) their invocations of subjectivity in modern art and criticism; and (3) the articulation of the relations between subjectivity and their accounts of complexity – aesthetic value – in the paintings under consideration. A striking agreement exists between all three over the primacy of consciousness as subject *and* object in modernism. Greenberg argues, for example, that the 'ultimate source of value or quality in art' is not skill, or 'anything else having to do with execution or performance', but rather 'conception alone'. (He is talking here about artists, but the conceptions of critics can surely not be left out of an analysis of his claim.) Conception has been given other names, Greenberg remarks – intuition, inspiration, invention – but it alone is 'decisive' and is what separates a truly great artist, like Barnett Newman, he asserts, from others who may well be able to imitate the look of his paintings exactly. It was Newman's decision to 'do' those paintings – 'far from easy to conceive', Greenberg observes – in the first place which is the difference, and 'their quality and meaning lies almost entirely in their conception'.[2]

Clark, in the opening pages of *Farewell to an Idea*, places particular emphasis on what he calls modern art's 'distinctive patterning of mental and technical possibilities'.[3] This is a work of self-interrogation and theory: paintings, Clark observes, 'should be cognitive – that is, investigative and totalizing . . . before they are decorative'.[4] Composition in painting – and criticism? – is therefore related to artists' – and critics? – mental composure or self-composition. This is a strong theme in Kantian philosophy: an ethic or ideal of rational freedom is embodied in both self-control and the control of artistic materials. Riegl had expressed the same belief by saying that the artist seeks to create another world which is his [sic] own free creation, to put beside the world which he did not make.[5] The idealism that this yearning represents contributes to the utopianism in modern art which particularly preoccupies Clark. It is figured, 'given form to', as I've explained, in the imag(in)ed totalities metaphorically represented in modern paintings. These totalities or ideals have been given many different names, and linked to various socio-political ideologies, since the late nineteenth century: Body, God, Nature, The People, Sensation, Visual Truth. Totality was also symbolized in mid-nineteenth-century French art writing by the concept of the 'tableau': an ideal wholeness of pictorial composition not simply made up of assembled fragments, but somehow both preceding production as an ideal but also potentially realizable within artistic production, bringing its completion or 'finishedness'. Clark suggests that great modern art yearns for and points to, but aborts time and again the realization of this totality, registering instead its own contingencies and ambiguities. Picasso's Cubism, for example, does *not* constitute a new visual language with which finally to understand the world, though *Ma Jolie* may look like, even 'pretend' to be, such a language. Pollock's drip-paintings, such as *Autumn Rhythm* (1948) or *Number 32, 1950*, in their abstractness may appear to 'cancel' figurative reference entirely or 'multiply' suggestions of figurativeness so as to forestall any single interpretation, but metaphors of 'oneness' inevitably return and drip-paintings come to be read as stable signs of Nature, or – a subset of that category – as Pollock's own bodily nature expressed in paint on canvas[6] [Plates 5 and 4].

Modern art's meanings, therefore, cannot be achieved without the presence and influence of critical language – as well as the subsequent related languages of art history. The pervading metaphors for understanding painting and criticism are generated *within, by*, this use of language. In the analyses of paintings and writings that follow I sometimes draw attention to the *formal mechanics* of this language – its figures of speech and rhetorical modes. At other times I 'look through' this language, as it were, to the world it creates. The former perspective has the purpose of identifying the presence and activity of rhetorical motifs in making a world of meanings for art, while the latter examines the consequences of this construction. If the two perspectives constitute separable forms of attention which I generate in order to make certain points about modern art and modernist criticism, then, in the 'real world' of social practice they have been, and are, bound up together. Signs, in this 'lived' sense – those both visual and verbal – cannot *precede* meaning. A useful parallel may be drawn between criticism and novel writing, which also sets to work a number of devices and conventions in order to invent a convincing world. This comparison is not meant, necessarily, *as a criticism*: art-historical writing is similarly 'fictive' in the sense that its discursive forms also offer contrasting and sometimes compelling ways of understanding the nature, place, and value of artists and artworks.

From my introductory discussion of the writings of Greenberg, Fried, Clark, Merleau-Ponty, Heidegger, and others it is clear that modern art and its explanation has been given extremely high value in philosophical and broad socio-political terms. Modern art, artists, and critics are implicated, and implicate themselves, in questions to do with truth, history, value, meaning, existence, and modernity. The novel form emerged and developed in the eighteenth and nineteenth centuries precisely as an experimental mode of writing that sought to engage seriously and creatively – through its new discursive forms – with all these questions. In the early twentieth century it set about the kind of 'self-criticism' of novelistic conventions that modern art, according to Greenberg, Fried, and Clark, had begun about half a century earlier.[7] Within the historical development of the novel form, therefore, conventions have been subject to radical questioning, testing, and re-formation – but they nevertheless remain indispensable. The same is true of conventions in writing about modern art.

Take the following examples. Look out particularly for the ways in which figures of speech are used here to attribute artists, paintings, and the often unspecified entity 'art' with certain kinds of apparent *intentions*, *capacities*, and *properties*. (I have indicated these attributions with underlinings.)

1   'Art <u>wants</u> to address someone, <u>it wants</u> something precise and extended to do; <u>it wants</u> resistance, <u>it needs</u> criteria; <u>it will</u> take risks in order to find them including the risk of <u>its own</u> dissolution' (Clark).

2   '. . . the essence of modernism resides in <u>its refusal</u> to regard a particular formal "solution", no matter how successful or inspired, as definitive . . . This is tantamount to the realization that if the <u>dialectic of modernism</u> were to come to a halt anywhere once and for all, <u>it would</u> thereby <u>betray itself</u>; that the <u>act of radical self-criticism on which it is founded</u> and by which *it perpetuates itself* can have no end' (Fried).

3   'Realistic, naturalistic <u>art had dissembled</u> the medium, using art to conceal art; <u>Modernism used art</u> to call attention to art. The limitations that constitute the medium of painting – the flat surface, the shape of the support, the properties of the pigment – were treated by the <u>Old Masters</u> as negative factors that could be acknowledged only implicitly or indirectly. <u>Under Modernism these same limitations came to be regarded</u> as positive factors, and <u>were acknowledged</u> openly' (Greenberg).[8]

The rhetorical device of *personification* saturates these statements: the inanimate entities 'art', 'paintings', and 'modernism' – the latter used with or without capital letters – are represented by all three critics as if they were human agents capable of having intentions, desires, needs, and abilities. Greenberg's phrase 'Old Masters' may refer, ambiguously, either to artists *or* artworks, or be read as a conflation of both. At the same time, some of these inanimate entities are represented as having what could be called a *constructed unity*, the components of which, however, are assumed, but not specified. This is the case, for example, with 'modernism' and its extension into another, qualified, constructed unity which Fried calls 'the dialectic of modernism'.

Clark and Fried themselves have commented on the pervasiveness of metaphoric devices in critical language – usually in order to point out what they regard as their misleading use. Sometimes Clark's and Fried's own statements identifying the use, by other writers, of personification and constructed unities ironically actually simultaneously reinstate, *that is, try to capture for their own use*, the same rhetorical figures. This occurs, for example, when Clark observes that most of what he calls '*modernism*'s pronouncements on matter and the production of meaning' have an 'a priori emptiness . . . Of course *modernism* usually vacillated between a crude voluntarism [personification] and an equally crude positivity ("in the nature of materials" and so on)' – 'positivity' here is synonymous with my notion of a constructed unity.[9] The term 'modernism' in Clark's statement here (which I italicize) is itself an effective personification, though one which appears to refer solely to critical writing – 'pronouncements' literally refers to actual speech – rather than to a conflation of such criticism with modern paintings and other materials, such as artists' statements. A much more ambiguous reference occurs, however, when Clark identifies something he calls the 'lyric'. By this he means, he says

> the illusion *in* an artwork of a singular voice or viewpoint, uninterrupted, absolute, laying claim to a world of *its* own . . . *metaphors* of agency, mastery, and self-centredness that enforce our acceptance of the work as the expression of a single *subject*.[10] [My italic.]

It is hard not to see these 'metaphors' (rather than 'pronouncements') as residing both 'in' paintings, such as in Picasso's Cubist or Pollock's drip-painting works [Plates 5 and 4], and 'in' modernist critical and art-historical accounts – including Clark's own. Where, indeed, do the voices 'in' a painting come from? 'Modernism', it should be clear, then, is itself a highly complicated rhetorical device. Its referents shift and collide, conflate and elide in ways that are sometimes intended and at other times unconscious – and, occasionally, merely a trick of the recalcitrance in language, by dint, for example, of the quirks of grammar.

It will become increasingly clear, too, how Greenberg, Fried, and Clark operate with different, sometimes opposed, and sometimes overlapping, senses of what a 'language' actually *is*.

Modernist criticism 'metaphorizes' its objects in a number of variable but always specifiable ways but its primary method is that of turning these objects into a fictive 'person' or 'subjectivity' equipped with a project – that is, a set of aims and objectives – that can be identified, discussed, and evaluated. Modernism's 'Solomon Grundy' subject was born in the mid-nineteenth century, grew and developed – perhaps beyond recognition – then atrophied, and appears to have died by the mid-1960s. Fried and Clark offer more considered views on the causes of the subject's death than Greenberg, and I shall come to these. Fried's concept of theatricality identifies, at the 'time of death', the growing prevalence of a 'corrupting' art he describes, in denigrating fashion, as 'literalist': bent, that is, on creating exploitative 'situations' and manipulating beholders. If Wilson's *20:50* may stand as exemplary of the traits of such literalism then it is because this installation involves a way of 'showing and seeing' the world that rejects and attacks, as far as Fried is concerned, the very moral and aesthetic bases of 'showing and seeing' that the modernist art of painting had erected [Plate 9]. Modernism, for Fried, linked painting's showing and seeing of the world to the task, simultaneously, of manifesting the material means of picturing: a necessarily *medium-specific* activity radically implicating the artist's subjective awareness. This was the basis of modernist painting's 'self-criticism'.[11]

After Manet, according to Merleau-Ponty, modern painters were released to find many other ways of showing the world, but these diverse ways were linked, in that all involved an acknowledgement of the activity of what could be called 'seeing-as-picturing'. Modern art is a history of continuous practice in this sense for Merleau-Ponty, and for Fried after him: its greatest exponents are linked in their knowledge of those before them who had engaged in the same critical and self-critical enterprise. Past great paintings of all ages remain a reservoir of 'sources' for the modern artist, but the psychobiological basis of seeing and picturing with – and from within – the human body remains an intrinsic component. For Merleau-Ponty, for example, Cézanne's paintings such as *Mont Sainte-Victoire* and *Still Life With Water Jug*, manage to 'embody' the kernel of this physicality of/to seeing, using brushes and paint applied to a canvas surface to represent that seeing-from-within-a-body [Plate 3]. Like Heidegger, Merleau-Ponty is engaged in a search for origins, believing that painters from *all* times have a special knowledge, experience, and ability to see and picture from within the body.

The terms 'seeing' and 'visibility' attain, accordingly, a freight of idealist and universalizing connotations within Merleau-Ponty's discourse.

For example, he declares that, in *whatever* civilization painting may have existed from whatever beliefs, motives, or thoughts, no matter what ceremonies surround it – even when it appears devoted to something else – from Lascaux to our time, pure or impure, figurative or not, painting celebrates no other enigma but that of visibility.[12] Notice Merleau-Ponty's use here of the term enigma – complexity in yet another guise! – to describe a phenomenon made possible because of one of the body's sensory faculties. The visibility of things is enigmatic because it is a consequence of all the things that go to make up human embodied-subjectivity. These include a consciousness and self-consciousness of bodily existence. The body, Merleau-Ponty states, 'sees itself seeing'. It is 'visible and sensitive for itself' but it 'is not a self though transparence, like thought, which only thinks its object by assimilating it, by constituting it, by transforming it into thought'. The subject, rather, is 'a self through confusion, narcissism, through inherence of the one who sees in that which he sees, and through inherence of sensing in the sensed – a self, therefore, that is caught up in things, that has a front and a back, a past and a future'.[13] These statements are themselves partly enigmatic, but Merleau-Ponty is pursuing through them the notion that human subjectivity, and visibility, and seeing, and picturing, are febrile, unstable, changing, unreliable things. Look at the lines of Cézanne's trees and mountain tops: they are broken, unsure, tentative, sometimes clear and then indistinct. Is that a branch or a smudge? Consider the apples, only half of which are 'there'; see a jug, clear enough, but notice the thick black lines around the plate and table cloth: what, and where, are they? Why is so much of the canvas 'empty'? In what ways can a painting, or a picture, actually be said to be 'empty'?

It is easy to see why Merleau-Ponty took to Cézanne: his apparently 'shifting views' of objects in the world offer an analogy to the shifting physical nature of looking – the eye in the head in the body moves, therefore the view seen 'moves'. The decline of Renaissance single-point rationalized perspective allows ideas and ideologies of Body and Sensation to breathe, and to feed, and feed off, diverse early twentieth-century notions of 'primitivism' in modern art.[14] Such modern paintings' seeings and picturings are valued by Merleau-Ponty, and a multitude besides, as creative acts of human liberation. An influential 'modernist-humanist' narrative of avant-garde art is erected on this seam of idealism and idealization. But there is a dark side, too: unstable, changing, incarnate avant-garde painting becomes understood, in a different reading, as the corruption, deception, and decadence of specific 'Jewish/Bolshevik' seeing and picturing, the physiological root of which is the 'diseased eye' that Adolf Hitler speculated on in 1937. These competing interpretations indicate that artistic visions and the worlds pictured within them are the subject of multiple, contested ideologies and values. Heidegger's own doubting phenomenology, like Merleau-Ponty's, is searching for answers to questions about the state of the world, as well as to the nature of seeing and the meaning and value of modern art. Van Gogh's shoes, which I discuss in Chapter 5, told another story for Heidegger – lecturing about modern art at almost the same time as Germany's Nazi Chancellor – about 'the truth in painting'.[15]

'World/Nature/Sensation/Subjectivity'[16]

Paintings by Manet, Cézanne, Van Gogh, Picasso, Matisse, Pollock, Rothko, Newman, Louis, Stella, and Noland will serve as my chief examples of great modern art. My 'reverse order' analysis begins in the next chapter with Fried's discussion of 'Post-Painterly' abstract art of the early to mid-1960s – Stella's 'shaped' pictures [Plate 6] and Noland's 'targets', which Fried relates to what he regards as the significant antecedent 'Colour-Field' paintings of Abstract Expressionists, Barnett Newman and Mark Rothko. Movement and style labels such as 'Abstract Expressionism', 'Colour-Field', and 'Post-Painterly' generally tell us more about the influence of certain art-historical narratives than they do about particular artists or artworks. Such terms are perhaps only significant to the extent that they represent victories in a competitive art-historical 'naming' game in which certain players got lucky at certain times, for particular reasons. 'Abstract Expressionist', for example, was a term applied by the critic Robert Coates in 1946 to a number of New York-based artists whom Harold Rosenberg decided, six years later, to call 'action painters'. Greenberg came up with his own rather clumsy name of ' "American-Type" painting' in 1955.[17]

On the whole, Greenberg, Fried, and Clark ignore these generalized nominations and the orthodox 'history of modern art movement' narratives that they instance. All three prefer to focus on specific artists and paintings. Greenberg, unlike Fried and Clark, worked for much of his professional life as a 'jobbing' critic, writing usually short reviews of exhibitions and books. His more discursive, extended, and 'theoretical' essays were relatively few and far between, but are much better known now in academic art history and art practice/theory contexts. These essays tended *not* to include much detailed discussion of particular artists, or paintings and sculptures.[18] In contrast, Fried and Clark work as professional art historians in universities, though Fried was for a time writing regular criticism during the 1960s, in between bouts of academic study and university employment. The terms 'critic' and 'criticism' have a range of meanings linked to this changing professional and institutional history after the Second World War, of which Greenberg's, Fried's, and Clark's writings are a part. Fried's output included early criticism in the conventional sense – reviews of exhibitions by artists and group show catalogue essays – but by the later 1960s US-based art magazines for which he wrote regularly, such as *Artforum*, had become much more intellectually demanding and oriented towards academic debate and publishing interests. All of Fried's and Clark's books have been conventionally 'art-historical' in the sense of being aimed primarily at scholars and students, often published by university presses.[19]

The subtitle to Clark's *Farewell to an Idea*, 'episodes from a history of modernism' – Clark tends to use 'modernism' in the same relatively neutral sense that I use the term 'modern art', that is, to refer to artists and artworks – acknowledges that his study is not some grand totalizing history, but rather a collection of, in some ways, rather disparate essays.[20] Connections between the essays, the first dealing with J.-L. David at the turn of the eighteenth century and the last with 1950s Abstract Expressionist painting, are left mostly implicit – there is no attempt to stitch them together into a single historical narrative. Clark's short introduction, however, offers the means to see their significant interconnection. Modernism, he observes, 'had two great wishes':

> It wanted its audience to be led toward a recognition of the social reality of the sign (away from the comforts of narrative and illusionism, was the claim); but equally it dreamed of turning the sign back to a bedrock of World/Nature/Sensation/Subjectivity which the to and fro of capitalism had all but destroyed. I would be the last to deny that modernism is ultimately to be judged by the passion with which, at certain moments, it imagined what this new signing would be like. Cézanne and Cubism are my touchstones, and Pollock in the world of his drip paintings.[21]

Consider Cézanne's 1904–1906 *The Large Bathers*, along with Picasso's 1911–1912 *Ma Jolie*, and Pollock's 1950 *Number 32, 1950* [Plates 5 and 4]. The first Clark might see as a vision of 'naked intensity in the wood'; *Ma Jolie* perhaps 'the image, the plan . . . of a post-human calculus'; and the drip-painting an artwork 'built out of statistical accumulations of thrown marks, or touch after touch of pure surfaceness, pure sensation'.[22] Their commonality lies in the totality or wholeness of feeling that Clark claims they promise to give image to – be it that of revealed sexual difference in *The Large Bathers*, the 're-materialized' Cubist portrait showing somehow finally the 'reality of seeing', or a revivification of human communication symbolized by Pollock's mark-making. At the same time, however, these paintings act to cancel or undercut their reference to these imagined, ideal wholenesses. In Cézanne's painting facial and body details smear and merge, gestures and dispositions collide, or fade, or thin – notice the woman on the far left has a curiously 'sharpening' torso. The licks of fire in the centre, to which hands reach, apparently 'extinguish' themselves into a mere smudge of colours and bare canvas. These pictures, then, show *represented* worlds not to be fully believed in. The handprints top right in Pollock's *Number 1A, 1948* similarly 'wave' at the viewer, indicating that a tangible, touchable, real world exists, but they remain stranded, annexed, cut off from the pictorial 'body' of other marks with scrambled indexical origins – more scribbled 'writings' without discernable sense.

Merleau-Ponty claims that Cézanne's pictures of Mont Sainte-Victoire materialize the realities of embodied visual perception: the 'world's instant' encapsulated somehow in a painting 'in a way that is different from, but no less energetic than, that of the hard rock above Aix' [Plate 3]. Like Clark, these paintings for Merleau-Ponty point both ways simultaneously – outwards towards a world, and inwards towards themselves as fabricated artefacts. 'Essence and existence, imaginary and real, visible and invisible – a painting mixes up all our categories in laying out its oneiric [dreamlike] universe of carnal essences, of effective likenesses, of mute meanings.'[23] Merleau-Ponty's revealed 'instant' of visible truth finds an echo in Greenberg's and Fried's agreement over their claimed ability to know 'at once' greatness in modern art, of a value revealed to be present *im*mediately – ' "full meaning" . . . most fully revealed at the first fresh glance'. Greenberg adds, though, in his next sentence that this revealed meaning apparently progressively fades (doesn't it?, he directly asks his reader) as 'continued examination destroys the unity of impression'.[24] Greenberg's modernism, this facet of it anyway, involves a form of doubting, a knowing and then – or somehow at the *same* time – knowing that one doesn't know. Paintings and critical appraisal seem to mirror to each other this doubt or scepticism.

Clark, on occasion, calls this scepticism in modern art a form of *contingency* – a courting of ambiguity and ambivalence. A not knowing 'where we stand' in relation to visual representation: an issue Manet problematizes in *A Bar at the Folies Bergère*, where the beholder of the painting is seemingly placed as the 'mirror-image' of the apparently mirror-imaged bourgeois man the waitress is, on the face of it, facing. But this, and the viewer's, position is doubtful: the angles and reflections don't tally, the surface and that scene/seen is uncertain. The artist's world of vision and visibility, Merleau-Ponty remarks, is 'demented because it is complete when it is yet only partial. Painting awakens and carries to its highest pitch a delirium which is vision itself.'[25] The same could be said of the critics' vision, and beyond that, even, potentially *all* beholders, when confronted with modern art's pictorial enigmas. Clark puts it differently: modernism, that is, certain paintings, 'conjure' new pictorial unities out of contingency's flux, presenting, as Cézanne's pictures might appear to do, a turn, or return, to the Body or Nature. But an undermining of meaning goes on at the same time. Who are those people, one a naked woman, in Manet's *Le Déjeuner sur l'herbe*, and what are they doing in that arcadian woodland glade, or is it really a suburban park? The painting, like its depicted subjects, *cannot* add up to a meaningful whole, to totality's tableau.

Or take Picasso's *Fernande* and Matisse's *Blue Nude. Souvenir of Biskra*. Put them next to Manet's *Olympia*. What do we have? Three women? [Plate 1]. Three representations of women, or is that Woman understood as a symbolic category? Or three representations of the portrait and nude genres, or some confusion of these? Or is the latter picture really Manet 'painting his relationship' to women, to Woman, and to Art? These paintings, in their different ways, are all scintillatingly materialistic: physical and about physicality, about surface and skin tone. Look at the panoply of painted and depicted surfaces in *Olympia*, from the sheen of her pillows and sheets to that mass of dark red hair – in illustrations often indistinguishable from the fabric of the screen-wall behind her. Matisse's nude is similarly nuanced. Notice the variety of blue and yellow hatchings on thigh and waist, the blues shimmering, reverberating, in an echo or shadow outside, next, to her body. Meanwhile, *Fernande*'s face, head, neck, and shoulders are themselves all a kind of exploded echo, dissociated fragments yet somehow cohering, dark orange, greens, yellows, and browns of hair and forehead. Body and Woman and Nude are 'conjured' here, but these putative totalities, as we know from contemporary critical reactions, did not provide a full or sufficient intelligibility. *Olympia* scandalized the Salon critics, picturing for them not an ideal of Woman for men, but a kind of unnameable class-specific 'working woman', whose relation to the painting's beholder was begged and nagged: what or who do you, the viewer, who ever you are, think you are consuming here?[26] What place of viewing her image does *Fernande* suggest or require? No actual single place? Well, yes – straight in front of the picture, because it *is* only a picture, not a visual map of some new way of understanding a woman or the world, and certainly not what John Berger wanted Cubism to be – dialectical materialism in painting, no less![27]

Modern artists want some way back, or forward, to the possibility of 'totality', claims Clark. Some of the names for this totality are 'World', 'Nature', 'Sensation', and 'Subjectivity'. Van Gogh's imagined totality might be what Clark calls a 'dream . . . of peasant leisure', something to be communicated directly within the artist's 'new and fully public language'.[28] *The Potato Eaters* might be said to picture an ideal of peasant community, while his now totemic work of Expressionism – another abstracting art-historical nomination – *Sunflowers*, comes to symbolize Sensation, or Nature Materialized. Listen, though, to Heidegger brooding on the intelligibility of modern art, and consider Van Gogh's *A Pair of Shoes* [Plate 2]:

> Is the work ever in itself accessible? To gain access to the work, it would be necessary to remove it from all relations to something other than itself, in order to let its stand on its own for itself alone. But the artist's most peculiar intention already aims in this direction. The work is to be released by him to its pure self-subsistence. It is precisely in great art – and only such art is under consideration here – that the artist remains inconsequential as compared with the work, almost like a passageway that destroys itself in the creative process for the work to emerge . . .[29]

'Pure subsistence'? The artist as a self-destroying 'passageway'? The security of the category of 'great art'? Heidegger manages to put his finger here on two modernist-critical axioms. First, that a modern painting deemed great somehow achieves a radical autonomy of meaning and value – freedom from its producer, and from the modest role of showing how a portion of the world looks. Second, that a canon of artefacts manage to deliver themselves as the realization and embodiment of this greatness in art. Heidegger's reading of (the 'owner' of) the shoes proposes, too, a very different meaning for the peasant in modern society, though dispute continues over his interpretation, and over the meaning and purpose of interpretation as the central art-critical and art-historical practice.[30] Whose 'shoes' are these? Whose painting is this? Whose interpretation is this? These disputes over ownership and authorship will be invoked throughout my study.

Clark also devotes an essay in *Farewell to an Idea* to the totality given the names of 'the People . . . the Party . . . the Plan'. He considers paintings by Kasimir Malevich, El Lissitzky, and other artists with socialist sympathies working in Russia after the Bolshevik revolution in 1917.[31] Totality in its various forms stands, then, for a dream, vision, or projection of unalienated wholeness – a promised plenitude of human existence seeking adequate visual representation. Such utopianism in modern art, Clark notes, breeds both exhilaration and despair, for neither a single painting, nor painting as a practice, in the end can manage to deliver such a plenitude. Hegel's 'unhappy consciousness' – the soul of man longing for union with God – metaphorically looms in Clark's understanding of the key 'episodes' in modern art's dreamings, and the exhilaration of its formal inventiveness subtends an underbelly of nihilism. Pollock's drip-paintings represent for Clark this mix of 'annihilation and totality', full of 'fierceness and sensuousness', torn between the exhilaration and the despair.[32] But it is to Fried's account of abstract artists working 'after' Pollock that I now turn.

Conviction, consciousness, and convention

If Clark stresses doubt and scepticism as the chief products of modern art's self-criticism then Fried, in contrast, emphasizes affirmation and belief in the value of certain artworks. This is true in all his accounts of the modern artists he designates as great. But artist *and* critic are both risk takers in Fried's understanding of the decision-making process over what to do, and what to say about what has been done in painting. Let me underscore the reflexivity of this process, in case the idealist conceit resurfaces that aesthetic judgement begins and concludes in an unmediated revelatory instant. *Both* the artist and the critic have to decide, deliberate, that a judgement over what to do, and what to say about what is done in painting, is right: that's where the 'conviction' – perhaps Fried's key approbatory term – comes in, and because more doing and judging will follow. Consider Louis's *Alpha-Phi* (1961) [Plate 8] and Noland's *Gift*. Remember the *size* of these paintings: Louis's is 'landscape'-shaped, about 2.5 metres by 4.5 metres, while Noland's is smaller, at just under 2 metres, and a perfect square.

Fried's argot of 'conviction' and 'feeling' is tied to the literal physical significance that relatively large-size paintings embody, although a large size in itself is no guarantee of anything, and certainly not high quality or value as far as Fried is concerned. The viewer's place in physical proximity to such paintings is also an influential factor. While one must stand relatively close to an 'easel'-size painting to have a sense of seeing everything on its surface in reasonable detail – while also seeing the artefact as a whole entity – large-size works bring a sense of being 'adequately' viewable from much further back, so that the painting's 'image' to the eye can actually appear quite small. The sheer physical significance of a large painting begins to be felt as one moves into its physical 'shadow', and as one moves further and further towards – 'into', it feels like – a section of the painting, and its extension beyond, around, and above, your own viewpoint and body becomes more emphatically felt.

The ways in which paintings as physical objects literally 'face' the viewer, and appear more or less 'striking' in their 'facingness' are an important aspect in Fried's much more recent discussion of Manet's art. The painting as artefact has a range of simultaneous referential objects, all of which are interlinked. As *index* the painting is 'of' the artist who produced it. As *sign* it exists to face a beholder or group of beholders. The artist becomes, too, one of the painting's beholders. These relations of production and reception or beholding, at once physical, social, intellectual, and moral for Fried, constitute the subject matter for modernism's self-criticism. The continuity of this self-criticism – 'painting consciousness' – is what links Manet to Pollock, and to Louis and Noland, among others, whose 'successful' paintings, for Fried, somehow achieve this 'conviction' in formal terms. Certain terms recur in Fried's lexicon of affirmative judgements, for example, Fried declares, what Noland found

> when he discovered the center of the canvas was nothing less than how to make paintings in whose quality and significance he could believe and this was not something he can be said to have had a choice about [why not?]. We are speaking here of modernist painting as a special kind of cognitive enterprise, one whose success, in fact whose existence, depends on the discovery of conventions capable of eliciting conviction – or at least of dissolving certain kinds of doubts.[33]

Noland believes these paintings are 'right', according to Fried, and Fried confirms this judgement. 'Conviction' connotes several different but overlapping meanings: (1) beliefs as principles; (2) truths confirmed by empirical experience; and (3) 'rightness' as a matter of both visual composition and moral judgement. The metaphors of litigation here are inescapable! Persuasiveness of case, the production of telling evidence, the matter of 'previous convictions considered', etc. 'Convictions' in court are also judgements that become, in their enunciation, 'fact': the truth, 'the whole truth, and nothing but the truth'. Discussion of the 'laws' of modernism recurs in the following chapters – metaphor is inescapable in criticism, as it is in any kind of writing.

In his judgements on abstract painting in the 1960s there is a way in which Fried's metaphoric armoury centres fundamentally on the crime-thriller 'whodunnit?' question: where is the artist 'in' these works, and how does the artist find a presence in pictures the formal aridity and sparseness of which can make Pollock's drip-paintings seem fecundly naturalistic and autobiographical? This was not, however, a new problem for either abstract artists in the 1960s or for those earlier critics, such as Clive Bell, who have retrospectively attracted the designation 'modernist'. The 'pure work' for Mallarmé in the 1870s, as Fried notes, implied the 'elocutionary disappearance' of the poet, 'who yields place to the words, mobilized by the shock of their inequality; they take light from mutual reflection, like an actual trail of fire over precious stones, replacing the old lyric afflatus or the enthusiastic personal direction of the phrase'.[34] Any authorial bodily reference or expressive indexicality seem absent from Stella's concentric lines in *Six Mile Bottom* (1960), as well as from Louis's parenthetical pourings in *Alpha-Phi*, which seem to ebb away out of the pictorial field altogether [Plates 6 and 8]. Significant antecedent visual-conventional sources for Stella's paintings, for Fried, include 'hard-edge' works by Newman – and he appears, like Greenberg, to be wholly uninterested in these artists' own spoken and written accounts of the significance of their pictures.[35]

Louis, according to Fried, for instance, was careful not to let his 'hand, wrist, and arm' get 'into' the picture in 'what he felt was the wrong way'. Fried's comment strongly suggests a reaction against the use of painterly devices that had enabled Pollock to place indexical traces of his body in his drip-paintings.[36] More than this, Fried claims that Louis had an imagination that was itself 'radically abstract', in such a way, Fried remarks, that bore comparison with no other modernist painter 'except perhaps' Matisse.[37] Cool intellectual hedonism that! Fried's critical language seeks out terms that, though seemingly offered as searchingly descriptive, contain ineffable judgements, and as such are impossible to match, via the normal comparative evidence of looking anyway, with what can be 'seen'. This is another way of saying, as Greenberg stated directly on one occasion (see Introduction, p. 31), that only those who 'see' *relevantly* and with the appropriate 'reflection' on their experience, can know where the art of high quality really is. Noland, along with Jules Olitski, are primarily 'painters of feeling', Fried declares, and though their pictures manifest the 'highest order' of what he calls 'formal intelligence', it is 'the depth and sweep of feeling which this intelligence makes possible'.[38] (Contrast this claim when considering Fredric Jameson's characterization of the 'postmodern' in art and culture as a 'waning of affect', brought about as part of what post-structuralist philosophy calls the 'death of the subject'. I return to this theme in the Conclusion.)[39]

Noland's and Olitski's paintings generate this quality of 'feeling' within a kind of dialectic with aesthetico-philosophical criticism. The 'collaboration' metaphor returns here, then, with pictorial 'resolution' – another legalism – as the desired end. Fried posits modernist painting's dynamic as a 'conflict' between 'material substance' (paint) and a 'material entity' (the picture support):

> It is a conflict in which the ultimate condition for the existence of painting in the world (that there be paint) is held against the ultimate condition for the existence of the world itself (that there be objects). Philosophy asked: What is an object of art? Now painting asks: Why should a painting be *of* an object at all, why can't color escape objects altogether?[40]

Fried's question is rhetorical. Painting and colour *have* escaped the role of depicting objects. This was not a development in modern art that had to wait until the 1960s, but Fried suggests that Olitski in particular has pushed modernism to a kind of limit – Olitski is 'the most highly evolved modernist we have'. Olitski exemplifies Greenberg's dictum quoted earlier that one can get away with anything in painting so long as the result is a good painting. Along with Manet, that is, Noland and Olitski are capable of making good paintings by virtue of '*how* not *what*'. A 'good painting' is good because of 'the way the artist painted it' and such excellence in art 'exists apart from style, depiction or any quality that can be put into words'.[41] These words of conviction and feeling, however, come from Fried's book on Manet, whose paintings I turn to now.

'Modernism' versus 'avant-garde'

Fried cites, in support of this claim that great art is about *how* not *what*, a statement the critic George Moore made in 1898 that Manet had been 'born a painter as absolutely as any man who ever lived'. Manet's intelligence, Moore continued, had never got in the way of his desire to 'put anything into his picture except good painting'.[42] This formulation is quite close to Fried's own, made in 1965, on Noland and Olitski quoted above (see note 38). Modern painters, that is, can potentially make great paintings out of *anything* – and certainly without having to depict and colour objects naturalistically. Manet's supercession of genre classifications, in pictures such as *Le Déjeuner sur l'herbe*, indicated this ability. Like his *The Angels at the Tomb of Christ* (1864), *Le Déjeuner sur l'herbe* 'crosses' genre in the way Clark claims that Pollock's paintings multiply metaphor. It is, at once and neither, a landscape, a still-life, a nude, and more – I consider Fried's account in some detail in my final chapter. This crossing and fusing of genre led to adverse, if intrigued, contemporary critical reaction: the painting was seen as enigmatic, well-painted in parts certainly, but not 'adding up' to any unified whole or totality. It contains no genuine tableau. Many of the words Fried uses about *The Angels at the Tomb of Christ* could be applied equally to how *Le Déjeuner sur l'herbe* was seen. It is 'incomprehensible, provocative, crudely drawn, hastily painted, in short, conceived and executed with blatant disregard for accepted norms of intellectual decorum, pictorial coherence, and technical competence'.[43]

In this it is 'of' the artist who painted it much more than it is 'of' any landscape, or still-life, or nude. The modern artist, Mallarmé had recognized, was becoming more and more the source of the work and origin of the work's 'meaning' – whatever that might be supposed to be. The producer, this development entailed, was as likely to be subject to castigation as his production would be if the latter was declared to be meaningless or shocking. Painter and painting were thus conjoined in an entirely novel way, and Manet particularly, according to Mallarmé, 'followed a . . . divergent course, seeking the truth, and loving it when found, because being true it was so strange, especially when compared with old and worn-out ideals of it'.[44] 'Conviction' and 'truth' are highly congruent if not synonymous terms in these uses, and they testify to the quality of *moral* questioning Fried will credit great modern art with, although the term 'moral' remains largely abstract and unexplored in his 1960s criticism. If Fried asserts the idea of 1860s French painting, especially Manet's, 'facing up' to – that is, challenging – the beholder, rather than offering the 'flatness' read by Greenberg, and later Rosalind Krauss, as a sign of modernism's seeming amoral 'opticality', then it must be because this painting's conviction, feeling, and search for truth is, in some way, inescapably moral.[45] If Clark has his own critique of at least a portion of Fried's account of modernism, then Fried also has his of Greenberg's. The doctrine of 'opticality' and its function in the aesthetic and social significance attributed to Impressionist painting by Greenberg and others is subject to particular attack by Fried. This is part of a broader retrospective critique Fried mounts of Greenberg's theorization of modernism as a whole. I discuss elements of this in the following chapters.

If 'moral', then Fried's notion of modernist 'conviction' and the search for truth must have socio-political implications too. *Olympia* and *A Bar at the Folies Bergère*, indeed, have become overloaded with such art-historical pathologies; both paintings have come to stand emblematically for various kinds of social history of art forensics focused on class and gender politics in late nineteenth-century Paris[46] [Plate 1]. Along with *Le Déjeuner sur l'herbe*, these paintings have all become seen as paradigmatic representations of modern life, modernity, and modernism. Though Gustave Courbet is usually credited with a crucial antecedent role in this development in French painting, it is the generation of Manet and the Impressionists who are responsible for what Robert L. Herbert, for instance, calls a 'casting out of history', and whose scenes of contemporary city and suburban life bring about a 'purification', a 'wrenching of art into the present'.[47] Arnold Hauser is definitive on the broad socio-political ramifications of the demise of the observance of genre hierarchy in modern art. Concentration in modern painting on portraits (for instance, the model in *Olympia*, the barmaid and male customer in *A Bar at the Folies Bergère*), and on pastoral and still-life scenes (*Le Déjeuner sur l'herbe* manages to suggest both) indicates the emergence, for Hauser, of a novel 'impressionistic psychology' leading to a 'new conception of psychological probability'.[48] These paintings both reflect and constitute modernity's re-ordering of human subjectivities, actions, and interactions. Fried and Clark would not demur, I imagine, from the broad tenor of this assessment. What it leaves out, of course, is the modernist critics' arguments defending the aesthetic value of these representations. Manet's paintings, Fried claims, apart from anything else, represent the artist's sense of relation to the world around him: *his* actions and interactions as a painter as well as, bound up with, those as a man. According to Fried, too, one of the interactions that particularly preoccupies Manet's painting – and subsequent great modern art – is the status of those beholding his paintings, and the new social relationships that are a part of that beholding.

Hauser claims that an even more profound development is set in train by the effective eradication of any hierarchy *within* the genres of a particular art, and of any *between* the arts.[49] This is an historical process that occurs over a period of perhaps eighty or a hundred years (roughly 1820–1900). Its result is that Van Gogh's *Sunflowers* (1888) and Cézanne's *Still-Life with Water Jug* (1892–1893) – 'lower' genre subject matter in earlier times – may eventually come to be seen as among the greatest works of modern art, peerlessly expressive 'of' their producers' unique 'artistic' visions and temperaments. Of course, there is more than a whiff of teleology in my 'eventually' here – for what I am trying to emphasize again are the retrodictively validating art-historical mechanisms to which the careers and oeuvres of the canonical artists get entrusted. The eradication of genre hierarchy is also both part symptom and cause of the decline of the power of state institutions for selecting and training artists, accrediting their 'professional' status or adequacy, and organising the exhibition and purchase of their works. This decline results in the obliteration of the distinction between what Hauser calls 'aesthetic orthodoxy and unorthodoxy'.[50] 'Art can get away with anything because there is nothing to tell us what it cannot get away with', remarked Greenberg.[51] Orthodoxy doesn't go away, however: it, too, becomes much more a matter of retrospective selection and validation. New forms of control and exclusion develop in the art schools, universities, galleries, museums, and government cultural funding agencies of nation-states in the twentieth century.[52] 'Modernist art theory' was itself an offspring of this process – Greenberg's 'Modernist Painting' essay, along with Fried's 1965 *Three American Painters* catalogue and 1967 'Art and Objecthood' essay became its core curriculum by the early 1970s – representing, curiously, both modernist criticism's apogee as an explanatory discourse, and somehow, at the same time (in retrospect!) a tacit intimation of its demise.[53]

Now that genre hierarchy and aesthetic orthodoxy appear to be done away with, Hauser concludes, something approaching what he calls a 'democracy' of artistic life comes into being.[54] Once 'academies', 'salons', and 'schools' are things of the past, art history will begin to populate its conceptual terrain with modern art 'movements', 'groups', and 'avant-gardes'. And its overarching nomination is 'Modernism' – which, in this capitalized usage, is converted into an abstract and inert art-historical 'period' or 'epoch', able to hold its own with all the other neutral-sounding period terms, as part of the familiar sequential litany: 'Renaissance, Mannerism, Baroque, Rococo, Neo-Classicism, Realism, Modernism'. More 'convictions' – that is, judgements – turned into fact! I will have more to say on the positive and negative meanings of Hauser's word 'democracy' later in this book, because, for example, Greenberg's 1939 defence of what he then called 'avant-garde culture' – not 'avant-garde *art*' – turns importantly on what he wants 'democracy' to signify, in the context of impending war in Europe and the implications of fascism and capitalism for the future of art.[55] The question of democracy, and its relations to post-Second World War advanced capitalism, is surely also pertinent to any attempt to make real sense of Fried's attack on the corrupting 'theatricality' and 'literalism' of art and culture in the late 1960s. I return to this issue in Chapter 2.

It is 'modernism', however – not 'avant-garde art' – which by 1960 becomes Greenberg's preferred term for the tradition of artists, art-making, and criticism he had spent the previous twenty years writing about. The clearly retrospective tone to 'Modernist Painting' indicates that Greenberg is pretty happy to see, and help, his object of attention become *historical*, and consequently safely art-historical. The millenarian flavour to his essay is bound up with this desire, for when things are 'history' it means, apart from anything else, that they are, in some sense *over*, *finished*. 'Modernist art ... takes its place', Greenberg concludes in his essay's penultimate paragraph, in what he calls the 'intelligible continuity of taste and tradition' which is art's enduring history. He may have had a sense of some personal and professional conclusion around the time of the commission, writing, and delivering of this talk for US government radio later to be published in numerous journals and books. Pollock, a friend in earlier times and himself becoming 'canonical' by 1960, had quite recently died.[56] 'Modernism' in Greenberg's essay, and in almost all of Fried's studies, is a term stripped of the sharp political connotations that 'avant-garde' still attracts. In one sense, 'modernism' became preferred too because, by the 1960s, it also didn't carry the negative connotations of the derivative apophthegm 'avant-gard*ism*', then coming into usage to suggest an inauthentic or delusional playing with radicalism, a mere show of 'bohemian' attitudes and dispositions of 'rejection' or 'opposition' to bourgeois society.[57] Only some of the artists by then 'canonically modernist' had understood their works to be avant-garde in any dissident political sense, and for many of those the rejection of bourgeois society anyway involved self-imposed 'exile' of various kinds, *not* a continuous confrontation of, or attempt to change, society through art or anything else.[58]

By the early 1950s, too, a revulsion against orthodox political activity *but also against both contemporary capitalist and Soviet state-socialist society* had taken place among artists in the US, evident in some of the statements by Abstract Expressionist painters (see Introduction, p. 27). This development was linked to the fortunes and failures of the American socialist left during the 1930s, the impact of revelations concerning the purges in the USSR under Stalin, and the resurgence of state-sponsored anti-communism in the period after 1945.[59] There were exceptions to this reaction against artists' involvement in political activism – Ben Shahn, for instance – and Greenberg himself continued to write about art, capitalism, and socialism in the period after the Second World War, for instance in his long and now almost unknown essay 'The Plight of Culture', published in the magazine *Commentary* in 1953.[60] But Pollock's *Number 32, 1950* (1950) [Plate 4], Newman's *Adam* (1951–1952), and Rothko's *Light Red Over Black* (1957), if they can be said to image putative 'worlds', or project new visual 'languages', do so within a rigorous regime that excludes the depiction of objects and narratives from any recognizable human environment. The meanings these pictures might convey, or suggest, that is, are necessarily based on a kind of ellipsis: a 'leaving out' of depicted human things and situations still represented, if obtusely, in most earlier modern art. This returns me to the problematic of complexity – modern painting's representation of occluded totalities: fragments torn from, 'of', and alluding to, an imagined or lost ideal wholeness. Standard art-historical accounts of Rothko and Newman remain awash with this kind of, usually, metaphysical interpretation, and some of the artists themselves said enough to provoke and confirm this reading.[61]

Pollock's drip-paintings, Clark claims, work to block as much as they might promote this rampant 'metaphorizing', though it is inevitable, he decides, that such 'reading in' takes place – abstract art's 'annihilating and totalizing', Pollock's included, is asking for it.[62] Fried and Greenberg have a different stance, as well as some differences between them. The critic who might be called the '"post-political" Greenberg' – that is, Greenberg after the 1940 essay 'Towards a Newer Laocoon' – represents modernist painting as a tradition of positive achievements and ever-advancing formal developments stripping the medium down to the bare bones of its material conditions and means. Clark's 'negations' and 'failures' make no sense at all in this purview – these embarrassing terms, like Clark's sleeve-worn Marxism, belong to 'avant-garde', not 'modernism'. By '"post-political" Greenberg' I mean the critic who jettisons his previously declared socialist and Marxist sympathies, *not* the Greenberg who will candidly note the links between modern art after 1945 and US economic, political, and military power in the world. Essays such as 'The Decline in Cubism' (1948), 'The Situation at the Moment' (1948), and '"American-Type" Painting' (1955) indicate eloquently enough Greenberg's continuing sense of how a new world *and* pictorial order had emerged together.

Finally, consider Greenberg much earlier on (1940), and then in contrast, to Fried (1965):

> It was to be the task of the avant-garde to perform in opposition to bourgeois society the function of finding new and adequate cultural forms for the expression of the same society, without at the same time succumbing to its ideological divisions and its refusal to permit the arts to be their own justification. The avant-garde, both child and negation of Romanticism, becomes the embodiment of art's instinct of self-preservation. It is interested in, and feels itself responsible to, only the values of art; and given society as it is, has an organic sense of what is good and what is bad for art.[63]
>
> (Greenberg)

> ... modernist art in this [twentieth] century finished what society in the nineteenth began: the alienation of the artist from the general preoccupations of the culture in which he is embedded, and the prizing loose of art itself from the concerns, aims, and ideals of that culture. With the achievements of Cubism in the first and second decades of this century, if not before, painting and sculpture became free to pursue concerns intrinsic to themselves. This meant that it was now possible to conceive of stylistic change in terms of the decisions of individual artists to engage with particular formal problems thrown up by the art of the recent past, and in fact the fundamentally Hegelian conception of art history at work in the writings of Wölfflin and Greenberg, whatever its limitations when applied to the art of the more distant past, seems particularly well-suited to the actual development of modernism in the visual arts, painting especially.[64]
>
> (Fried)

If abstract paintings by Louis, Stella, Noland, and Olitski abandon the use of colour in the depiction of objects – in fact, abandon the depiction of objects altogether – then it is also true that Fried abandons the mention of certain referents still present in Greenberg's 'transitional' essay from twenty-five years earlier. Exchange Greenberg's 'opposition to bourgeois society' and 'ideological divisions' for Fried's 'general preoccupations of the culture' and 'the concerns, aims, and ideals of that culture'! That, finally, is the journey from avant-garde to modernist painting. In Chapter 2, I examine Fried's account of the artists and paintings he thought marked the climax of this journey, as I begin to write my way back to modernism's modern art.

Pure formality

1960s abstract painting

Art Fiction Five

A   'It's just colours, isn't it? On very large canvasses. I mean the size
     of them is meant to . . . well, impress you, but there isn't anything
     else there, is there?'
     Z   'How come you keep asking questions which suggest you
          want to find something out but at the same time you are just
          endlessly dismissive and cynical?'
A   'I don't think that's fair. I just don't know what to say – or what to
     see either. Or how to behave in the gallery for that matter. You seem
     to know all the etiquette.'
     Z   'It isn't anything to do with "etiquette" – that's just another
          of your disguised putdowns. All I know is that I want to
          find out about these pictures and you need an open mind to
          do that. But I haven't already judged the art in advance like
          you have.'
A   'I haven't "already judged" it! I don't know what I'm supposed to
     even do to start looking at it!'
     Z   'You just look. That's a start. And maybe think about the
          titles – they're obviously there for a purpose. "Adam", for
          instance. Now what does that suggest to you?'
A   'Well, Adam is in the Bible, isn't he? Adam and Eve. The Garden
     of Eden, Satan and sin, I suppose. But how does that help looking
     at that slightly wavy brown stripe?'

Z   'The title doesn't tell us what's in the painting, does it? It's not a picture of Adam, is it? So perhaps it has a symbolic meaning instead.'

A   'What do you mean "symbolic"?'

Z   'That the title alludes to something not shown that might help us to make sense of what we see. It is just brown and red paint in a few bands but it might have a meaning to it.'

A   'Well presumably the artist knew what it meant, didn't he? Artists must know what they're doing, or no one else will, will they?'

Z   'Well, before modernism artists were given commissions, weren't they? Told what to paint. It was the way they did it that made their paintings interesting. But after Manet artists could do whatever they wanted – nobody told them what to do.'

A   'Is that why art became abstract, then? Because they had nothing to paint anymore?'

Z   'They did have things to paint – symbolic things. It's just harder for us to know what the meanings are.'

A   'What about critics? What's his name – Greenberg. He wrote about Newman, didn't he?'

Z   'Indeed. He had a whole theory of modernist painting. And then Michael Fried developed one.'

A   'So critics became the explainers of abstract painting, then?'

Re: form

Looking at early 1960s paintings by Louis, Stella, and Noland I think it is fairly easy to see why these artworks might attract the negative label 'formalist' [Plates 8 and 6]. They are just paint on canvas, aren't they? Louis simply pours some acrylic colours down each side of an otherwise 'empty' canvas. Stella presents an otherwise apparently undifferentiated grey canvas punctuated by a series of concentric black lines which echo the indented shape of the painting and meet in a central black oblong bar. Noland positions a round 'target' form of white, blue, and two tones of brown acrylic on a yellow background of square canvas. Their titles – 'Alpha-Phi', 'Six-Mile Bottom', 'Gift' – at first reading, don't help much. They may contain references that have some personal significance for a particular viewer, but without further knowledge of their possible significance as far as the artists were concerned they seem random – if, in terms of their own literary abstractness, perhaps somewhat pretentious. These paintings might then pejoratively be called 'formalist' meaning they seem empty of significant meaning, having no recognizable or interesting 'subject matter' or 'content'. That is to say, they are *merely* coloured shapes and patterns. If one was to conclude this, then all further questions or observations concerning the character of these paintings – or the reasons why their producers bothered to make them, and why critics such as Fried bothered to write about them – might appear redundant.

Fried discusses problems to do with notions of 'formalism' and the 'formal critic' in retrospective comments published in his introduction to *Art and Objecthood*. From its origins as a term initially used in his 1965 catalogue essay *Three American Painters* to describe criticism that wanted to identify its interests as 'formal' – concerned, that is, with 'visual form' in abstract painting – the label 'formalist' began to be applied, with both good and bad connotations, to works being made by a group of artists at the time that Fried's essays were themselves being written.[1] I have mentioned that Fried became particularly friendly with Stella and Caro and will return to the question of the significance of these relationships for his criticism later in this chapter. Fried describes his involvement with these and other artists via critical exchange, involvement in curatorial activities, and other forms of intellectual and social interaction. If not actually 'collaborative' in the sense of an organized, consciously planned project of work, these relationships, for Fried – then a man still in his early twenties – were clearly highly formative.[2] But if Fried's conception of modernism was constituted partly on the basis of this interaction and friendship with certain painters and sculptors in the early and mid-1960s, then he acknowledges that his movement *away* from interaction and friendship with Greenberg also played an important part.

Fried's original evaluation of paintings by Stella, Noland, and Olitski – as well as his 1998 review of this evaluation – is intrinsically bound up with a loosening of intellectual ties with his critical 'father figure'. Developments in Fried's assessment of Greenberg's understanding of modernism can also be identified in his discussion of other already established artists whose paintings were examples of what Greenberg in 1964 had dubbed 'Post Painterly abstraction': these artists might be identified, then, as Fried's 'Jackson Pollock', 'Barnett Newman', and 'Morris Louis'[3] [Plates 4 and 8]. Another facet of Fried's appraisal of Greenberg's ideas was developed, indirectly, through his attack on those artists he called the 'literalists', better known in art history as the 'Minimalists'.[4] However, the crux of Fried's dispute with Greenberg is really to do with the meaning of 'modernist self-criticism'. In one sense Fried wants radically to redefine the term self-criticism – that is, uncouple it from a usage by Greenberg that Fried claims fundamentally reduces its value as a means to explain how artists, historically, have viewed past art, and how they decide to act on these views in their own practice. Fried's manoeuvre, in effect if not in intention, depicts Greenberg, pejoratively, as a 'formalist' who crudely construes the relations between artists and artworks and relies on confusing and inappropriate figures of speech. Bear in mind, however, what *alternative* metaphors Fried will himself offer.

Modernist painting is 'self-critical', Greenberg claims in his essay of that title, in that it draws attention to its formal conditions and means. Painting understood both as a collective practice carried out over a period of time and *actual* paintings – for instance Manet's *Le Déjeuner sur l'herbe* and Newman's *Adam* – 'used art to draw attention to art'. The 'task of self-criticism became', Greenberg asserts, 'to eliminate from the specific effects of each art any and every effect that might conceivably be borrowed from or by the medium of any other art'.[5] Note but ignore for the time-being the personifications and constructed unities here that I pointed out in the previous chapter, as well as Greenberg's later remark in the same essay that this 'self-criticism' is 'spontaneous' and carried out in a 'largely subliminal way' – that is, that the artists themselves are not, and seemingly *cannot* be, aware of their art being 'self-critical'.[6] Greenberg's definitive paragraph on visual form follows immediately after his assertion that Manet's were the 'first modernist pictures' by virtue of the way his paintings 'frankly' declared their flat surfaces:

> It was the stressing of the ineluctable flatness of the surface that remained ... more fundamental than anything else to the processes by which pictorial art criticized and defined itself under Modernism. For flatness alone was unique and exclusive to pictorial art. The enclosing shape of the picture was a limiting condition, or norm, that was shared with the art of the theater; color was a norm and a means shared not only with the theater, but also with sculpture. Because flatness was the only condition painting shared with no other art, Modernist painting oriented itself to flatness as it did to nothing else.[7]

Greenberg restated this position two years later in his essay 'After Abstract Expressionism'. Here he includes some terse qualifications that may have helped to trigger Fried's critical reaction. Remember also that Fried, at this time, is beginning to associate himself with artists 'after' Abstract Expressionism, and wanted to define this 'afterness' in his own way. Self-criticism in painting, Greenberg says, is an attempt to determine 'the irreducible working essence of art'. This 'essence', he claims, 'consists in but two constitutive conventions or norms: flatness and the delimitation of flatness'.[8] 'Delimitation' here suggests both a 'marking' – *delineation* – as well as a 'fixing of boundaries'. In this statement Greenberg conflates two categorically distinct things. First, 'flatness' meaning literally the physical character of a stretched support, which in this sense is not actually a 'convention' or 'norm' at all, but rather a *condition* – though the agreement made to carry on painting on such stretched flat supports could be called a convention, or indeed the agreement to carry on making these stretched flat supports for painting on. Second, 'flatness' meaning the marking – metaphorically, a 'fixing of boundaries' – of the canvas *in such a way* as to draw the viewer's attention to the physical condition of flatness. This marking might be done either intentionally (that is, 'self-critically' or 'self-consciously') or unintentionally.

Fried is unhappy with Greenberg's use of the term 'essence', especially, I suggest, because he conflates – at best confuses – these two separate and separable aspects to painting. Fried adamantly stated in his *Three American Painters* catalogue essay, agreeing on this with Greenberg, that modern painting's 'evolution' has been *away* from 'considerations of subject matter toward an ever more exclusive preoccupation with problems and issues intrinsic to the art'. However, in retrospect Fried identifies major problems with this idea of 'intrinsic'.[9] The 'essence of painting', Fried had declared in his 1980s exchange with Clark, though he was then quoting an earlier statement he had made, 'is not something irreducible. Rather, [it is] the task of the modernist painter . . . to discover those conventions which, *at a given moment*, alone are capable of establishing his work's identity as painting'[10] (my italic). In his accounts of Stella, Noland, and Olitski, for instance, Fried identifies *shape*, *colour*, and *facture* as newly isolated and significant conventions within these artists' paintings. I shall come to these shortly. Fried regards the identification of such features, by certain artists at certain times, as no less than the key to asserting what he calls modernist painting's 'nontrivial' identity. Contemporary artists sift *what might become* such significant conventions from their observation of recent modernist art – thus potentially giving earlier art new significance by highlighting these conventions in their own paintings. Pollock's drip-paintings, for instance, Fried claims, have had this regenerative value since the 1950s, as later so-called 'Colour-Field' paintings – such as those by Newman and Rothko – have enacted a 'continual reinterpretation' of Pollock's 1947–1950 works, as well as confirmed the value of those Pollock paintings as 'the fountainhead of an entire tradition of modernist painting'.[11]

Fried remarks that what his critique of Greenberg's idea of essence amounts to is *not* a rejection of the belief that certain norms or conventions are intrinsic to painting. Flatness and the delimitation of flatness are, he says, 'something like the *minimal conditions for something's being seen as a painting*'[12] (Fried's italic). Rather, he chooses to place emphasis on the shifting significance of these conventions as far as modernist artists are concerned. At different moments in modernism's history certain conventions, that is, have been isolated, re-understood, and made newly significant: they have been put to work as a 'compelling conviction', and thus have produced successful paintings. Fried calls this recognition an attempt to 'historicize the concept of essence'. In order to underline its importance he draws on a statement about the nature of language taken from Wittgenstein:

> If you talk about *essence* . . . you are merely noting a convention. But here one would like to retort: there is no greater difference than that between a proposition about the depth of the essence and one about – a mere convention. But what if I reply: to the *depth* that we see in the essence there corresponds the *deep* need for the convention.[13]

Newman and Rothko, for instance, might be said to exhibit a 'deep need' to reject the convention of 'gestural-painterliness' evident in Pollock's drip-paintings – a rejection that Stella, Noland, and Olitski take much further in their paintings. If Pollock's drip-paintings from the late 1940s still metaphorize nature, if in an abstract manner – suggesting some discernable organic world through multiple drawing, pouring, and dripping facture techniques, including, on occasion, handprints and other expressive bodily indices – then it is conceivable that a Post-Painterly 'abstracting-further-from-this-abstraction' might appear to leave artists with nothing except the apparently 'pure' properties of line, shape, and colour [Plates 4 and 6].

Such problems of pictorial form might be re-conceptualized as problems of object. In 'After Abstract Expressionism', Greenberg suggests that observance of what he calls the two norms of painting – flatness and its 'delimitation' – were enough 'to create an object which can be experienced as a picture'.[14] This had led to a situation, paradoxically, he observes, in which a far wider range of objects might legitimately be considered to be 'pictures' than had previously been allowed under the designation. Marks on walls, brickwork, partially stripped wallpaper, for example, might lend themselves, Greenberg notes, 'to being experienced pictorially or in meaningful relation to the pictorial: all sorts of large and small items that used to belong entirely to the realm of the arbitrary and the visually meaningless'.[15] A stretched or tacked-up canvas already exists as a 'picture', his own logic dictates, but 'not necessarily as a successful one'. Greenberg then observes, in qualification – immediately after this last statement – that artistic 'conception' *alone* is the key to great art. However, the more paintings and sculptures 'after Pollock' become concerned apparently solely with problems 'intrinsic' to form, Fried notes, the more danger there is that they might come to resemble the mid-1960s 'literalist' objects founded, he asserts, on the exploitation of situations and the corruptions of theatricality [Plate 9].

According to Fried, Robert Morris, one of Minimalism's first exponents, confirmed the intention to provide and orchestrate the 'experience of an object in a *situation* – one that, virtually by definition, *includes the beholder*'.[16] Fried considers the discussion that another 'literalist', Tony Smith, recounted, when on a car ride accompanied by three students on a New Jersey freeway in the mid-1960s. If the concrete road itself, and the airstrips and drill-grounds they passed, were not 'works of art', Smith had asked, then what were they? 'What, indeed', Fried declares, 'if not empty, or "abandoned" *situations*?'.[17] Greenberg, according to Fried, had no closer group of followers in the mid-1960s than these 'literalists', because they had taken to heart the letter and the law of Greenberg's 'reductivist' definition of modernism. In wanting, that is, to create artefacts that had no truck whatsoever with illusionism they abandoned altogether the idea that artworks should *represent*. Instead they simply *presented* objects *themselves* – literally, in what Fried calls a 'hypostatization'.[18] Stella's painting practice, too, had had to negotiate this possible destination, given his searching interrogation of shape and colour conventions. His black and metallic stripe paintings – including *Six Mile Bottom* – indeed had been 'formative', Fried asserts, for the 'literalists' [Plate 6]. Olitski's hybrid 'painting-sculpture' artefact *Bunga 45* (1967), a series of conjoined painted aluminium tubes, had also been readable in such a 'literalist' manner. But Stella had pulled back from 'literalism', Fried concludes, in favour of a renewed 'commitment to the enterprise of painting', demonstrable in his later irregular polygon paintings, such as *Effingham III* and *Union III* (both 1966).[19] These paintings, Fried claims, are 'as radically illusive and intractably ambiguous as any in the history of modernism'.[20] Those terms 'illusive' and 'intractably ambiguous', central to the problematic of complexity, are offered as terms of high approbation.

Paintings by Stella, Noland, and Olitski, in their respective emphasis on the conventions of shape, colour, and facture – Olitski adopted and elaborated spray-painting techniques – work to reaffirm the central significance that Greenberg, in 'Modernist Painting', had attributed to Picasso's Cubist paintings, understood as a 'practical-critique' of the role of pictorial structure in the modernist art produced between Manet and Cézanne [Plates 6, 5, 1, and 3]. Cubism had demonstrated what Fried calls a 'growing consciousness of the literal character of the picture support and a draining of conviction in traditional illusionism'.[21] Whatever differences emerged, then, between Greenberg and Fried in the 1960s, they continued to share the belief that modernist art and criticism together constituted what the latter calls 'a special kind of cognitive enterprise'.[22] It is impossible to separate this conviction from the sense both critics also had that modernist art, as such an enterprise, also constituted a special kind of value. However, although Fried subjects Greenberg's notion of modernism to some fundamental criticism it is Clark's account of negation in modern art which threatens to undermine the roots of Fried's own perspective.

Value and vision

Clark and Fried certainly agree on the significance of Pollock as a great artist, but they differ on the meaning and legacy of his paintings. Clark sees Pollock as at the end of a series of episodes in great modern painting, while Fried believes the baton of greatness Pollock carried is handed on to Louis, Stella, Noland, and Olitski in the 1960s. Pollock's drip-paintings are radically important for modern art, Clark argues, in that they take the 'rudimentary elements of depiction' – line, colour, handling (facture) – and attempt to 'free' these from their 'normal associations with the world we know'.[23] There is a parallel here with Fried's claim that modernism 'evolves' through the isolation of, and transformation in, the use of a convention or set of conventions. But Clark will not accept the element in Fried's account of Pollock – and in modern art generally – which posits some experience of, or meaning for, art apparently *outside* or *unrelated to* broader society and history.

Clark quotes what he regards as a critical passage from Fried's *Three American Painters*, which grounds Fried's defence of Stella's, Noland's, and Olitski's art within an account of the significance of Pollock's paintings:

> In a painting such as *Number 1, 1948* there is only a pictorial field so homogeneous, overall and devoid both of recognizable objects and of abstract shapes that I want to call it *optical*, to distinguish it from the structured, essentially tactile pictorial field of previous modernist painting from Cubism to de Kooning, and even Hans Hofmann. Pollock's field is optical because it addresses itself to eyesight alone. The materiality of his pigment is rendered sheerly visual, and the result is a new kind of space – if it still makes sense to call it space – in which conditions of seeing prevail rather than one in which objects exist, flat shapes are juxtaposed or physical events transpire.[24]

Now Clark acknowledges that Fried himself demonstrates some tentativeness in this passage, but is clear, Clark notes, that 'optical' here is 'a word called on to do an immense amount of rhetorical work'. Later phrases in the passage, Clark decides – for instance 'addresses itself to eyesight alone', 'rendered sheerly visual', 'conditions of seeing prevail' – 'are fine as long as they are not meant to conjure up some bogus ontological threshold which Pollock's line magically crosses. (A lot of terrible 1960s criticism thrived on this sort of thing.)'[25] A few pages later Clark once again quotes Fried on Pollock, saying that the painter's 'concern in his art was not with any fashionable metaphysics of despair but with making the best paintings of which he was capable'. Clark calls this a 'false distinction propped up nicely by the scareword "fashionable"'.[26] Clark here is pressing Fried on the question of the relationships between 'greatness' in art, the life experiences of artists, the significance of the wider world in art-making, and the ways in which critics explain to themselves, and to others, their processes of judgement.

Clark wants great modern art – and, to re-emphasize, he is generally in close agreement with Fried and Greenberg on who the great modern artists are – to be understood as a product of decisions made by artists *within this whole nexus of factors*, not in a separated sphere of art reserved for what Fried calls 'a special kind of cognitive activity'. When modernist painting becomes, however, as remorselessly abstract as that produced by Newman, Rothko, Louis, Stella, Noland, and Olitski in the later 1950s and 1960s, Fried's resort to the apparently descriptive language of 'opticality' or pure vision *seems* intelligible, though its effect – and perhaps its intention – is precisely to confirm the autonomy of both modernist painting and criticism. 'I shall point to the difficulties', Clark argues in his exchange with Fried, 'involved in the very notion of art itself becoming [that is, being seen as] an independent source of value'.[27] The metaphors critics use are fine, Clark seems to be saying, as long as no one – and especially not the critics who deploy them – begin to think these convictions are actually bald descriptions of fact.

Clark uses the term 'negation' to suggest how the greatest modern paintings, through their appropriation of compositional conventions, manage both to allude to yet, at the same time, disputatiously interrogate the world beyond art. The 'flatness' of Manet's *A Bar at the Folies Bergère*, for instance, *is*, on the one hand, a negation of academic painting's illusionistic conventions. But for Clark 'flatness' *simultaneously* contains, or signals, a range of other meanings, values, and experiences beyond the pictorial or aesthetic narrowly conceived. 'Flatness', for instance, might metaphorically stand for modernity's social ennui or alienation, and the characteristic banalities of gesture and expression that govern human interaction – such as buying or tendering a drink in a bar – based on commercial exchange.[28] 'Negation' also implies a cancelling, or 'crossing-out' of meaning, a sense which Clark develops in order to account for Pollock's drip-paintings, to which I turn in the following chapter. Fried, however, understands Clark's use of the category of negation in relation to artistic modernism as an orthodox Marxist conceit: by it, Fried says, 'artistic modernism must be understood as something like a reflection of the incoherence and contradictoriness of modern capitalist society'.[29] It is only the term 'reflection' here that I suspect would upset Clark, who has always been at pains to show – like Raymond Williams – that representation is an active, constitutive process: art is a social 'visual behaviour', as Warburg put it, like any other human activity, and part therefore of a whole way of life.

Contrary to Clark, Fried sees the whole span of modernist painting, up to and beyond Pollock, as a full 'positivity' of achievement and development:

> Unintelligibility in Manet, far from being a value in its own right as mere negation of meaning, is in the service of aims and aspirations that have in view a new and profound and, for want of a better word, positive conception of the enterprise of painting. I would make the same sort of argument about the violation or ordinary spatial logic in Cézanne [Plate 3], or the distorted drawing and bizarre colour in Matisse, or the near dissolution of

sculptural form in Picasso [Plate 5], or the embracing of abstraction and the exploration of new means of picture-making in Pollock [Plate 4], or the use of industrial materials and techniques in [David] Smith and Caro.[30]

Within Fried's accounts of this lineage of positive achievement a cluster of terms and phrases recur as signals for the autonomy of, and autonomous value he wishes to grant to, modernist art: the 'optical', the 'sheerly visual', 'addresses . . . to eyesight alone', 'conditions of seeing', to which can be added 'the purely visual', and 'the optical mode of illusionism'.[31] The terms 'pure' and 'purity' populate Fried's essays on 1960s abstract painting and have a ghostly presence too in his discussion of modernist art's theatrical opposite, 'literalism', to which I return later in this chapter. 'Pure' and 'purity' cannot avoid connotations of moral significance – something of which Fried himself was clearly aware when he chose to use these terms, along with the even more baiting and, full of innuendo, 'grace', about which he has commented retrospectively.[32] This cluster of terms, however, has partial precedent in Greenberg's writings and Fried is prepared to make them another vehicle for distinguishing his account of modernism from that of his one-time critical mentor.

Greenberg deploys the idea of purity, for example, in 'Modernist Painting', though he surrounds it with his own scare-quotes. We are in the presence, once again then, of a serviceable metaphor threatening to congeal into fact:

> The task of self-criticism became to eliminate from the specific effects of each art any and every effect that might conceivably be borrowed from or by the medium of any other art. Thus would each art be rendered 'pure', and in its 'purity' find the guarantee of its standards of quality as well as of its independence. 'Purity' meant self-definition, and the enterprise of self-criticism in the arts became one of self-definition with a vengeance.[33]

Remember, Greenberg composed this essay at the very end of the 1950s, at a time when he could look back to Manet's art, see Pollock's 1947–1950 drip-paintings, *and* be aware of the then recent emergence of the 'post-gestural' abstract painting associated with Louis and Stella [Plates 6 and 8]. 'Modernist Painting's' perspective *is* inevitably retrospective, and terms like 'pure' and 'purity' can seem to be appropriate *metaphorically* to the fullness or completeness of abstraction in these 'post-Pollock' paintings. Greenberg acknowledges this through his use of scare-quotes. Later in the essay he is explicit about the relationship of his account to very recent art. Though he mentions no names, he says that the 'latest abstract painting tries to fulfil the Impressionist insistence on the optical as the only sense that a completely and quintessentially pictorial art can evoke'.[34] 'Optical' and 'pictorial', Fried declares, are certainly at the point of conflation in Greenberg's usage.[35] But beyond this important issue, even more significantly, lies the central problem of modernist critical judgement: 'aesthetic experience'.

Beholders, of course, experience paintings by looking at them, but I have established that this encounter is necessarily informed by the whole gamut of previous experiences, knowledge, and wider interests that beholders bring to their viewing of art. Such experiences, knowledge, and wider interests help to propel them into an art gallery in the first place. 'Seeing', then, though, as Merleau-Ponty stresses, an embodied, bio-perceptual capacity, is *also*, simultaneously, an activity shaped by intellectual and ideological factors, as Clark insists. This is true for artists, as well as for all other viewers and critics of art – artists are, after all, viewers of their own works, and that of others. It is hard to read the following statement by Greenberg, also from 'Modernist Painting', and *not* conclude that he is talking about decisions – that is, conscious, premeditated, and informed acts of choice – taken by the artists he mentions:

> With Manet and the Impressionists the question stopped being defined as one of color versus drawing, and became one of purely optical experience against optical experience as revised or modified by tactile associations. It was in the name of the purely and literally optical, not in the name of color, that the Impressionists set themselves to undermining shading and modelling and everything else in painting that seemed to connote the sculptural. It was, once again, in the name of the sculptural, with its shading and modelling, that Cézanne, and the Cubists after him, reacted against Impressionism, as David had reacted against [Jean Honoré] Fragonard. But once more, just as David's and Ingres' reaction had culminated, paradoxically, in a kind of painting even less sculptural than before, so the Cubist counter-revolution eventuated in a kind of painting flatter than anything in Western art since before Giotto and Cimabue – so flat indeed that it could hardly contain recognizable images.[36]

Fried confirms and completes this reading, in one sense, by stating in *Three American Painters* that abstract paintings by Pollock, Newman, and Louis demonstrate the emergence of 'a new, exclusively visual mode of illusionism' – illusions, that is, 'of space experienced in sheerly optical terms'[37] [Plates 4 and 8]. That is, the placing of paint on canvas *by and in itself* creates a sense of 'space', but *not* space alluding to, or figuring, some actual physical or human world – rather this is the simply visual, or optical, 'in front of' and 'behind' effect that any mark on a surface creates. Fried raises the stakes by then describing this apparent development in modernist painting as a shift in what he calls its 'phenomenological center . . . in the direction of an increasing appeal to vision *alone*'[38] (my italic). As if, that is, this 'vision' could itself be detached from, or exist outside of, the world of experience and knowledge that informs and allows seeing to happen at all. This imagined and idealized 'vision alone' might well be thought to have a kind of purity. Fried, however, will himself later take issue with Greenberg's claim that the Impressionists were antecedents – originators, in fact – in the development of what might be called, with a nod to Krauss's study, modernism's 'optical consciousness'.[39] In doing this, Fried is prepared to stand closer to Clark than he might otherwise want to present himself, and certainly much nearer than Clark and he stand in their respective understandings of Pollock and the significance of abstract painting in the US after 1945.

The same year that Greenberg delivered his radio broadcast of 'Modernist Painting' he published an essay on paintings by 'post-Pollock' artists Louis and Noland. The large fabric canvasses by Louis, 'soaked in paint rather than merely covered by it', notes Greenberg, in some sense *became* paint in themselves [Plate 8]. This effect, combined with the white-grey bare areas, often actually covered with a thin gesso layer, 'produced a sense not only of color as somehow *disembodied*, and therefore more *purely optical*, but also of color as a thing that opens and expands the picture plane'[40] (my italic). This openness of colour Louis had gleaned, Greenberg says, from sight of paintings by Still, Newman, and Rothko. His facture, or technique of applying paint, had also developed from a knowledge of recent paintings by Helen Frankenthaler. It was the absorbency of watercolour paint used in her pictures, such as *Mountains and Sea* (1952) that had allowed the mark to become 'free' from its tactile associations. 'Abstract colour' and what Greenberg calls 'emphasis on the exclusively visual' led, when a painting was successful, to a reaffirmation of 'the limitedness of pictorial space as such, with all its rectangularity and flatness and *opacity*'[41] (my italic). In restoring, then, to my discussion of 1960s abstract art and criticism something of the wider world of experience and knowledge that both

Greenberg and Fried were determined to keep at a distance from it, I need to turn again to the meanings of complexity and 'opacity' – one of its metaphors given here a highly circumscribed meaning and value by the author of 'Modernist Painting'.

Re: 'composition' and 'decomposition'

Look at the work of these 'Post Painterly' abstract artists again, inheritors of the legacies of Pollock, Picasso, and Manet [Plates 6 and 8]. Fried and Greenberg mostly ignored the titles given to these works, which came in a fairly limited variety of categories.[42] These include what might be called (1) the 'theological/metaphysical' category, such as Newman's 'Adam'; (2) the 'literature/philosophy' category, such as Stella's 'Six Mile Bottom' – a quotation from a poem – and Louis' 'Alpha-Phi'; and (3) the 'simply colours or numbers' category, such as Rothko's 'Light Red over Black'. If Fried's concern was with how these paintings were 'of' modernism and 'of' their makers' convictions and feelings, this did not include an interest in how their titles might be said significantly to be 'of' their makers too. In one sense Greenberg and Fried could simply dismiss these titles as inherently *literary* – 'non-visual', that is – and therefore wholly irrelevant. Pollock had been criticized by Greenberg on this score too, though the 'gothic-ness' he identified in paintings before the 1947 watershed was, more importantly, also a judgement on the formal character of these paintings.[43]

The titles of paintings by Louis, Stella, and Noland, however, can be seen as allusions to meanings for these works beyond what Fried calls their 'sheerly visual' or 'purely optical' character. For *all* these titles are metaphors of sorts: mental instruments, that is, for thinking about the paintings to which, conventionally, they refer. Some (hypothetical) modernist critic, for instance, might like to resist the idea that flatness is anything other than a reference to the *literal* shape of a canvas – say, that of *A Bar at the Folies Bergère* – and the *relative* flatness of spatial effects caused by the way paint has been applied to this surface. No metaphoric leap there, the critic might conclude, to a painting signifying something of the experience of boredom and alienation in capitalist society; to giving 'flatness' back its metaphoric scare-quotes. 'Gift' or 'Adam' tell you nothing important, this critic might also conclude, about the abstract paintings to which these names refer. Clark, I suggest, would demur from this judgement as a matter of principle. For him no painting can portray 'flatness' of any kind without it being the bearer of what he calls some 'awkward, empirical quiddity'. Brute 'fact' and 'metaphor', that is, are intrinsically bound up together: painting as a communicative medium is what Clark calls 'the vehicle of a complex act of meaning'.[44] The recognition and exploration of the consequences of this necessary complexity, for which 'opacity' is another term, is at the root of the disagreement Clark has with the critical-modernisms of Greenberg *and* Fried.

Clark, like Kant, recognizes that composition in art is linked to social and self-composition. However, if Greenberg and Fried themselves continually stress the positive achievements of control and self-control based on 'conception' and 'conviction' that they think the great painters and paintings of modernism exhibit, Clark in contrast emphasizes the opposite: 'negation', and what he calls, in his 1980s exchange with Fried, modernism's 'decomposition'. Clark *does*, generally, believe these same artworks – up to Pollock's drip-paintings, anyway – are great and deservedly canonical, but the terms of his evaluation are radically different and, at points, sharply antagonistic to those of Fried. The limitation of this evaluation to something narrowly called 'aesthetic' is particularly problematic for Clark.[45] This reflects the fundamental differences between Clark and Fried regarding the nature of the process involved in explaining *why* and *how* modern paintings get made, and the circumstances within which that making – and subsequent critical readings of such paintings – occur. For Clark, a multitude of interests *always* attend on, influence, sway, the making and critical reading of artworks, and an adequate account of agency in artistic production – *all* the 'hows' and 'whys' – requires the understanding of a range of socio-historical factors effectively bracketed out of analysis within both ('post-political') Greenberg's and Fried's modernist perspectives.

For Clark, negation was what he calls a reasonable 'strategy' adopted by avant-garde artists as part of a 'response to' and 'refusal' of bourgeois civilization since 1871. Modern art's inveterate turning over of conventions, its courting of controversy and institutional opprobrium since Manet is precisely what Clark says he admires, and what he believes is 'usable' in modernism. But the 'ruthlessness' of this negation, Clark wonders, may in the end not offer anything else *other than* 'the spectacle of decomposition'.[46] It is this doubt over the value of modern art's negations that spurs Fried to rail so vociferously against Clark's entire formulation: it seems to be based on the judgement, Fried concludes, that modernism has an essential 'futility'.[47] Certainly Clark stresses that the 'work of negation' carried out by the avant-garde has been 'untidy', but this is unsurprising given that it has occurred within the 'particular conditions of "ideological confusion and violence" under capital' – Clark is quoting Greenberg from 'Avant-Garde and Kitsch' here.[48] Negation in modern art, Clark asserts, is intelligible in relation to a set of 'social facts' conditioning artistic production: the decline of ruling class elites, the absence of a supportive social base for art, and the vanishing of a bourgeoisie for whom contemporary high art might be made. Negation in art, understood as a Warburgian social 'visual behaviour' then, is *part* of this 'wider decomposition'.[49]

Put Clark's following account of modern art's episodic negations, then, against Fried's notion of modernism as a tradition of positive achievements (originally quoted above, see note 30):

> [Practices of negation] . . . are simply inseparable from the work of self-definition . . . inseparable in the case of Pollock [Plate 4], for certain, or Miro or Picasso [Plate 5], or for that matter, Matisse. Modernism is certainly that art which insists on its medium and says that meaning can henceforth only be found in *practice*. But the practice in question is extraordinary and desperate: it presents itself as a work of interminable and absolute decomposition, a work which is always pushing 'medium' to its limits – to its ending – to the point where it breaks or evaporates or turns back into mere unworked material. That is the form in which medium is retrieved or reinvented: the fact of Art, in modernism, *is* the fact of negation.[50]
>
> (Clark)

> . . . unintelligibility in Manet [Plate 1], far from being a value in its own right as mere negation of meaning, is in the service of aims and aspirations that have in view a new and profound and for want of a better word, positive conception of the enterprise of painting. I would make the same sort of argument about the violation or ordinary spatial logic in Cézanne [Plate 3], or the distorted drawing and bizarre colour in Matisse, or the near dissolution of sculptural form in Picasso [Plate 5], or the embracing of abstraction and the exploration of new means of picture-making in Pollock [Plate 4] or the use of industrial materials and techniques in [David] Smith and Caro.
>
> (Fried)

Both Clark and Fried, it should be clear, *are* talking about value – why something should be regarded as good, important, significant. Both *do* have an account of how modern art understood as 'practice' or 'enterprise' involves a sequence of artists and artworks – one necessarily before the other, and before the next. Manet stands at the beginning of this practice, Clark and Fried agree, and Pollock somewhere towards its end. Where they differ, then, is on the question of how this practice of art and artists makes sense, achieve value, in relation to the socio-historical world beyond; *whether, indeed, that world needs to be represented at all, and if so, in what ways* in an adequate account of the significance of this art. Clark's account, stressing negation, 'absence of finish or coherence, indeterminacy . . . producing gaps and silences, making [modern art's medium] stand as the opposite of sense or continuity, having matter be the synonym for resistance' is an 'anti-modernist-criticism' in its refusal of the intellectual closures that characterize Greenberg's and Fried's values and judgements.[51]

At the root of these values lies the claims Greenberg and Fried both make about their experience of artworks, and the apparent detachment of these experiences – in fact, their claimed radical autonomy – from the interests of the world beyond. Their judgements about quality and value in art, and ideas about the relevance of detail in their explanation of these virtues, are driven by their understanding of aesthetic experience as 'immediate, intuitive, undeliberate, and involuntary'. (Though as I demonstrate in Chapter 6, Fried's 1960s essays concerned with contemporary abstract painting differ markedly from – perhaps to the point of some incompatibility with – his 1997 account of Manet, where he attempts a kind of partial rapprochement with Clark over the status of social-historical explanations of 1860s French painting.) Two factors in particular seem decisively to influence Fried's reading of 'post-Pollock' painting: (1) its radical abstractness centred on the 'newly stressed' conventions of colour, shape, and facture; and (2) his personal relationships with some of the artists involved. Questions of subjectivity and inter-subjectivity are inevitably raised by this second issue. They cannot, moreover, be divorced from questions of meaning and value 'in' artworks.

Before 'Complaints of an Art Critic' Greenberg had described something of the paradigmatic modernist aesthetic experience in an essay entitled 'The Case for Abstract Art', published around the time he was commissioned to write the radio talk that became 'Modernist Painting'. I have emphasized with italic several key terms and ideas in the following quotation that recur in following chapters. Consider again, when reading this passage, paintings by Louis, Stella, and Noland [Plates 6 and 8]. When becoming visually engaged with a painting of high value, Greenberg reports:

You are summoned and gathered into one point in *the continuum of duration*. The picture does this to you, willy-nilly, regardless of whatever else is on your mind; a mere glance at it creates the attitude required for its appreciation, like a stimulus that elicits an automatic response. You become all attention, which means that *you become, for the moment, selfless* and in a sense *entirely identified with the object of your attention* . . . For the cultivated eye, the picture repeats *its instantaneous unity like a mouth repeating a single word* . . . This pinpointing of the attention, this complete liberation and concentration of it, offers what is largely a new experience to most people in our society.[52] [My italic.]

One can imagine the seductiveness of this sense of 'complete liberation'! There is no reason to doubt that Greenberg would have wished this experience to be one that everyone could have. It is hard not to consider parallel discussions of what is usually called 'religious experience'. That is to say, this is a report of the experience of a kind of personal transcendence – with the sense of becoming some 'thing' or some 'one' else, for a time. Four years later, in a catalogue essay on recent paintings by Louis, Noland, and Olitski exhibited at the Norman MacKenzie Art Gallery in Regina, Canada, Greenberg asserted the value of the same three artists Fried would write about two years later in his catalogue essay *Three American Painters*. These radically abstract paintings, Greenberg observes, were 'first and foremost, [made] for the sake of feeling, and as vehicles of feeling. And if these paintings fail as vehicles and expressions of feeling, they fail entirely.'[53] 'Feeling', to clarify, means 'the emotional side of a person's nature (contrasted with the intellect)' (*Oxford Paperback Dictionary*). It is precisely Greenberg's feelings that are the subject of his discussion in 'The Case for Abstract Art'. Presumably, also somehow relevant to his experience of these feelings is the experience that led these artists to produce these works 'with feeling' and, as Fried tells us many times over, with concomitant 'conviction' and 'sensibility'.[54]

Fried pushes Greenberg's account of aesthetic experience one step further in his 1966 essay 'Shape as Form' – this article is partly a defence of modernism against what he believes is the corrupting influence of 'literalism's' theatricality. 'Real' enjoyment of art, or enjoyment 'of what is really there', Fried asserts, cannot be separated from judgement and the question of quality. The 'work of modernism', he claims in a footnote, has '*become*' that of finding this aesthetic quality[55] (my italic). To repeat, Fried declares that the purpose of modernist art has 'become' that of finding aesthetic quality, which carries the implication that before this moment modernism had other objectives. In that time 'before', artists, presumably, had a range of interests and experiences relevant to the production of art, but these became *irrelevant* once art 'became' about finding aesthetic quality. Given this fundamental redefinition of, or restriction set on, modernist art's purpose – a radically important redefinition or restriction rather oddly announced only in a footnote, and, bracketing for a moment the problem of *when* this redefinition or restriction was supposed to have occurred – it is easy to see how Fried's idea of the 'formal critic' became necessary.[56] This term merely confirms that aesthetic quality and value lay now, Fried believes, *only and entirely* in the matter of abstract art's formal character. This formal character was, at the same time, however, necessarily the bearer of the subjective feelings and character of the artwork's maker *and* those of the artwork's critical interlocutor. What implications might there be for such judgements of aesthetic quality when maker and interlocutor were friends?

Subjectivity, inter-subjectivity, and 'the society of the spectacle'

Fried has apparently been candid in retrospect about his relationships with artists during the 1960s. 'I might never have written art criticism at all,' he reflects, 'had I not met Frank Stella at Princeton [University]; my debt to him and to the other artists . . . is unpayable.'[57] In November 1961, Fried acted as best man at Stella's wedding to the critic Barbara Rose. When Fried speaks of 'conviction' and 'feeling' as the chief qualities of paintings and sculptures by Stella, Noland, and Caro, it is difficult to see how this judgement could not be bound up *in some way* with the high regard he has for these men as his contemporary friends and acquaintances. This is not to doubt, however, that Fried was convinced that his evaluations were wholly and only about 'quality' in these artists' paintings and sculptures – that he had, to use Greenberg's formulation, truthfully reported his 'experience' of aesthetic judgement. Fried's friendship with Caro appears to have been erected on his affirmative appraisal of the value of the sculpture *Midday* (1960), which Fried remembers seeing alone at the sculptor's house for several minutes before its producer appeared. Fried declared to Caro, he recalls, that the sculpture was 'nothing less than a masterpiece' and that its maker was 'a great sculptor'. Fried relates that Caro 'seemed genuinely pleased. Our friendship took off from there.'[58] Reminiscent in some ways of the subjective rapture that Greenberg talks of in 'The Case for Abstract

Art', Fried explains that his response to Caro's work was self-revelatory: 'it was thrilling to discover in myself', he recalls, 'so intense, spontaneous, and convinced a response to [Caro's] work'.[59] Notice that these terms, 'thrilling', 'intense', and 'spontaneous', and the high tone relating his feelings, are close to the recurring terms and high tone Fried deploys in his 1960s critical essays to characterize the material and formal qualities of the artworks he examines. Chief among these terms are 'commitment', 'conviction', 'compulsion'.

In the following examples of Fried's use of these terms in relation to paintings by Stella, notice how his critical rhetoric implicates, simultaneously, producer, product *and* beholder; intention, artefact, *and* interpretation [Plate 6].

> [By] the viability of shape, I mean its power to hold, to stamp itself out, and *in* – as verisimilitude and narrative and symbolism used to impress themselves – compelling conviction . . . It is only in their work that shape as such can be said to have become capable of holding, or stamping itself out, or compelling conviction . . . shape . . . become[s], one might say, an object of conviction, whereas before it was merely . . . a kind of object.[60]

> In those paintings – the asymmetrical chevrons of 1964 – the exact dimensions of the support became important . . . that if the edge of the bottommost chevron did not *exactly* intersect the upper corners of the canvas, the relation of all the chevrons – that is, of the depicted shapes – to the shape of the support became acutely problematic and the ability of the painting as a whole to compel conviction was called into question . . .[61]

> Stella discovered both the depth of his commitment to the enterprise of painting and the irreconcilability with that commitment of what may be called a reductionist conception of the nature of that enterprise . . .[62]

Fried is surely talking here as much about the psychological composition, and value, of maker and critical interlocutor, as about the maker's paintings. His attack on the theatricality of 'literalism' brings the moral – and implicitly social – facet of his critical perspective fleetingly into the open and I shall come to this in a moment.

Fried's earlier eulogistic remarks about Louis, however, who died in 1962 at the age of forty-nine, suggest that the 'formal critic's' terms of description and evaluation were always intertwined with such moral and social judgements, though they were not always represented *as such*. Louis had been an artist, Fried asserts, of exemplary 'integrity, discipline, and seriousness'. His enterprise as a painter, 'unless inspired by moral and intellectual passion was fated to triviality and unless informed by uncommon powers of moral and intellectual discrimination was doomed to failure'.[63] The forcefulness of Fried's own convictions and seriousness are crystal clear in his criticism of 1960s abstract art. There comes a point, in fact, when his sense of the utter, unremitting truthfulness of his account of the development of modernist art – about what it had 'become' to be about, about what art was good and bad, and why – is enshrined, at least for some of the time, in the rhetorical language of scientific objectivity. Fried claims, for example, that 'shortly before 1960' there had occurred the '*discovery* . . . of a new mode of pictorial structure' in modernist art[64] (my italic). Louis's early death had deprived the world of 'the now unimaginable possibilities for the future of painting' that the 'natural unfolding of his genius' would 'have opened up'.[65] Noland's commitment to 'making color yield major painting' had led the artist to '*discover* structures' (my italic) able to 'compel conviction', while Olitski's spray paintings '*in fact* represent what is almost certainly the most radical and thoroughgoing attempt in the history of modernism to make major painting out of nothing but color'[66] (my italic).

The millenarianism evident in these statements exudes a claimed authority of judgement – indeed, the term 'authority' and the related notion of 'taking possession' recur in Fried's critical language at this time – in a manner that mirrors the self-certainty of Greenberg's nostrums in 'Modernist Painting'.[67] The objectivist language and tone of both Greenberg's essay and Fried's later appraisals of 1960s abstract art have, in retrospect, an academicizing mark of death on them: the world (of art) was about to change again, and threaten with redundancy this 'experience', 'conviction', and 'sensibility'. The marriage of heightened, self-consciously subjective feeling with the language of objectivist 'formal' description in modernist criticism, however, didn't start with Greenberg and Fried, though it achieves its apotheosis with them. Clive Bell and Roger Fry, for example, gave them a run for their money several decades earlier.[68] What they all share is the certainty that a precious kind of experience and a connected way of life – with distinct moral and social implications – is under threat of closure. 'Good' and 'bad' may be the terms of a sequestered aesthetic realm of experience and judgement, but they bleed inevitably into questions of moral and social goodness and badness too.

Fried has claimed, in retrospect, that the later 1960s and early 1970s saw the death of what he calls 'evaluative criticism'. This practice, bound up with modernist art, was to be replaced, he concludes, with 'cultural commentary, "oppositional" position taking, exercises in recycled French theory, and so on'.[69] It is unfortunate that Fried cannot resist this pejorative judgement but *not* because he is, despite the intended insult, right about what happened to criticism after about 1970 – he isn't – and I will say why in my conclusion. The tone of his comment is unfortunate because it denigrates the seriousness of many others whose attempts to understand *and value* art were certainly as ingenuous and searching as the best of Fried's own criticism in the 1960s. The mordancy of his attack on the forms of cultural theory that came after modernist criticism was matched, however, by his attack on the practices and artefacts that appeared to be coming after modernist art.

Fried comments on his critical essays from the 1960s that, in retrospect 'I feel they were written by another person (or at least in another world, that of America in the age of the Vietnam War, the struggle for Civil Rights, the assassinations) . . .'[70] In 'Art and Objecthood' (1967), Fried asserts that another war was going on – that 'between theater and modernist painting, between the theatrical and the pictorial'. If the Minimalist Donald Judd had commented that contemporary art, shorn of an anachronistic subjectivism, now needed only to be 'interesting', then Fried, retorting that the problem with 'literalist' art was that it might be *'merely interesting'*, declared that modernist art, to be successful, needed to retain conviction.[71] Art-making is 'not only a moral condition but a pictorial task'. It was 'under modernism', Fried claims, here conflating artworks and critical discourse, that 'the fact . . . this is so has been made lucid and explicit'.[72] The rise, by the mid-1960s, of Pop and Minimalist art, Greenberg thought, had been accompanied by a decline in the quality of what he called 'painterly abstraction' which was producing by then, he says in 1964, 'some of the most mannered, imitative, uninspired, and repetitious art in our tradition'.[73] Though paintings by Stella, Noland, and Olitski might point the way forward for art of high value within the modernist tradition, as far as Fried was concerned, Pop and Minimalism's 'theatricality' bore an ominous and more serious danger. Wilson's *20:50* installation, I've suggested, has an inheritance traceable back to that moment [Plate 9].

Fried is clear that he saw this time – the late 1960s – in terms of 'a sense of inner combat'. The mood was definitely 'theological': his 'Art and Objecthood' essay opened with a quotation, from Perry Miller on the meditative journal-keeper Jonathan Edwards, carrying the implication that the revelatory experience of great art was akin to the experience, no less, of knowing God through His works and the world He has made.[74] Fried recalls that he and Carl Andre around this time had been involved in what sounds like a kind of *Exorcist*-type contest over the artistic future of their then mutual friend Frank Stella. 'In a sense,' Fried notes in retrospect, 'Carl Andre and I were fighting for his soul, and Andre and I represented very different things.'[75] Andre, that is, represented the path to 'literalism', while Fried held aloft the beacon of modernism. Fried's recollection, I suggest, is itself fairly *theatrical*, that is, 'exaggerated and designed to make a showy effect' (*Oxford Paperback Dictionary*).

Modernist art and 'literalism' opposed each other in three separate though related respects, as far as the author of 'Art and Objecthood' was concerned. These aspects I will call (1) objective, (2) hermeneutic, and (3) temporal. In my Conclusion, I shall reconsider Fried's account of 'literalism'. My aim here is only to sketch out some of its basic details, and to offer a few observations on its implications and relevance to the chapters to follow. 'Theatricality', for Fried, means a *conflation* and *confusion* of different artistic media and in this sense he follows Greenberg's injunction in 'Modernist Painting' that only the individual arts – for instance, painting and sculpture – defined in terms of their basic material conditions and conventions can ever be the source of true value as art-forms. 'Theatre' in this sense is inherently pejorative: what is 'theatrical' has a basic inauthenticity. Although Fried's usage has some of its origins in Diderot's criticism, there is a surviving ordinary derogatory definition for the term meaning, as I've just said, 'exaggerated and designed to make a showy effect'. It is interesting to note that Greenberg himself refers to 'theatre' – Fried often picks up terms Greenberg has used previously and develops or redeploys them.[76] Any such mixing of conditions and conventions – 'hybridization' became a widespread term for this deliberate 'post-modernist' practice after 1970 – would lead necessarily, Fried claims, to the 'degeneration' of art: '*What lies* between *the arts is theatre.*'[77] My first aspect, 'objective', then, refers (a) to an understanding of the *material constituents* of an artistic practice, such as painting – e.g. paint, the flat support, painting implements; (b) to an understanding of the *conventions* of such a practice – e.g. the uprightness of the support when placed on an easel, or placed flat on the ground; the varying means of applying paint – via brushes or pouring, etc.; dividing the support into areas where paint is applied or the support left bare; use of line, pattern, figuration, etc.; and (c) to the *intentions and aims* of the producer, given their acceptance of (a) and (b), that is: the *effects* the producer wishes to bring about. An installation, such as *20:50*, in its use of a wide variety of materials, would thus qualify as 'theatrical' in Fried's understanding of it.

In 1967, however, Fried had in mind the kind of objects created by Donald Judd, such as *Untitled* (1963–1975). This artefact – not clearly identifiable as a sculpture, and certainly not as a painting – combined painted wood and metal suggestive of an angled platform upon which was balanced a frame containing a series of dividing struts. Like Andre's *Equivalent Eight* (1966), objects such as this were neither examples of one art-form nor another. These artefacts, Fried declares, 'cannot be said to *acknowledge*' the literalness of the materials from which they had been made (my italic):

> they simply *are literal*. And it is hard to see how literalness as such, divided from the conventions which, from Manet to Noland, Olitski, and Stella, have *given* literalness value and have *made* it a bearer of conviction, can be experienced as a *source* of both of these – and what is more, one powerful enough to generate new conventions, a new art.[78]

This literalness, Fried claims, 'amounted to a new genre of theatre'.[79] Think of *20:50* here again in relation to what Fried says about the place of the beholder, and the beholder's body, in relation to such theatrical objects. It is not the address to the beholder's body, per se, Fried notes, that is one of the bases of his attack upon 'literalism' – for all art implies some physical relation to a positioned, embodied, viewer – rather it is that:

> literalism theatricalized the body, put it endlessly on stage, made it uncanny or opaque to itself, hollowed it out, deadened its expressiveness, denied its finitude and in a sense its humanness, and so on. There is . . . something vaguely *monstrous* about the body in literalism.[80]

This statement in its entirety may not seem true to one's experience of *20:50* but it confirms the sense I mentioned in my Introduction that this installation somehow *requires* a body 'within it' to make it do what it does as an installation – that is, it literally 'puts a body on its stage', and is most intelligible as the artefact it was intended to be when one sees a person literally within it. The beholder might be the person within it, or another watching from outside the space of the installation. In either case the installation has made the beholder's body – its physical location – key to the experience and meaning of the artefact. Somehow this installation, and 'literalist' art generally, manages to install the beholder 'inside the work': sometimes literally and sometimes metaphorically. The interpretation, or 'hermeneutic' – my second aspect – of theatricality in art, has this 're-placing' of the beholder's body as one of its conditions.

In going beyond the limiting, specifying conditions and conventions of an art-form such as modernist painting, and in articulating the beholder's body as key to the experience and meaning of the work, 'literalism's' theatricality is nothing less than what Fried calls 'the negation of art'.[81] His use of the term that Clark himself will deploy fifteen years later, in his 1980s exchange with Fried, has none of the dialectical qualities Clark's use was designed to bring with it. 'Literalism's' negation of modernist art merely reflects what Fried calls 'a sensibility *already* theatrical, already (to say the worst) corrupted or perverted by theater'.[82] 'Literalism' has no value and as 'the negation of art' it is a dead end. Further, Fried appears to imply that 'literalism' is merely the thin edge of the theatricality wedge: that a whole culture and society is, or soon will be, corrupted by forms of representation that objectify, conflate, and deaden authentic expressiveness. Modernist painting – for instance, Stella's – has been able for a time to 'defeat or suspend its own objecthood', Fried claims, by making shape crucial. But this is shape belonging to painting which 'must be pictorial, not, or not merely, literal'[83] [Plate 6]. 'Non-art'-ness lies in this literalizing of materials, and as Fried suggests, sometimes Stella's paintings themselves had come very close to being seen literally as objects, *not* paintings.

Theatricality, being, and temporality

If 'literalism', then, was constituted upon a radical objectification of materials and a hermeneutic of the 'theatricalized' body, for Fried a third basic component related to the sense of time its experience conveyed. Greenberg and Fried both agree that great modernist art apparently achieves its affect all 'at-once', 'like a sudden revelation' – the quasi-religious tones are salient. Fried claims that it is as though the experience of modernist painting and sculpture:

> *has no* duration – not because one in fact experiences a picture
> by Noland or Olitski, or a sculpture by David Smith or Caro in

no time at all, but because *at every moment the work itself is wholly manifest* ... It is this continuous and entire *presentness* amounting, as it were, to the perpetual creation of itself, that one experiences as a kind of *instantaneousness*, as though if only one were infinitely more acute, a single infinitely brief instant would be long enough to see everything, to experience the work in all its depth and fullness, to be forever convinced of it.[84]

(This preoccupation with duration recurs in Fried's account of Manet's painting, to which I refer in the final chapter. It is bound up with the critic simultaneously 'thinking through' his own subjective relation to the artworks in question, and Fried speculating on Manet's own understanding of them.) 'Literalism's' temporality, in contrast, he says, is 'essentially a presentment of endless or indefinite *duration* ... the experience in question *persists in time* ... *simultaneously approaching and receding*, as if apprehended in an infinite perspective'.[85] It is not clear here whether Fried is talking about his *own* experience of looking at 'literalist' artefacts – which might thus be reduced to the simpler formulation that 'as he was bored the looking seemed to take a long time' – or musing on the intentions and aims of 'literalism's' producers; or indeed, some combination of both. Nor is it clear why this experience of apparently 'indefinite duration' is necessarily a bad thing, which appears to be Fried's implication.

It is also difficult to extrapolate from 'literalism's' objects to the wider 'society of the spectacle' which Fried's critique of theatricality's corrupting effects might be thought to allude to. While objectification and body-fetishism have clear places within diverse accounts of societal 'spectacularization' – from Marxist, feminist, and postcolonial studies perspectives, for instance – critical-theoretical discussion of temporality is far less clear-cut. An equally persuasive case might be made for arguing, for instance, that theatricality within the 'society of the spectacle' radically disconnects, segments, and isolates experience of time, denuding it of *any* continuity or coherence.[86] Perhaps, then, Fried's account of 'literalism' and his decidedly brief comments on its broader socio-historical analogues should be treated circumspectly – maybe even as simple prejudice, and certainly not as proto-analysis. At any rate, the final two sentences of 'Art and Objecthood' became epigrammatic of Fried's overall stance:

I want to call attention to the utter pervasiveness – the virtual universality – of the sensibility or mode of being that I have characterized as corrupted or perverted by theater. We are all literalists most or all of our lives. Presentness is grace.[87]

'Presentness' is the term Fried chooses finally to signal the 'at-onceness' that the quality of modernist art apparently reveals to the adequately sensitive viewer. This term is confusingly close, as I've noted, to the term Fried uses to characterize the negative quality which he believes pervades 'literalism' – 'presence', or what he also calls 'object-hood': the crude, unconverted materiality to those artefacts 'between' the arts, bereft of true conventions that can spawn an authentic artistic legacy.[88]

If 'Art and Objecthood' looks forward pessimistically to an impending degeneration in art the result of a set of conditions and forces that is not actually spelt out or considered by Fried in any persuasive detail, then it also looks back on the history of modernist painting that had, by the mid-1960s, produced what Fried thought of as its newest and most radical heirs – the paintings of Louis, Stella, Noland, and Olitski [Plates 8 and 6]. However, the notion and value of 'truth in painting' that Fried makes central to his essays on these artists had been raised by Heidegger about thirty years earlier. It was precisely the material 'thinglyness' of artworks that concerned Heidegger, along with the question of how critical meaning and aesthetic value might be dependent upon this quality. Heidegger's tones, like Fried's, manage to sound both speculatively interrogative and crypto-religious:

> Our aim is to arrive at the immediate and full reality of a work of art, for only in this shall we discover real art also within it. Hence we must first bring to view the thingly element of the work. To this end it is necessary that we should know with sufficient clarity what a thing is. Only then can we say whether the art work is a thing, but a thing to which something else adheres; only then can we decide whether the work is at bottom something else and not a thing at all . . . Truth is never gathered from objects that are present and ordinary. Rather, the opening up of the Open, and the clearing of what is, happens only as the openness is projected, sketched out . . . makes its advent in thrownness.[89]

Heidegger and Fried share a predilection for sometimes obtuse abstractions used to designate fundamentals. Both are focused, though, on modern art as a carrier of ontological and epistemological truth, and both puzzle away at the question of how the origins, development, and conventions of modern painting are to be understood and valued. Though Heidegger's essay 'The Origin of the Work of Art' has Van Gogh's shoes painting as its ostensible subject – which I consider in Chapter 5 – his concept of 'thrownness' will serve as a conduit to the artist who is at the centre of attention in the next chapter.

For Fried, 1960s abstract painting was borne of fecund critical reaction to Pollock's drip-paintings [Plates 6 and 8]. It was attention to, and subsequent movement away from, the formal conventions addressed in these pictures that crucially motivated modernist painters in the late 1950s and early 1960s. It is these artists – some becoming the critic's friends – whose paintings pushed modernist art, Fried claims, into a new phase of its development. Depictive or indexical traces of a world beyond modernist painting's formal conventions apparently were dissolved in pictures by Louis, Stella, Noland, and Olitski. The 'formal art critic' became a possibility. But for Clark, Pollock's drip-paintings represent a critical negation which attempted precisely to deal with – that is, figure – the world *beyond* art, although this was certainly a world which included the meanings that 'art' had been, and might be, given in the culture at large. 'Annihilation and totality', as Clark has it, were both 'thrown' into the drip-paintings. This bad complexity, understood as an occluding, negating, resisting, value overturns Fried's, and Greenberg's, sense that modernism in the visual arts represents an unalloyed tradition of positive achievement.

'Thrownness' translates, in a suitably crude manner, the concept of *geworfenheit* developed in Heidegger's *Being and Time* (1927). It is an existential characteristic of *Dasein* – the 'being in the worldness' that humans have no choice but to experience. 'Thrownness' suggests something of the brutal 'that's-the-way-it-is'-ness of human existence: the conditions and circumstances people find themselves in. It also implies the responsibilities that people must take on in those conditions and circumstances, the ways in which people must become self-responsible and make the world take on value and meaning.[90] 'Thrownness' may be seen as a metaphor for both structure and agency in the world that humans inhabit, and as a means of understanding the relation of their 'formation' to their ability to 'form'. Pollock's drip-paintings could be said to figure all this, and it is to them, and their critical interpretation, that I now turn.

Chapter 3

Pollock, or 'abstraction'

Art Fiction Four

Lighting up a cigarette, Jon said that showing that kind of blow-up of a Pollock painting was an interesting 'laboratory experiment', but didn't have any historical value. No actual persons, apart from art history students and their lecturers, had ever seen a portion of Number 1A 1948 *that big. It made the stripes of yellow aluminium paint in the corner look like runny egg yoke. Paul chipped in that you'd have to learn to call it 'aluminum', as T.J. Clark had said, sounding like he was doing an Elvis impression, in the video interview with Fried they'd all seen before the seminar. Jorge, from Berlin for the year, said that he didn't have a clue what the lektor had been going on about – what could it mean to say that Pollock had tried to make his painting 'resistant' to the readings that were to be made of it after his death? That was just a paraphrase of Clark's argument, explained Lingo, who was writing his dissertation on 'Pollock and Metaphoricity'. How do you get from looking at the canvas – or rather looking at some dodgy slides of it – to the sorts of philosophical explanations the books gave you? The two didn't seem to fit together, said Paul. You either look or read. Writing essays on Pollock was essentially a matter of trotting out the clichéd 'descriptions' with a dash of fashionable Theory for good measure, added Jorge, who had to do it in his second language to boot. This kind of cynicism and ignorance Lingo couldn't stand – he'd actually gone to MOMA in New York to see the Pollocks. Lined up for a Ph.D. at the Courtauld Institute and needing to get a government grant to pay for his fees, he'd been taking everything that semester very seriously. The focus of his dissertation, he explained to his friends, would be the signif-icance of the handprints – whether they were Pollock's, or a woman's, and why they were on the outside of the painting. He's saying 'no' with them, he claimed, they're 'stop' signs, saying, in effect, 'keep back', or 'don't enter'. How can you prove that?, asked Jorge. It wasn't a matter of proof, replied Lingo. More a matter of tipping the balance of persua-sion with some effective quoting from the appropriate theoretical sources. You pompous a-hole, Paul had retorted. Getting on in academia was all about learning the right languages, and then getting others to learn yours, smiled Lingo. He was half-way there, he believed. 'Appropriate' was a classic academic term, for example, which you could make mean any-thing you liked: now that was persuasion! As for* Number 1A 1948, *Greenberg's, Fried's, and Clark's fingerprints were the ones that were really 'all-over' it – know what I mean?*

'Annihilation and totality'?[1]

Clark's 'Pollock' is not the sign for fecund wholeness and positive achievement that Fried dreams of in *Three American Painters*. The mater-ials 'thrown' into the drip-paintings, and into *Untitled (Cut-Out)* (1948–1950), are far too messy and hard to read for that. 'Pollock', then, becomes a site for the contest between Clark's account of modern-ism and Fried's. Some of the terms in this dispute should now be familiar: abstract art understood by Clark as a kind of 'resistance', 'refusal', or 'negation'. A means, no doubt 'convoluted' – and deliberately so, he believes – through which to figure a world beyond art, and to figure a meaning for art beyond something narrowly and aridly called 'aesthetic'. The value of Pollock's paintings, for Clark, lies precisely in this *convo-lution*: that is, in its 'coiled' and 'twisted' complexity (*Oxford Paperback Dictionary*). The drip-paintings appear to offer some kind of world, but it is 'scrambled', and doesn't constitute a resolved wholeness or totality – though some clues as to the elements of the totality it suggests *are* visible. This imagined, idealized wholeness or totality – a pictorial *complexum significabile* – has been given different names in modern art at different times, notes Clark, and several will fit Pollock's paintings well: Body, Nature, the Unconscious, even 'Art itself'.[2]

Look again at *Number 1A 1948*. The painting is much bigger than a person with their arms outstretched. If you move in close it appears to enclose you. Silver and black enamel paint streams trace a net of thickening and thinning density, peppered by occasional spurts of yellow and globules of red-brown. 'Behind' this wire cloud of paint and painting is a seeming yellow-white bareness, carrying within it, however, discontinuous flicks of black, brown, and white. As you move – and your eyes move – across the surface of the painting the variety of 'micro-climates' in the cloud become obvious: separate and separated galaxies of marks and tones. Move in very close and the sharpness of paint lines becomes crystal salient, along with the way thickened rivulets have soaked into the canvas texture, taking on something of the appearance of detail in an aerial photograph – lines of paint like solitary roads or paths. Move to the top-right, stretching up, to see the hand prints. The variations of pressure and movement applied in each print are – or appear – clear: thick black to almost thin outline trace only, the twist of the wrist suggested by the angles at which the fingers lie, or point.

Now look at *Untitled (Cut-Out)*. This is a much smaller picture – barely 2½ ft by 2 ft. Its shape and small size immediately suggests a 'portrait': some pictured 'body'. What there is, though, is an absence where the likeness should be, a roughly cut outline of a toy-like creature, with head cut half off, dragging a club foot. Surrounding this shape is a dark and dense drip-painting world in orange, yellow, black, and grey, the smudges and lines of which trespass 'onto', 'over', 'through' the body shape. This figure seems upbeat, despite the dulling crudity of physiognomy: doing a little dance perhaps, or saying 'hello! – look at me!' *Number 32 1950* also has its mouth open and is shouting loudly ('I am a very large painting!') [Plate 4]. Black enamel paint forms into clusters like letters, or is it fish? Or perhaps iron-filings pulled together by the force of magnets hidden behind the picture? Move up close, again, and see that the paint is clearly absorbed over much of the surface – bled into the canvas: more galaxies and road maps, where one tends to see the trees rather than the wood.

Any attempt at describing these pictures seems to need the use of metaphors of one kind or another, or several kinds mixed together or 'convoluted'. Pollock will simply throw in too many suggestive figures for reference to things in the world to be avoidable. In contrast, Louis, Stella, Noland, and Olitski seem to have gone out of their way to avoid including these signs, and if they do – say, Noland's so-called 'targets' – the reference itself is somehow 'bloodless' and abstracted. Clark's argument is that Pollock wants to have metaphor in his paintings, or better, perhaps, wants to signal 'metaphoricity': that painting will be read as pointing to this, or to that. Perversely, wanting to show metaphoricity means denying power or authority to specific metaphors, in case they take over and harden into a world:

This is what links [Pollock] to Cézanne [Plate 3]. His work is a constant action against metaphor: that is to say, against any of his pictures settling down inside a single metaphorical frame. He wants to cross metaphor, to block connotation by multiplying it. He aims so to accelerate the business of signifying that any one frame of reference will not fit. Figures of dissonance cancel figures of totality: no metaphor will get hold of these pictures' standing for a world, though we think each picture does stand for one – it has the requisite density.[3]

Clark is candid here in his rhetorical inferences: Pollock 'wants' and 'aims' to do this, he presumes. Whereas in his studies of Courbet and Manet Clark tended to rely on contemporary critical readings as evidence for the meanings of artworks, his essays in *Farewell to an Idea* lean much more heavily on biographical materials. This is another important difference between him and Fried and Greenberg. Here are some of the statements Pollock made which Clark cites:

1   'The pictures I contemplate painting would constitute a half-way state, and an attempt to point out the direction of the future, without arriving there completely.'

2   'I try to stay away from any recognizable image; if it creeps in, I try to do away with it . . . to let the painting come through. I don't let the image carry the painting . . . It's an extra cargo – and unnecessary . . . Recognizable images are always there in the end.'

3   'I saw a landscape the likes of which no human being could have seen . . . When you're painting out of your unconsciousness . . . I think the unconscious drives do mean a lot in looking at paintings . . . I just can't stand reality . . . We're all of us influenced by Freud, I guess . . .'[4]

It would be crass to say that as modern art becomes increasingly abstract, its critical interlocutors increasingly resort to the words of its producers as a way to ground their explanations. Fried and Greenberg have little interest in any of the words, or titles, used by the artists they consider significant. In one sense, they even 'take the words out of the mouths' of the artists, denying, as Greenberg does in 'Modernist Painting', for instance, that artists *could* rationalize the dynamics at work in modernist 'self-criticism'. This was, remember, 'altogether a question of practice, immanent to practice, and never a topic of theory

... I want to repeat that Modernist art does not offer theoretical demon-strations.'[5] But the 'word' was then put straight into the paintings themselves, as Greenberg muses: for those with a suitably cultivated eye 'the picture repeats its instantaneous unity like a mouth repeating a single word' (reference in Chapter 2, note 52).

Clark sees neither the unity, nor the clarity, of a single message in Pollock's paintings. The 'figures' in these paintings – that is, marks, lines, patterns, shapes, *all* pictorial incident – both suggest but simulta-neously deny unity and clarity of meaning. Pollock is concerned to show 'what gets in the way of likeness', how the combination of disparate figures prevents metaphor 'congealing' into 'totalization'.[6] *Untitled (Cut-Out) does* figure a likeness, weirdly (un)formed as it is, but it does it through the device of literally removing – 'abstracting' – part of the picture. This literally cut-out figure 'will displace the figurative ... and then give the weightless, placeless homunculus just enough character for it to be someone, after all'. This painting is one of Pollock's 'triumphs', Clark declares, noting that Fried had also written eloquently about it.[7] It is at this point that Clark makes his comment that certain pictures 'most need interpreters, even ruthless ones. And not just inter-preters, collaborators'.[8] Modern art throws up bizarre artefacts like this, he means, and unless someone takes them seriously, bothers to argue for their value, they will be consigned to oblivion. Modernism, in this recuperative sense, *is* its criticism.

But Clark's 'modernism' is one of decomposition, negation, refusal, and resistance to signs of totality and full plenitude. Bourgeois hege-mony, he says, 'may be a tired catchphrase' – and may still set Fried yawning embarrassedly – but it names the complicated 'mapping and extension of experience over the centuries' from at least 1500 onwards. All that is left outside of it by the twentieth century, Clark asserts, is 'the dislocated, the inarticulate, the outdated, the lacking in history, the solipsistic, the *informe*'.[9] This is Pollock's territory (and Freud's): a search for an 'outside' to bourgeois consciousness through a critique of visual representation. Picasso's Cubism is importantly antecedent to Pollock, for Clark – 'a depiction *of* illusionism, or of illusionism without a "world" to represent'[10] [Plate 5]. I consider this claim in Chapter 4. Pollock's drip-paintings, then, picture for Clark, the:

Unfounded ... There is a kind of experience, these pictures say, that is vestigial, by the looks of it – unusable, marginal, uncanny in the limiting sense of the world – but that at least the parent culture leaves alone. It is the kind of experience modern painting has often been forced back on: the only kind, so it believes, not colonized and banalized by the ruling symbolic regimes.[11]

'These pictures say' and 'it believes' are made to do a lot of work in this statement! They are Clark's own only half-submerged metaphors for explaining, or cajoling, the 'purpose' and value (out) of these artefacts. They implicate Pollock as a thinking, intending agent, as well as Clark's own world of experiences and knowledge brought to bear in his encounter with these paintings. He just will go and make abstract art be political! Pollock's chosen materials and markings force the issue, the 'cantankerousness . . . inconsistencies, scrawling, episodes of rhetorical excess – crushed glass, chicken wire, whorls of paint squeezed convulsively from tubes, twine'. Pollock has thrown worldly elements into the picture, but the picture, with what Clark calls its 'discomposure', lacking 'visual totality', doesn't add up to a recognizable world.[12]

Clark knows that he and Fried stand on different sides of an argument here. Pollock features as a kind of 'floating signifier' in their 1980s exchange, waiting for someone to put a secure net over him. What Clark wants to stress is negation and doubt in and over these paintings; what he calls 'the violence with which the normal repertoire of likeness is annihilated', and the question of whether 'any other ground for representation had been secured, or could possibly be secured, in the process'.[13] This is a bit elliptical but it might signal, among other things, that Clark does not see Pollock's creations as any font for Stella's or Noland's or Olitski's paintings. Whatever 'direction of the future' Pollock thought he signalled in his pictures, he didn't signal *that* one. Clark turns back to the issue of the import of 'negation' towards the end of his essay on Pollock. He restates its embarrassingly salient political significance once again. Pollock's art, he declares, in its resistance to bourgeois hegemony,

> turns back to the root conditions of its own abstractness, and tries to give them form. The form it chooses is refusal of aesthetic closure; cutting out, interruption, efforts at infantile metonymy: dissonance meaning mimesis, meaning sensuousness *as well as* 'Gothic-ness, paranoia, and resentment' – the one set of qualities in the form of the other.

As such, these pictures may be taken as emblems for one of the key 'episodes' in modern art that Clark examines: he will never talk, like Greenberg or Fried, of a modernist 'tradition', the tone of which is both far too self-satisfied and historically dubious.[14]

The 'gothic-ness' Clark refers to here is a reference to Greenberg's comment on Pollock from 1947. Greenberg was irritated by how that romantic literary metaphor of feeling and world got figured in Pollock's early – becoming abstract – paintings, though he does not mention any specific pictures. It tugged with it what he calls the 'violence, exasperation and stridency' reminiscent of novels by William Faulkner and Herman Melville.[15] But in this essay Greenberg is also highly complimentary about Pollock's paintings – and was ridiculed for this at the time – describing him as 'the most powerful painter in contemporary America and the only one who promises to be a major one'.[16] In a way, Greenberg, like Clark, will come to see Pollock's greatness as somehow wrapped up with, and within, his pictures' 'annihilations' of likeness. Twenty years after the 'gothic-ness' gibe Greenberg reflected that Pollock's art

> speaks for itself. Or it will do eventually. Till now it has been, for the most part, extravagantly misunderstood. [A reference, perhaps, to Fried's reading, two years earlier, in *Three American Painters*?] And what has been most misunderstood in it is its sophistication. Pollock's sophistication was of the ultimate kind which consists in an instinct for the relevant. He had also what Keats called Negative Capability: he could be doubtful and uncertain without becoming bewildered – that is, in what concerned his art . . . People who knew Pollock were . . . misled by his diffidence with words. They may also have been misled by his indifference to phrases and 'ideas' . . .[17]

How 'Clarkian' this is! Pollock's painting is eloquently 'negative', 'doubtful', 'uncertain' – articulately speaking its own negatives, or it will, 'eventually'! Shades, almost, of Clark's invocation of Mikhail Bakhtin's socio-linguistics. Language and Pollock's art both anticipate a public life to come, Clark (and Greenberg) claims: a new set of meanings to be acquired or to evolve. Future contexts for meaning somehow manage to get figured *into* Pollock's paintings, Clark asserts – here perhaps at his most apodictic – and thus, in these paintings, 'context is text', the two 'entangled', therefore convoluted and complex.[18] Clark cites the use of some drip-paintings as background – read 'context' – for Cecil Beaton's photographs of *Vogue* models in evening dresses. This was the most likely future, and meaning, for abstract art, then: as decorative backdrop.[19] Pollock knew about this emergent 'society of the spectacle' – he had been photographed himself for it, by Hans Namuth, in 1950. For that matter, Greenberg's 1967 essay, promising that Pollock's art would eventually 'speak for itself', was also published in *Vogue*!

Is there even perhaps a hint of 'Friedian' – as well as Freudian – 'theatricality' in the drip-paintings? Clark describes *Number 32, 1950*, for example, as 'mimesis, as handwriting, as theater of some sort'[20] [Plate 4]. If the *Vogue* context was a fate for these paintings that Pollock might have anticipated and wished somehow to block or disavow, is it possible that the scrawling, cantankerousness 'signs of discomposure'[21] of these paintings might have been intended to signify ugliness and inelegance, 'a kind of peremptory violence done . . . with the sticks and dried bushes' saying: 'stay away from me!'?[22] These pictures, that is, end up sometimes seeming beautiful *despite* themselves. What lessons might be learned, then, about Pollock's art – and modern art as some kind of whole, for that matter – from the various fates these paintings were to suffer?

'Addressed to eyesight alone'?: modernism's contested meanings

Not just modern art, Clark asks, but *any* 'art of real complexity' is going to get used, 'recruited, and misread', isn't it? This seems to be a matter of its innate capaciousness, or, to put it another way, ambiguities.[23] So many synonyms, then, for complexity, which means value. Within modern painting, however, ambiguity is tied, as far as Clark is concerned, to the task of 'resistance' and 'refusal'. The identification of 'real complexity in the work of representation', he declares, is the test that this resistance has been effective.[24] Pollock's drip-paintings are part of this work carried out by avant-garde artists since the mid-nineteenth century. Clark argues that Courbet, Manet, Picasso, and Pollock have all made paintings which produced meanings that exceeded the 'normal understandings' of the culture: 'The test of art was held to be some form of intransigence or difficulty in the object produced, some action against the codes and procedures by which the world was lent its usual likenesses.'[25]

From the example of Manet's paintings onwards, Clark claims, this 'intransigence' was given a variety of pejorative names by critics. The 'fragmentary', for instance – connoting the morceau/tableau distinction that I shall come to fully in Chapter 6. Or the superficial 'formlessness' associated with the emphatic flatness of Cézanne's paintings [Plate 3]. Or 'ugliness', in paintings by Matisse and Van Gogh [Plate 2]. In 1945 Greenberg notes that Pollock was 'not afraid to look ugly', adding the somewhat gratuitous dictum that 'all profoundly original art looks ugly at first'. He doesn't say whether such 'profoundly original art' was also usually, rarely, or randomly good; or whether the ugliness always, rarely, or randomly disappeared – like acne – in time.[26]

Nearly a year later Greenberg *did* claim that Pollock's paintings would become, in time, 'a new standard of beauty', because their present ugliness was only relative to 'contemporary taste'. Something of this ugliness perhaps lay in what he called Pollock's 'violent and extravagant art', anticipating his own 'gothic-ness' charge made about a year later.[27] Pollock, at this moment, for Greenberg, is a man who flaunts his masculinity in his paintings: something Clark appears to agree on, but decides wanes in the 1947–1950 drip-painting phase.[28] Greenberg puts this in a startlingly direct, because sexual, manner. Pollock's emotion, he says, 'starts out pictorially; it does not have to be castrated and translated in order to be put into a picture'.[29]

Fried turns to this question of 'translation' in *Three American Painters*, where he observes what he calls the 'almost complete failure of contemporary art criticism to come to grips with Pollock's accomplishment'.[30] Fried's aim in this essay is, to repeat, *retrospectively* to establish the particular interpretation of Pollock – and particular interpretation of modernism – that will ground his account of the significance of paintings by Stella, Noland, and Olitski. If Clark argues that the value of the drip-paintings lies in their negating 'convolution' of signs and metaphors, offering an occluded totality that *might* stand for a world but simultaneously annihilating that representation's intelligibility, then Fried makes Pollock's art the register of another complex contradiction. His name for this is 'figuration'.

Consider again *Number 1A, 1948* and *Untitled (Cut-Out)*. Fried is concerned with the function of line, and 'outline', in these, and other, drip-paintings. In the works he produced in the 1947–1950 phase, Pollock created paintings 'founded on the negation not only of traditional tactile illusionism but of traditional drawing as well'.[31] Note Fried's use of 'negation' in this assertion. Compare Pollock's pictures with Cézanne's [Plate 3], or Matisse's depictions of human bodies. According to Fried, in the drip-paintings:

> line is no longer *contour*, no longer the *edge* of anything. It does not, by and large, give rise to positive and negative areas: we are not made to feel that one part of the canvas demands to be read as figure, whether abstract or representational, against another part of the canvas read as ground. This is tantamount to the claim that . . . line has been freed at last from the job of describing

contours and bounding shapes – that it has been purged of its figurative character . . . the illusion established in these paintings is not of tangibility but of its opposite: as though the dripped line, indeed the paintings in their entirety, are accessible to eyesight alone, not to touch.[32]

Fried calls this the development of Pollock's 'opticality', meaning by the term that, in these paintings, the task of making reference to physical objects or experiences in the world has finally been abandoned. He acknowledges that Pollock 'returns' from this development after painting *Out of the Web: Number 7, 1949* (1949), concluding that Pollock realized this 'solution' 'could not be improved upon and repetition would have debased it'.[33] But whose 'solution' was it? And to whose problem?: Pollock's or Fried's? The 'solution', understood as a way to make (sense of) abstraction in the drip-paintings, certainly enables Fried to plot causative connections in his account of modernist art 'leading up' to Pollock and 'leading on to' Stella, Noland, and Olitski.

These causative connections are 'formalist' in art-critical and art-historical character, as his notion, and dream, of a pure 'opticality' suggests. Clark's attack on this idea has already been discussed (see Chapter 2, p. 71). Fried temporarily adopts the role of positivistic modernist art historian, dextrously wielding style labels and art-critical jargon like pseudo-explanatory coshes: Pollock's earlier paintings, such as the *White Cockatoo* (1948), represent, he notifies the reader, an 'awkward compromise among three stylistic modes: first, Synthetic, or Late Cubism; second, what might be called naïve abstract illusionism or naïve abstract figuration, in which an abstract shape or figure is seen against a background situated an indeterminate distance behind it; and third, the allover, optical, nonfigurative abstraction of Pollock's best . . . work'.[34] This is stark naked art-historic*ism*, designed as scenic backdrop to bolster the claims he makes about the significance of the 1960s abstract painters who, according to Fried, absorb Pollock's 'solution' and move on to their own focus on the pictorial conventions of shape, colour, and facture.

Fried's 'Pollock', then, is all positive achievement or 'good complexity' pushing modernism onwards and upwards, and the 'negation' he does register is simply in the service of further achievement. His concept of 'opticality' is a kind of yearning for, or dreaming out loud about, abstract art's pristine, 'purged' significance and value. Fried, by this point around 1966–1967, has pushed his hubristic idealism into a kind of hyper-drive that Greenberg generally avoided.[35] Compare and contrast Fried and Clark – my 'bad complexity' theorist – talking here about Pollock, but also about their accounts of modernism:

1   Pollock seems to have been on the verge of an entirely new and different kind of painting, combining figuration with opticality in a new pictorial synthesis of virtually limitless potential . . .

2   If a painting is to be abstract at all – this seems to me the drip paintings' logic – then it ought to be so through and through, down to the last detail or first gestalt: it ought to be made into the opposite of figuration, the outright, strict negative of it.[36]

What would the 'outright, strict negative' of figuration be, or *look like*? And what could it mean? No common ground is possible between Clark's idea of 'negation' and Fried's 'synthesis of limitless potential'. Clark, as I have suggested, simply can have no truck with the clichéd positivities of something called 'modernist tradition', with the strong odours of teleology and historicism the term carries for him, and which clearly infuse Fried's 'formal art criticism' in the mid-1960s. It is *this* Fried that Clark has little time for and gets irritable and angry with, not the later 'art-historical' Fried who seemingly abandons art criticism, seeking instead to locate Manet in the 'generation of 1863'.[37]

Clark will not let any reductive or idealist art-historical explanation of Pollock stand, and certainly not any modernist art-historical explanation secured on a restriction of criteria and evidence to questions and matters of Friedian 'visual form' or Greenbergian 'artistic conception'. The problem of the meaning of the drip-paintings will not be solved, Clark declares, 'by claiming that what Pollock and Miro took from the Surrealists, by some miracle of probity, was a set of techniques which they quickly cleansed and turned to higher purpose, rather than a whole strategy of release, exacerbation, emptying, and self-splitting'.[38] 'Negation' in modern art is thus an inherently unstable destructive and 'self'-destructive phenomenon, or what Clark also calls the '"can't go on, will go on" syndrome'. Adducing nineteenth- and twentieth-century examples from music (Mozart and Beethoven), literature (Rimbaud and Baudelaire), and visual art (Matisse and Pierre Bonnard), Clark describes modern artistic 'development', 'practice', or 'episodes' – whatever analytic and narrative terms are chosen, as some will always have to be – as labile, necessarily risking attenuation, and courting unintelligibility.

To ignore or underplay these characteristics is simply to misunderstand the historical place of avant-garde art and artists in the modern world. And that of modern art's critics, one might add! Both Pollock and Fried – the latter here in his guise as the 'formal art critic' – one could say, paraphrasing Clark, appear to believe in the idea of a 'beginning again or putting an end to representation': both notions are what he calls 'kinds of simplification and overload'.[39] If Fried sees 'conviction' and 'feeling' in the compositions of great paintings as a mirror of those qualities present in the mental-moral composition of such art's producers, then Clark – negating again! – wants none of this. Subjectivity in modernism is not true; it is precisely a *fiction*:

> The marks in [Pollock's] paintings . . . are not meant to be read as consistent trace of a making subject, but rather as a texture of interruptions, gaps, zigzags, a-rhythms and incorrectnesses: all of which signify a making, no doubt, but at the same time the absence of a singular maker – if by that we mean a central, continuous psyche persisting from start to finish.[40]

Clark quotes Pollock himself on the artist's desire that his unconsciousness will – or rather, perhaps, could or should? – erupt through the painting; that abstract painting might be 'a way to be certain of having truly divested oneself of the "I"'.[41] This might be to take the 'writing' in *Number 32, 1950*, for example, absolutely literally – as the mute formal traces of a voice, that is, with no speaker [Plate 4]. Abstraction is negation in this sense too: in disposing of its 'parasitic relation to likeness' it subtracts stable identity and meaning. Could *this* be what Clark means by the 'opposite of figuration'?[42] Perhaps. But this negation still has, or wants, a place, *not* a non-place, Clark declares. Pollock, or 'abstraction' – the two are terminally confused, it seems – wants some other 'means of signifying experience. It might be able to put itself in a different relation to the world.'[43] Modernism, then, for Clark, is, if anything, a *situation*, not a 'tradition'.

Its best practitioners, he asserts, meaning Manet and Picasso and Pollock, are involved in a 'war' between their use of technique and what they want 'control and assessment' to mean. 'Spontaneity' is given particular value by Pollock, its presumed occurrence a sign that his unconscious has spoken – or call it Pollock's 'sexuality'. Clark notes that Greenberg believed the artist's 'uncastrated' emotions got into his earlier pictures, though Clark believes this is Pollock somehow 'translating' class issues into those of gender.[44] I shall move on to Clark's account of Abstract Expressionism shortly, where he offers in polemic form the outline of a political-economy of post-1945 American painting. Ideology and social class are inescapable themes in this account and, like Fried on Manet, Clark believes that Pollock is, in effect, trying to 'paint his relationship to the world' – an effort which somehow must entail figuring both consciousness *and* self-consciousness.

However preposterous this hypothesis might appear, its pursuit must be grounded in some description of how these paintings *look*. Clark introduces the concept of 'vulgarity' in his attempt to pursue this question, which he links to social class, and to death. After all, he observes, modernism has always been about endings of one kind or another – be it Beethoven 'scratching out Napoleon's name on his Eroica symphony', or Rimbaud departing from Marseilles for the Orient. 'Every modernism has to have its proximate Black Square.'[45] Pollock and Franz Kline have a repetitive compulsion, Clark says, traceable in formal not biographical terms. It is a 'constant (fruitful) drive towards emptiness, endlessness, the non-human, and the inorganic'.[46] The compulsion is thrown *there*, somehow, in the sheer scale of *Number 32, 1950*, and in the metallic paints and sundry debris that find their way into *Number 1A, 1948* and *Untitled (Cut-Out)* [Plate 4]. But these are parts of some 'world', too, if not a human one. The critic Parker Tyler, Clark asserts, put his finger on this when he'd remarked, apropos of the drip-paintings, that something 'which can not be recognized as part of the universe is made to represent the universe in totality of being'.[47] Some recalcitrant wholeness will always try to creep in!

The scale of the drip-paintings, that is, is ambitious, and the language they use aspires to be public and declarative. Not just a world, indeed, according to Tyler's humanism, but a whole universe somehow manages to get figured. If Fried, in contrast, plots an alternative significance for Pollock in his dream-world of 'formal art criticism', then Greenberg, like Clark, sees a more mundane positing and posturing of subjectivity, sexuality, and carnality. And, like Clark, Greenberg sees Pollock and American abstract painting after the Second World War as meaningfully part of, and part response to, the historical and social situation. The same could be said for the place of the critic.

Criticism's subjectivities

Pollock came out of a situation of isolation that, according to Greenberg, writing in 1948, all American artists had to 'embrace and content' themselves with. (The following, however, might represent the standard description of the lot of avant-garde artists since the mid-nineteenth century):

> Isolation is, so to speak, the natural condition of high art in America ... Yet it is precisely our more intimate and habitual acquaintance with isolation that gives us our advantage at this moment. Isolation, or rather the alienation which is its cause, is the truth – isolation, alienation, naked and revealed unto itself, is the condition under which the true reality of our age is experienced. And the experience of this true reality is indispensable to any ambitious art.[48]

Note Greenberg's personifications here! At one level he seems to be talking about the US nation and its relations with Europe at the beginning of the Cold War. But then this isolation is given some kind of brooding subjective identity, it is 'naked and revealed unto itself', somehow half-person (artist?) and half-thing (artwork?). If Bohemia had been what Greenberg calls only an 'anticipation' in nineteenth-century Paris, then it has come into actuality in 1930s New York. Though the easel painting 'is on its way out', abstract pictures 'rarely go with the furniture' and 'the canvas, even when it measures 10 ft × 10 ft, has become a kind of private journal'.[49] (Clark will open his essay on Abstract Expressionism with a photograph showing abstract paintings by Hans Hofmann going – or is that not going? – with the furniture in an apartment.) By 1961, with the market for Pollock's paintings 'soaring', Greenberg is musing on the way Pollock posthumously has become, like Van Gogh, an exemplification of the *artiste maudit*, 'the damned or cursed artist, self-destructive in his impatience with the ordinariness of life, self-consuming in the service of his art'.[50]

Modern artistic subjectivity can slide, then, into solipsism – as Hauser had suggested – and it is easy to see how Pollock's drip-paintings entertain this kind of reading. Clark's note on the paintings' 'drive towards emptiness, endlessness' indicates how a form of self-consumption in art may come, finally, to signal 'death' – death, that is, as the final, killer, metaphor for a complete absence of meaning or communication. Pollock's paintings may figure or gesture towards some ideal totality – call it Body or Nature – but their other side, remember, is what Clark calls 'annihilation': a meaning-freezing cancelling and negating of world, figured both in actual paintings, and in the practice/situation of modernist painting understood as 'social relation' between artist and others. Clark reminds his readers that the nineteenth-century poet and critic Flaubert had dreamed of

> a book about nothing, a book dependent on nothing external, which would be held together by the internal strength of its style

> . . . a book which would have almost no subject, or at least where the subject would be almost invisible, if such a thing was possible.[51]

Pollock is in the grip of a similar determination, Clark believes, to dispense with 'externals and visibilities', in order to fasten more strongly on to his paintings' 'objectivity'. What results, he says, is a 'deadlock . . . between a language so fine and cold that it hopes to annihilate the emotions it describes as it describes them, and an absolute subjugation to those emotions and the world of longing they conjure up'.[52] Clark, unlike Fried, does take Pollock's titles seriously. However tacky or tawdry – read 'petty-bourgeois' – in their references, they indicate this 'longing' Pollock has for subjective enchantment, transcendence, immersion, 'entering-into-wholeness', new states of being to be passed into: *Sea-Change* (1947), *Cathedral* (1947), *Full-Fathom Five* (1947), *Alchemy* (1947), *Autumn Rhythm: Number 30* (1950), *Number One* (1948), *Number One* (1949), *One: Number 31* (1950), *Lavender Mist* (1950). Pollock shared this longing for enchantment, Clark notes, with Matisse: both produce an 'art of high negativity – books about nothing [no-things?], paintings done with consciousness deliberately on hold'. Pollock had called this 'painting out of your unconsciousness'.[53]

But how do *critics*' subjectivities and longings translate 'into the picture'? Through the usual rhetorical means: rampant personification and objectification of – that is, constructing unities for – terms like 'modernism'. Clark asks, for example, what 'else . . . *did modernism expect* from the public realm' in which Pollock's drip-paintings would be seen? Apart from Beaton's *Vogue* models, what 'else *did it* [modernism] *think* art was for?' The 'fact' or 'fear' of appropriation, Clark declares, '*is internalized by* modernism and *built into its* operations: it is part, perhaps even cause, of modern painting's way with its medium'[54] (my italic). Clark immediately follows these personifications with the statement that this fact or fear anyway was 'certainly' Pollock's way with his medium. Clark, like Fried and Greenberg, operates this rhetorical device of conflation, giving subjective identity and will to abstractions ('modernism' principally), as well as to artefacts such as paintings. So we hear that, for instance, abstract 'painting *intended* to set the world aside', while only 'those Abstract Expressionist canvases will do that are *truly consumed with their own* empty intensity, with painting as posturing, with a ludicrous bigness and lushness and generality'[55] (my italic). Whose meanings, then, are at stake in these interpretations?

The standard art-historical answer is, of course, those 'of' the artists themselves. Abstract Expressionist paintings, however, deliver a metaphoric brick wall, or the opposite: a gateway to anywhere. Think of Newman's *Adam* (1951–52) and Rothko's *Light Red Over Black* (1957) here, as well as Pollock's drip-paintings. Fried fashions an *optical* 'Pollock' and 'Newman' that fit into his account of the development of modernism reaching its apogee with the 'post painterly' abstract artists discussed in my previous chapter. Greenberg's understanding of Pollock and those he calls the 'American-Type' or 'painterly abstraction' painters is, by comparison, catholic. He certainly stresses the formal significance of their paintings within the logic of his 'Modernist Painting' framework, and particularly singles out Pollock as the great talent in the later 1940s. But, as I have noted, Greenberg also recognizes and writes about the significance of the social and political circumstances in which Pollock and the other Abstract Expressionists emerged and became successful in the period after the Second World War.[56]

The question of *whose* meanings and identities are at stake in accounts of Abstract Expressionism is particularly problematic because of the attention paid by art historians and cultural critics, during the period after 1970, specifically to the ideological or propagandistic use of American abstract painting as, as one writer famously put it, 'a weapon of the cold war'. This so-called 'revisionist' history has produced many books and essays, and continues to be fruitful and important as a means specifically to understand the contemporary reception of exhibitions of Abstract Expressionist work in the Americas and throughout the world.[57] But Clark largely ignores this whole tradition of inquiry – at least as a means to understand what he believes Pollock's art was really about and why it is important. His essay on Abstract Expressionism – categorically separated from, and by and large *un*related to, his evaluation of Pollock – *does* grapple with the social, political, and ideological implications of American abstract painting, but in a manner largely detached from the specifics of Cold War historiography and the literature devoted to this in the visual arts.

Clark is clear in this essay's introductory remarks that his concern is fundamentally with what he calls an 'attitude to the painting in question'. This has become possible again, he claims, now that about forty years has passed since the demise of Abstract Expressionism:

> Awe at its triumphs is long gone; but so is laughter at its cheap philosophy, or distaste for its heavy breathing, or boredom with its sublimity, or even resentment at the part it played in the Cold War. Not that any of those feelings has dissipated, or even should, but . . . it begins to be clear that none of them – not even the sum

of them – amounts to an attitude to the painting in question. They are what artists and critics went in for because they did not have an attitude – because something stood in the way of their making Abstract Expressionism a thing of the past.[58]

Clark's long essay on Pollock certainly amounts to – much more than anything else – an 'attitude' towards his paintings, though it is also an engagement with Fried's 'Pollock'. There is something Friedian, in fact, in Clark's reference to making Abstract Expressionism 'a thing of the past'. In his account of how Manet distances himself from all previous art, effectively making it into a reservoir of sources for his own contemporary and future modernist use, Fried develops this idea at some length. I discuss it further in Chapter 6.

But Clark's attitude *is not, and can never be* simply 'towards' the paintings in an unproblematic sense. The whole of my previous discussion has highlighted how Clark's 'Pollock' is also an interpretation of modernism and modernism's situation. This is rooted in Clark's Marxist perspective on the development of modern society and culture. Indeed, Clark offers, partly within his account of Pollock's art, a dissection of Fried's 'formal art criticism' – premised, as this neologism explicitly was, on the ideal of examining only the pristine and pure 'works of art themselves'. The corroding subjectivism that Hauser and Greenberg both see as intrinsic to the character of the self-consuming *artiste maudit* – be it modelled on Van Gogh or Pollock – finds form in modern artworks, and Abstract Expressionist paintings, Clark notes, take this to a higher level, with their 'ludicrous bigness and lushness . . . consumed with their own empty intensity'.

What Clark calls the 'cheap philosophy' of Abstract Expressionism – whether this is a reference to Harold Rosenberg's 'Action Painting' existentialism, which Greenberg abhored, or the artists' own metaphysical pronouncements, or both – provided the basic materials for the *ideological* connotation that this painting attained in public discourse in America during the 1950s and 1960s.[59] Abstract Expressionism comes to emblematize, Clark asserts, 'the absurdities of individualism in pure form – unbreathably pure, almost, a last gasp of oxygen as the plane goes down'.[60] But which 'plane' is this? Is it Gary Power's plane going down, while spying, in 1960 or Dr Strangelove's B52 bomber crashing in 1964? If Newman's and Rothko's canvases signal, for Clark, this bloated and vacuous individualism – though he reserves his real venom for Hans Hofmann – then what is it that separates all these painters from Pollock?

Clark's answer is 'negation', or bad complexity: a self-cancelling of metaphor in the drip-paintings that does not occur in the work of the other Abstract Expressionists who manage competently and crassly to represent their abstract sublime wholenesses – whether it is the ideals of God, or Being, or Expression, or Art itself. Pollock is not completely immune to this reading, Clark concedes. The ' "Action-Painting"-existentialism' tag is inevitable, because 'part of Pollock *is* tawdry. (It is just that Rosenberg could not see any other part).'[61] Greenberg gets Pollock 'right' – that is, identifies him as by far and away the best of all the post-war American painters – because, like Clark, he sees that the drip-paintings – like modernism – are 'materialist deep down', and Pollock is prepared to dwell, like Picasso and Matisse before him, 'in the world of immediate sensations'.[62] Greenberg, I've noted, identified this painting's attendant sexual and emotional American stridency. The titles of the mid-1940s pictures are indicative here, too: *Male and Female* (1942), *She-Wolf* (1943), *The Moon Woman Cuts the Circle* (1943), *Gothic* (1944), *Totem Lesson 2* (1945), *Two* (1945). The 1947–1950 drip-paintings pull away from these titles and their pictures' narrative-figurative symbolisms *towards* the dissonant convolutions of 'annihilation and totality'. The paintings that manage to achieve this state – for instance, *Number 1A, 1948* and *Untitled (Cut-Out)* – are the ones that are great, as far as Clark is concerned, because they both posit a world and brilliantly disavow it at the same time.

At several points Clark acknowledges openly the operations and contingencies of his own subjectivity in seeing and accounting for Pollock's paintings. It is as if this acknowledgement is required because abstract painting in particular appears to admit so many different and possibly contradictory readings. Such contradictions occur *within* specific readings as much as between them. Take Pollock's *One: Number 31* (1950). Clark says that its paint has been 'more poured than thrown, and more splashed (rained) than poured. Spotted. Sprayed. Which does not mean that its surface looks straightforwardly liquid. Finding words for the contradictory qualities of Pollock's surfaces is, you see already, a tortuous business.'[63] On encountering *Number 1A, 1948* in the Museum of Modern Art in New York, Clark declares 'catching sight of it, I am struck again by the counter-intuitive use it makes of [its] dimensions. To me it always looks small . . .'.[64] Of a particular section of its surface in relation to the shape of the painting, he notes:

> The central black whiplash with its gorgeous bleep of red, and
> the final black spot to the right of it, seal the belonging of every

thing to the easel size and easel-shape. I do not understand why these – of all shapes and velocities – do this kind of work. Still less why the incident should strike me, as it does each time I see it, as condensing the whole possibility of painting at a certain moment into three or four thrown marks.[65]

Here I am more interested in Clark's declared self-bafflement than with anything else. With these remarks he is, in a way, putting himself manifestly 'into' these pictures, and conspiring to erode – or, at least, complexify – the distinction between an attitude 'towards these paintings' and towards everything else, including his own doubting self.

Listen again to the observations that Newman and Still made in order to dramatize their sense that their abstract pictures were 'victims' of such critical interlocution – of critics getting 'into' the pictures:

> Harold Rosenberg challenged me to explain what one of my paintings could possibly mean to the world. My answer was that if he and others could read it properly, it would mean the end of all state capitalism and totalitarianism.
>
> (Newman)

> My contempt for the intelligence of the scribblers I have read is so complete that I can not tolerate their imbecilities, particularly when they attempt to deal with my canvases. Men like ... Greenberg, etc. ... are to be categorically rejected.
>
> (Still)[66]

There is an air of desperation about both statements here – Newman's 'could read it properly' seems particularly hopeless. I detect a similar, though much reduced anxiety, in Clark's self-reflective statements. At one point he even says he knows his opinions on Pollock are 'banal' and that he hates what has become his 'confessional' tone. At the same time he declares his belief that the drip-paintings have come to epitomize 'our and their time'.[67] All these statements are ways of affirming that value is inevitably subjective, and that this subjective quality to value-judgements is somehow more nakedly visible when one considers abstract art. But this recognition does not constitute an admission from Clark that his account is not *truthful*.

Though Clark says he relishes the fact that Pollock 'in Greenberg's words, was a "goddamn Stalinist from start to finish"', as far as he is concerned 'I know my interest does not count much in understanding what [Pollock] did as [a] painter ...'.[68] Clark is hinting here, I believe, at his own a priori beliefs and responses, deep down beneath layers of negation and doubt. These beliefs and responses have somehow managed to find (recognize?) themselves on the surface of certain paintings. Clark is partly talking about himself, then, when he says:

> art will eternally hold us with its glittering eye. Not only will it forego its role in the disenchantment of the world, but it will accept the role that has constantly been foistered upon it by false friends: it will become one of the forms, maybe *the* form, in which the world is re-enchanted.[69]

This 're-enchantment' is an ideological phenomenon, as Clark fully knows. The term 'false friends' also suggests the Marxist Georg Lukács' notion of ideology as a 'false consciousness': a mistaking of one thing for another, a getting things upside down. Clark begs a lot of questions with this statement. In one sense he appears to wish to exempt Pollock from this ideological reality, yet in another he knows – and says clearly – that Pollock's 'bad complexity' is bound up with the ideological role his paintings, as part of Abstract Expressionism, came to play in the Cold War period. Their susceptibility to ideological manipulation is part of what Clark means by their 'tawdriness'. The ideological character of Abstract Expressionism – the extent to which it might be said to 'belong at the deepest level . . . the level of language, of procedure, of presuppositions about world-making' to the American bourgeoisie, 'who bought it and took it on their travels', as Clark puts it, is the focus of my last section.[70]

Dreamings and disasters

The essence of Clark's argument is that abstract painting in America after 1945 was called upon to represent the ideology of individualism in a nation-state that had *ceased to have* a robust traditional national bourgeoisie. There simply was no class of substantial enough size, power, knowledge, and ambition, he states, able to maintain a 'high culture', or to defend such a culture's virtues within the circumstances of post-war US consumer capitalism. Clark's claims are, as I imagine he would accept, speculative and fairly blunt: his essay is short and produces neither the evidence nor detail of explanation required adequately to defend its central historical assertions about the nature of US society.[71] Clark signals this tentativeness by attaching question marks at various points to his own theses. It is, then, a matter of *to what extent* Abstract Expressionism might be said to belong – in terms of its 'language', 'procedure', or 'presuppositions about world making' – to the national bourgeoisie that did exist in the US after 1945. By 'bourgeoisie' Clark refers to a range of agents, institutions, and forces: those both private and those controlled by, or bound to, the state in terms of, for example, funding, or personnel, or ideological orientation. Institutions such as the Museum of Modern Art in New York, whose activities during the Cold War organizing the exhibition of American painting abroad has been well-documented, effectively operated both as a private institution *and* as a de facto organ of the State Department. Clark, however, is not interested either in elaborating state-theory or in exploring the significance of state activities within cultural analysis.[72] Clark's query begs some very important questions. For instance, to the extent that it might be determined that Abstract Expressionism *did not* 'belong' to this bourgeoisie, one is bound to ask, then who (or what) *did* it belong to? Or was that part of its existence unrelated to the bourgeoisie precisely a matter of it 'belonging' importantly to no-one or no thing? Was that, perhaps, where its claimed autonomy, and autonomous value as art, lay? Pollock is certainly the artist from this time – say 1948 to 1962 – whose paintings, Clark believes, manage to wrest the *most* autonomy possible in this conjuncture.

Given these analytical lacunae, Clark's essay has a necessarily highly rhetorical cast to it, focusing on the question of what kinds of value might be attributed to Abstract Expressionist paintings. Unlike Fried, however, and from a retrospective position not available to Greenberg, Clark presses the question of the significance of abstract painting within the broad social and historical circumstances of the US during the Cold War. The essay acknowledges the necessity of registering these issues while nevertheless specifying, as I have noted he does at the outset, his primary interest in an 'attitude toward these paintings'. However, despite the serious problems of socio-historical analysis Clark's essay throws up, due to its very unelaborated account of class and social formation in US society after 1945, and his lack of engagement – at the level of detailed analysis – with the revisionist history of Abstract Expressionism, his account remains important as a *rejection* of, and a *rejoinder* to, Fried's representation of an 'optical' Pollock and Newman.

Clark is firm on the principle that should govern accounts of Abstract Expressionism. That is, that these paintings occupy

> a place in a determinate class formation; one which, though long prepared, took on the specific trappings of cultural power in the

years after 1945 ... We mean that the practice somehow partici-
pates in that class's whole construction of a 'world'. We are talking
of overlap and mutual feeding at the level of representational
practice – at the level of symbolic production (ideology).[73]

The 'large', 'lush', 'empty' canvases of Abstract Expressionism generate
what Clark calls 'vulgarity' and this term is the one he will stolidly
defend as the appropriate designation for the value of these paintings.
The meanings to this term, as Clark examines and develops them in his
essay, never settle down into a unitary valence or significance – they
point, simultaneously, to this art's goodnesses and badnesses that are
bound up together. Clark is resolute in affirming this:

> My chapter title, 'In Defense of Abstract Expressionism,' is not
> meant ironically. I ... [offer] ... what I think is the best defense
> possible of this body of work, and of course I am aware that in
> doing so the noun 'vulgarity' has turned into a term of value,
> *whether I wanted it to or not*. If the formula were not so mechan-
> ical, I would say that Abstract Expressionist painting is best when
> it is most vulgar, because it then grasps most fully the conditions
> of representation – the technical and social conditions – of its
> historical moment.[74] [My italic.]

In one way, 'vulgarity' – like negation, or opacity, or ambiguity –
contains the same sense of a 'contradictoriness' *within* the artwork it
specifies: a contradictoriness which is difficult, productive, and valuable.
'Vulgarity' is another name, then, for this great art's bad complexity.
But I must emphasize my own tentativeness at this interpretation of
Clark's term and how he deploys it – his essay seems to me to be
genuinely troubling, and troubled itself, at the level of his discussion
of judgement. The sub-clause I have italicized in the last quotation
indicates this. Vulgarity, for Clark, what ever else it is, *is* Abstract
Expressionism's way of being truthful about the (awfulness of the) world
in which it has been made. As sympathetic critics have pointed out,
however, Clark's exegeses in *Farewell to an Idea* – particularly in this
essay – seem much more rooted in his own meditations on looking at
paintings than in combining such meditations with comprehensive
consideration of various kinds of historical evidence. The latter procedure had been the basis for his studies of Courbet and Manet.[75] A much
less generous verdict would be to say that Clark in this essay is simply
'reading in' his own meanings with a vengeance.

Abstract Expressionist paintings, Clark asserts, 'take part in a particular triumph and disaster of the petty bourgeoisie' in the US. This ever-broadening class, he claims, has had ceded to it the responsibility, Clark claims, of representing the ideals of an increasingly marginal high bourgeoisie. Vulgarity is the 'necessary form of that individuality allowed the petty bourgeoisie' and it is manifest in this painting in terms of a 'ruthlessness of (self-)exposure, the courting of bathos, the unapologetic banality'.[76] One can take Abstract Expressionism, then – at the level of the claims made by its artists and some of its critics about its existential, spiritual, or metaphysical pretensions – either extremely seriously or with an extreme scepticism. Abstract Expressionism raised the stakes on the philosophical value and meaning of art to ridiculous, 'unbreathably pure', levels – Newman's retort to Rosenberg indicates this. One can understand why Greenberg and Fried chose simply to ignore this whole welter of interpretation and self-interpretation.

Clark's 'vulgarity' thesis, however, rejects Greenberg's and Fried's modernist-critical positivities as much as it does that of the theological and humanist positivities superintending the psycho-spiritual pronouncements. These all boil down to versions of good complexity judgements. Fried's is more interesting intellectually, based on a much more careful looking – and speaking about looking – but it shares with the 'petty-bourgeois individualist' judgement the view that this art is made to represent 'the leftovers of the cry for totality', even though the petty bourgeoisie makes what Clark calls, without further explanation, a 'ludicrous mishmash' of this representation.[77] Time, then, to name some names. Rothko, Hofmann, and Adolph Gottlieb make their paintings 'under the sign or spell' of individuality, believing, Clark asserts, 'utterly (innocently, idiotically) in its power'. Rothko's paintings represent a kind of 'hectoring absolute of self-presence . . . in face of the void'.[78]

Clark reserves much of his poison for Hofmann's paintings – of which Greenberg seems to have remained inordinately fond.[79] In works such as *The Garden* (1956), Clark observes, Hofmann demonstrates his true 'tastelessness'. 'Tastelessness' appears to be used by Clark as a synonym for vulgarity at this point:

Tasteless in its invocations of Europe, tasteless in its mock-religiosity, tasteless in its Color-by-Technicolor, its winks and nudges toward landscape format, its Irving Stone title, and the cloying demonstrativeness of its handling. Tasteless, and in complete control of its decomposing means . . .[80]

Note the recurrence here of the motif of 'decomposition' – the term denoting a negating, self-critical process evident in the modern art Clark values most. The implication is that Hofmann and the other Abstract Expressionists are extremely competent and *truthful* in their painting, though of course they cannot theorize its significance in the terms Clark chooses to use. Vulgarity, to paraphrase Greenberg, is a process immanent to Abstract Expressionist painting, and never a topic of theory!

The key idea, Clark states, is that vulgarity in abstract painting represents betrayal, on 'the part of those who by rights ought to be in the vanguard of good taste'. Vulgarity, that is, 'roughly' equals Greenberg's own notion of 'kitsch', or ersatz culture. A spattering of judgements follow: Newman, Clark concludes, was 'never vulgar enough' – or only vulgar with his titles, such as 'The First Man was an Artist', 'The Sublime is Now', or 'The True Revolution is Anarchist!'. Gottlieb, in paintings such as *Black, Blue, Red* (1956) – abstract evocations of atom bombs detonating and the like – was the most vulgar: Clark says his art 'goes straight for the cosmological jugular, straight for the pages of *Time* or *Life*'.[81] If Asger Jorn was the best painter in Europe after 1945, as Clark maintains – 'best' because his tampering with and framing of garish effects manages always to pull his canvases 'back into the realm of painting' – American abstract painting, in contrast, is done without irony, in order to 'keep the corpse of painting hideously alive'.[82]

Another 'ending' to modernism is being proposed here, isn't it? Clark's 'attack' on Abstract Expressionism adds up to saying that 'it' knows that modernism's game is really over, its meretricious and overblown sentiment 'all the time coquetting with Death'. But, as Clark knows, modernism has always had a thing about endings and cancellations, as well as with beginnings and first lights. That is to say, modernist critics have been responding to modern art in these terms since the late nineteenth century. Think of Clark on vulgarity in Abstract Expressionist painting, but listen to Mallarmé and consider Olympia [Plate 1] and the barmaid at the *Folies Bergère*:

> The reproach which superficial people formulate against Manet, that whereas once he painted ugliness now he paints vulgarity, falls harmlessly to the ground, when we recognise the fact that he paints the truth, and recollect those difficulties he encountered on his way to seek it, and how he conquered them.[83]

Think also of Greenberg in 1939, for that matter, worrying away about the past, present, and possible future transactions between 'avant-garde culture' and its own creaturely opposite, 'kitsch'.

Clark, like Greenberg, holds that Pollock in his drip-painting phase of 1947–1950 is an artist of greatness far beyond the abilities of any other in his generation. They both agree this is mostly down to the materialism of Pollock's practice – though this materialism can be defined in various ways and from it can be drawn limited or more extensive implications. By contrast, Abstract Expressionism, loaded with its 'cheap philosophy' – the intellectual rotten core of its vulgarity – is antimaterialist by definition. Pollock's materialism, for Clark, in paintings such as *Number 1A, 1948* or *Number 32, 1950* draws attention to 'the social reality of the sign', while at the same time suggesting a turn back, or forward, to some primary reality of Nature or Subjectivity [Plate 4]. 'Metaphoricity' gives and takes. Despite the 'Gothic-ness', Greenberg praises Pollock's art around 1947 as 'still an attempt to cope with urban life: it dwells entirely in the lonely jungle of immediate sensations, impulses and notions, therefore is positivist, concrete'.[84] This materialism is inevitably psychobiological, given Pollock's exposure to Freud, though Clark notes that we have to respect the banalities of this field of reference in Pollock's own statements as well as his deadly earnestness. Some of what Clark calls the 'slapstick' around representations of sexuality in pictures such as *Two* (1945) and *Male and Female* (1942) we shall have cause to revisit in my discussion of Cézanne in Chapter 5.

Pollock's *Untitled (Cut-Out)*, along with *The Wooden Horse: Number 10A* (1948) represent for Clark a very different quality and value, and give some clue to the political significance of his category of vulgarity. In proposing some return to likeness, a crude figuring of human or animal form, Clark claims these two artworks lean, as 'modernism in general leans on the artless and childlike'. Though these conventions are already clichéd, they may still turn out to have some power in their 'artlessness'. This 'artlessness' is what Clark defines as a characteristic of the 'popular' as opposed to the 'vulgar'; a means through which to avoid 'the pathos of bourgeois taste' and its crass petty bourgeois individualist derivatives. If Pollock's best paintings conjured 'kinds of simplicity, directness, naivety, sentiment and sentimentality, emotional and material force, in spite of everything about art's actual place and function that put such qualities beyond its grasp', then so, Clark claims, did Picasso's Cubism, the subject of my next chapter.[85]

Chapter 4

Cubism's complexities

Art Fiction Three

'Can you wait just a minute, please, I haven't finished yet.'

Rosy put down her bucket and leaned on the top of her mop. 'I 'ave to be done in 'ere by 6, you know, sir, or I will be late finishin' up. The Turners always take twice as long 'cause those rooms are more popular. I don't want to miss my bus.' She turned and noticed a new smudge mark on the adjoining Braque she'd have to attend to.

'Well, really. I wonder sometimes who this gallery is really run for. I have to finish these notes and take at least five more photographs. Can't you clean over there first?'

'What's so special about that one, then?' said Rosy, 'This one 'ere looks almost the same but no one ever bothers to take photographs of it.'

'Ma Jolie is one of Picasso's most important Cubist portrait pictures – perhaps the most important. Braque's paintings were really a kind of exercise in parallel thinking but the quality is unmistakably weaker.'

Rosy thought for a minute. Haughty though this curator was, at least he bothered to talk to her. She rarely looked at the pictures any more, there was so much wiping and polishing to do. Standing back, though, she looked at the Picasso and the Braque and tried to imagine what he meant by 'quality'. 'Can't see anything there in either of 'em – bits of faces and shoulders, I suppose. Why did they make 'em so hard to see?'

'I haven't really got time for this, I'm afraid. Look in the gallery guide, there's a section on them both in there. Give me another ten minutes here and I'll be through.' Rosy squeezed the dirty water out of her mop through the red bucket's sieve. She'd make a start over the other side of the room. 'Thank you sir.'

Glancing again at the painting she realised how dark it was – funny that a picture called 'Jolly' should look so miserable, she thought. The glass over it made a bit of difference – reflecting the lights in the room, sometimes so you could see a bit of yourself in it, if you looked at the glass and not at the paint beneath. After a bit of polishing, though, the surface came up a treat.

Theatricality, vulgarity, *kitsch*

If, in their accounts of American abstract painting in the period after 1945 Fried and Clark both press the idea that modernism finds itself opposed by developments in the wider culture that threaten to corrupt and destroy art of 'real complexity' and value, then Greenberg himself makes a similar claim in his 1939 essay 'Avant-Garde and Kitsch'. Published in the then far left New York-based intellectual and political journal *Partisan Review*, Greenberg's well-known article includes a section concerned with a discussion of the hypothetical experience 'an ignorant Russian peasant' might have had when confronted by a Cubist picture by Picasso and a narrative battle scene by the late nineteenth century Russian social realist painter Ilya Repin.[1] Bear in mind the family resemblance between this proposed 'ignorant peasant' and the various walk-on parts for 'charwomen', 'drunken toilet cleaners', and 'manual labourers' introduced by Gombrich, Heidegger, and others in my earlier chapters. I know that Greenberg is entertaining this hypothetical character initially imagined by another contributor to *Partisan Review*, but he nevertheless goes along with the conceit. Consider Picasso's *Ma Jolie* (1911–1912) in the following discussion, while Bonnencontre's *Three Graces* (*c*.1900) – this time not seen through Gombrich's 'wobbly glass' – can reasonably stand for *some* of the illusionistic qualities Greenberg imagines the virtually contemporaneous Repin picture would manifest [Plate 5]. Remember, too, Greenberg's and Fried's autobiographical accounts of aesthetic experiences cited earlier (e.g. Introduction, pp. 29–32).

I want to concentrate on a section of Greenberg's analysis focused on what he imagines would be the difference in the 'ignorant peasant's' experience of the two paintings. Of course, Greenberg is arguing that the Picasso painting is infinitely superior to the one by Repin:

> The ultimate values which the cultivated spectator derives from the Picasso are derived at a second remove, as the result of reflection upon the immediate impression left by the plastic values. It is only then that the recognizable, the miraculous and the sympathetic enter. They are not immediately or externally present in Picasso's painting, but must be projected into it by the spectator sensitive enough to react sufficiently to plastic qualities. They belong to the 'reflected' effect. In Repin, on the other hand, the 'reflected' effect has already been included in the picture, ready for the spectator's unreflective enjoyment. Where Picasso paints *cause*, Repin paints *effect*. Repin predigests art for the spectator and spares him effort, provides him with a short cut to the pleasure of art that detours what is necessarily difficult in genuine art. Repin, or kitsch, is synthetic art.[2]

Greenberg's 'cultivated' and 'sensitive' spectator 'reflecting' on his [sic] 'immediate impression' here bares some comparison with his later description of the critic who has learnt to experience modern art *relevantly* (Introduction p. 31). Notice, too, that the 'ultimate values' 'of' the Picasso painting, Greenberg claims, are *not* present in the work – art simply *cannot* be the source of its own value! Clark declares – but are generated 'at a second remove', incited by, but the product of 'reflection' upon, the painting's 'plastic values'. Greenberg's last sentence on the 'necessarily difficult' in 'genuine art' suggests, too, the occluded totality – the 'not seen' – which is the sign of complexity/value. *Cause* hints at the materiality of painting as a practice of representation being 'drawn attention to', through the Cubist devices that fragment and erode the emergence of a clearly intelligible depiction. (Gombrich's Bonnencontre nudes, seen through multiplying layers of cracked glass approximate, as I've noted, the look of a Cubist picture.)

By *effect* Greenberg means the clever illusionistic depiction of things in the Repin painting shown 'in the way in which he [the 'ignorant Russian peasant'] recognizes and sees things outside of pictures – there is no discontinuity between art and life'. The painting, that is, through its apparent narrative realism, immediately invites the 'ignorant peasant's' participation in the illusory world the picture 'miraculously' conjures.[3] However, if the Repin picture is bad because it is 'kitsch' – by which Greenberg means it relies parasitically upon the debasement

of genuine art's conventions and techniques – then compared with magazine illustration painting the social realist artist is lucky. That is because
'the peasant is protected from the products of American capitalism, for
he would not stand a chance next to a *Saturday Evening Post* cover
by Norman Rockwell'. (Twenty years later Greenberg will find himself
writing about the 'difficult' virtues of Picasso and Pollock for this very
magazine.[4])

In different, though related ways, theatricality, vulgarity, and
kitsch all represent the hostile 'outside' against which Fried, Clark, and
Greenberg propose their defences of modernism. In each case, too, note
that the characteristics specified by the negative term are seen by each
of the three critics to be insinuating themselves – or threatening to –
into authentic modernist art. For Clark, more disturbingly and ambiguously, it appears that Abstract Expressionism's value ('best when it is
most vulgar'), *is* that it tells the vulgar truth, vulgarly, about what
happened to US society and the remnants of bourgeois 'high art' values
there when consumer capitalism and its ideological surrogate, petty
bourgeois individualism, tightens its grip during the 1950s. If you can't
see how this disaster gets figured even in paintings by Pollock, Clark
declares, then you must have 'a tin ear for agony'.[5] Greenberg, back in
antediluvian 1939, was wondering about this future, though from the
tone of 'Avant-Garde and Kitsch' it is clear that he thought the prospects
for culture and democracy in US capitalist society were very bleak.[6]
High art was on the point of being abandoned by those – the ruling
class – to whom it belonged.

The period in the late 1930s and early 1940s saw Greenberg's
explicit commitment to socialist political beliefs and an engagement with
the Marxist intellectual tradition that profoundly influenced his understanding of the place of culture and modern art under capitalist
economic and social conditions. 'Avant-Garde and Kitsch' and 'Towards
a Newer Laocoon' (1940) are his two essays most indebted to this
engagement, though in the latter the political, ideological, and socio-
historical elements within his developing perspective on modern art are
already becoming implicit or latent, rather than stated directly. An
elegiac poem he wrote, also in 1940, 'Ode to Trotsky', remained unpublished throughout his lifetime.[7] Clark is definitive on the position he
believes Greenberg came to adopt in this period, though the *terms* in
which this belief came to be expressed changed drastically between
'Avant-Garde and Kitsch' (when Greenberg's political perspective and
socialist beliefs were articulated openly) and the 1961 'Modernist
Painting' (when 'self-criticism' becomes, in effect, a code-word for visual

art's dissidence in the face of the wider capitalist culture) 'Greenberg ... does believe ... that art can substitute *itself* for the values capitalism has made valueless. A refusal to share that belief ... is finally what I am urging.'[8]

This statement helps to clarify Clark's position, developed in later essays, on Pollock and Abstract Expressionism. His ambivalence over the significance of Pollock – wanting to see his drip-paintings as great artworks, but seeing also their 'tawdriness', finally seeing them somehow *as both at the same time* – and his argument that the value of Abstract Expressionism lies in its truth-telling vulgarity, confirm this earlier declaration that abstract art after 1945 should not be understood to stand autonomously apart from the capitalist conditions that have engendered and supported its production and critical reception. That is why, for Clark, modernism as a critical practice of 'resistance' or 'refusal' of bourgeois society *ends* with Abstract Expressionist painting in the 1950s.

Now consider *Ma Jolie* [Plate 5] and *Woman with Pears (Fernande)* again. Cubist paintings, for Clark and Greenberg, occupy a particularly significant position within modernism understood as a resistance to – or dissidence in face of – the wider, encroaching capitalist culture. Although in usual art-historical terms the Cubist phase of Picasso and Braque's work is limited to the decade between about 1907 and 1917, there is a way in which modern art in the interwar period is portrayed virtually tout court as 'Cubist' in nature and purpose. One (partial) exception is Matisse, seen as the only real challenger, or match, to Picasso, and source of another 'primitivism' of vision and execution. I use 'primitivism', however, in the broader sense implied in Clark's discussion, cited earlier, of the 'outsides' to visual representation in bourgeois hegemony. Primitivism in this usage, then, refers to everything in art left out of this hegemony by 1907, the year of Picasso's *Demoiselles d'Avignon*: 'the dislocated, the inarticulate, the outdated, the lacking in history, the solipsistic, the *informe*'. I noted in the previous chapter that Cubism, according to Clark, is 'a depiction *of* illusionism, or of illusionism without a "world" to represent'.[9]

Yet there she is, Fernande Olivier, Picasso's model and lover, all twisting neck and raised eyebrows, with lips pursed and flesh the same tones as the pears behind and below her on the table. The portrait is slightly bigger than life-size, but close enough. The viewer's eye readily joins up the separated suggested lines of her figure and curves of her upper torso and turned neck. Look too closely and the figure fragments, but move back and there it is again, posed in front of a stage (surely?) with green curtains: there *is* a kind of whole or totality represented there. It is far less clear who or where the beautiful 'woman with the zither' ('Ma Jolie') *is*; 'she' is far more spread out, exploded around the canvas which is similar in size to *Woman with Pears (Fernande)*, though its more oblong shape perhaps makes it look bigger [Plate 5]. Line does much more work to approximate her figure here than do coloured patches of modelling, and the body and musical instrument elements are equally scattered across the picture. The game of making your eye see a likeness here is much more obviously something one has to enter into as a game, and a game you know in advance you will really lose: the surface as a whole pushes you back into your own space, throwing you back on, into, your own resources, as Greenberg suggested. It has (presents) its surface 'difficulties'.

If Greenberg believes this difficulty is characteristic of genuine art, and that it holds out something against kitsch's easy pleasures of painting *effect*, then Clark wishes overtly to politicize this judgement. On the face of it, he claims, there is an analogy between seeing Cubism as the 'imagining' of a radically new kind of description of reality in Western painting and 'some overall recasting of social practice (the kind that happened in Giotto's and Piero's centuries)'. This is self-declared rhetoric, however, and Clark will retreat to another, bathetic, position soon after, but the rhetoric serves a point: it enables Clark to confirm – in case any one had suspected it, he says – 'a last residue in my text of Marxist determinism or worse'.[10] Cubism, Clark decides, though presented *art-historically* as the 'classic moment of modernist painting' actually only pretends (or 'counterfeits') such a new description of reality, and therefore cannot be part of any corresponding 'recasting' or revolution in society as a whole. Clark, though he doesn't actually say it, would put John Berger's implication that Cubism was dialectical-materialism in painting into the deep trashcan of insane historicist musings.[11]

In his 1982 essay on Greenberg, however, Clark is definitive on the significance of what he calls the critic's position of 'Eliotic Trotsky-ism' – that is, Greenberg's late 1930s 'cultural Marxism' elaborated in 'Avant-Garde and Kitsch'. This presented, Clark states, 'a justified, though extreme, pessimism as to the nature of established culture since 1870'. This pessimism has attracted the name of 'ultra-leftism', and characterizes the perspective, a 'version' of which Clark himself thinks is correct, and which is 'a good vantage for a history of our culture'.[12] If capitalism up to 1890 still supported a bourgeoisie 'confident in its powers' but also scrupulous and original in its dialogue with science and ways of appraising experience and articulating values, then by the 1930s and the Slump, Clark claims, the bourgeois intelligentsia has begun to disappear. Along with this process begins the decline of high art, tied, as Greenberg famously observes, to the bourgeoisie by 'an umbilical cord of gold'.[13] Kitsch is one symptom produced by this broader culture and society of 'late capitalism':

> By which I mean the order emerging from the Great Depression ... a period of cultural uniformity: a levelling-down, a squeezing-out of previous bourgeois elites, a narrowing of distance between class and class *and* between fractions of the same class. In this case, the distance largely disappears between bourgeois intelligentsia and unintelligentsia: by our own time one might say it is normally impossible to distinguish one from the other.[14]

Cubism, by this historical reckoning, is placed squarely between capitalism's last confident phase of growth and belief 'in the commodity as a (perplexing) form of freedom', and the decade that sees capitalism brought to its lowest ever point and the concomitant rise of fascism and Stalinist communism across Europe.[15]

Moving on, I shall consider how, for Greenberg, Clark, and Fried, Cubist painting, and that of Matisse, registers something of this moment, and how this is related to its attainment of the status, within art history at any rate, as *the* 'classic modernism'. However, Greenberg, writing around 1950, finds himself torn between two ways of seeing the legacy of Cubism in modernist painting after 1940, when the centre of power, he notes, has moved decisively to the US. In one sense, he reflects, American painterly abstraction – meaning the art of Pollock, de Kooning, and Arshile Gorky – has not broken with 'the Cubist and post-Cubist past' as much as extended it 'in an unforeseen way ... Theirs represents', he states, 'the first genuine and compelled effort to *impose* Cubist *order* – the only *order* possible to ambitious painting in our time – on the experience of the post-Cubist, *post-1930 world*'[16] (my italic). Greenberg may be meaning by 'Cubist order' here shallow pictorial *space*, paintings that acknowledge the *boundaries* of the support, and the absence of *convincing illusions*. But his choice of terms suggests a conflation of pictorial with recent-past and contemporary political and historical conditions in what he calls the 'post-1930 world'. 'Order' and 'impose', in particular, carry burdens of artistic, military, social, imperial, and ideological connotation. What were the Second World War, fascism, and Stalinism about if not disputes over 'space', 'boundaries', and competing 'convincing illusions'? For Greenberg, 'America' (and American art) is – as is still said today! – the 'best of Europe' plus indigenous experience and energies. Which make it *better*. At the 1950 Venice Biennale, he goes on regretfully to conclude, the critics were not humble in their praise of the new American painting: it looked, to the Europeans, Greenberg says 'new beyond freshness, and therefore violent'.[17]

Two years earlier he had been more reserved and sceptical. 'To define the exact status of contemporary American art in relation to the history of art past and present demands a certain amount of mercilessness and pessimism.'[18] The implication here is that American painting can't, as yet, shake off either its derivative ('late Cubist') Europeanness, or its indigenous 'American-Scene' parochialism.[19] Both hold it back from the achievements 'ambitious painting' seeks. The legacy of Cubism, that is to say, is both enabling and restricting.

'Classic Cubism'/'cool hedonism'

Fried states the same opinion most clearly – and also most predictably – in *Three American Painters* when he begins to rehearse the virtues of antecedent modernist art leading up to Stella, Noland, and Olitski. One may deplore, he declares, the critical attention to matters of visual form in the writings of Roger Fry and Greenberg, but the painters whom they most admire 'on formal grounds' – including Manet, the Impressionists, Georges Seurat, Cézanne, Picasso, Matisse – are 'among the finest painters of the past hundred years'.[20] Criticism of a contextual or socio-political kind, he claims,

> has shown itself largely unable to make convincing discriminations of value among the works of a particular artist: and in this century it often happens that those paintings that are most full of explicit human content can be faulted on formal grounds – Picasso's *Guernica* [1937, a painting depicting the fascist aerial bombing of the Spanish town] is perhaps the most conspicuous example – in comparison with others virtually devoid of such content. (It must be granted that this says something about the limitations of formal criticism as well as about its strengths. Though precisely what it is taken to say will depend on one's feelings about *Guernica*, etc.)[21]

Guernica, in this, by then already entrenched modernist-critical view, is the chief example of Picasso's own egregious post-Cubist painting: a picture containing the merest residue of genuine Cubism's formal inventiveness that has been grafted onto a clunking ideological-propagandistic narrative vehicle. Greenberg, by comparison, is far less doctrinaire than Fried on the valences of Cubist painting. He recognizes, as Clark does, its positive, world-engaged 'materialist' side.

What Greenberg calls the School of Paris's 'positivism', after 1920 – after the end, that is, of 'classic Cubism' – had not just been a matter of 'technical' advances [Plate 5]. Interestingly, Greenberg tendentiously notes – presaging Clark? – that it is around this moment that 'the suspicion arose that capitalism . . . no longer commanded perspectives of infinite expansion'. This intimation had influenced artists, like Mondrian, he suggests, to move towards a non-'physical' abstraction in their painting, because they saw that art, like capitalism, was now 'likewise faced with limits beyond which it could not go'. However

> artists like Matisse and Picasso . . . appear to have felt that unless painting proceeded, at least during our time, in its exploration of the physical, it would stop advancing altogether – that to turn to the literary would be to retreat and repeat; whether the physical was exhausted or not, there was no ambitious alternative. All this – the despair of the physical and the doubt whether anything but the physical remained – is dramatically mirrored in the painting Picasso has done since 1927 . . . whereas the surrealists and neo-romantics conceived of pleasure in terms of sentimental subject matter, Matisse, Picasso and those who followed them saw it principally in luscious color, rich surfaces, decoratively inflected design.[22]

After the watershed of 1920 Greenberg comes to prefer the paintings of Matisse to Picasso, in 1948 famously calling the former's art 'cold, undistracted, and full of arrogant purpose'.[23] More reverberative Cold War terms pepper Greenberg's criticism at this time – the 'cool', the 'ordered', the 'detached'. Whatever the 'genuinely violent and extravagant' in Pollock's painting, it must be harnessed, states Greenberg, to these controls and limits.[24] Picasso's 'classic Cubism' undoubtedly functions within Greenberg's criticism as the chief articulatory principle of modernist painting as a whole, the very canon of an equilibrium of formal energies and stylistic control, and balance between line and tone. Balance between, that is, depictive features and the explicit acknowledgement of painting's actual materials of making – paint placed upon the surface of the bounded and framed support.

If Clark stresses modernism as a negating, breaking, cancelling, *situation*, at its best reactive and responsive to (and figuring, however fitfully) a world outside of art, then Greenberg, overall, stresses – like Fried – modernism as a boldly 'carrying-on', building, achieving, *tradition* bound to all great art before the 1860s. It is no surprise, then, to hear Fried quoting *this* emphasis in Greenberg in a footnote to his book on Manet. Modernism is not a break with the past but rather 'a dialectical turn' made in order to 'maintain or restore continuity' and to maintain or restore 'standards, levels of quality'.[25] Greenberg, in his 1955 discussion of 'American-Type' paintings, continually brings his criticism back to their relation to Cubism and 'late Cubism' – and to the question of how far de Kooning, Rothko, or Pollock move beyond Cubism, or remain in its shadow. Greenberg's essay on Fernand Léger, published a year before ' "American-Type" Painting', lays out his understanding of the fundamental significance of Cubism for modernism as a tradition. If Cézanne had been one of the first modern artists to worry consciously about

> how to pass from the contours of an object to what lay behind or
> next to it without violating either the integrity of the picture surface
> as a flat continuum, or the represented three-dimensionality of
> the object itself, which Impressionism had inadvertently threatened
> . . . [then] . . . the Cubists inherited this problem, and solved it,
> but – as Marx would say – only, by destroying it: willingly or
> unwillingly, they sacrificed the integrity of the object almost
> entirely to that of the surface. This – which had, however, nothing
> intrinsic to do with aesthetic value – is why Cubism constituted a
> turning point in the history of painting.[26] [Plate 5]

Note, in Greenberg's reference to Marx here, a hint of the 'negation' (as destruction) motif central to Clark's account, though it may also be an implicit reference to Picasso's own well-known remark that his art amounted to 'a sum of destructions'.[27]

Like Clark, too, Greenberg shares a sense that Cubism, at its best, was a kind of artistic materialism, and had emerged just at the point in the early twentieth century when capitalism, science, and industry were on 'the crest of a mood of "materialistic" optimism'.[28] Picasso's materialism, for Clark, however – as I shall indicate in a moment – is overwhelmingly dark: a pictorial font of epistemological doubt and scepticism, implying doubt and scepticism about the times. The building blocks for this doubt and scepticism in the paintings are the devices of 'visual paradox' that set out to cancel the descriptive work the pictures appear to do. As in his discussion of Pollock, Clark will draw on Picasso's own statements and biographical details, detecting attitudinal instabilities: changes of mind about the 'finishedness' of groups of paintings – for instance, those the artist photographed propped up across a doorway at Sorgues in 1912 – analogous to the paradoxical visual-formal uncertainties that Clark claims characterize the pictures themselves.[29]

Ma Jolie [Plate 5] and *Man with a Guitar* (1912), Clark claims, manifest a 'base kind of materialism'. That is, these pictures draw us near to their actual painted surfaces in order to demonstrate illusionism's 'true (enviable) simple-mindedness – as the conjuring trick *it once had been*'[30] (my italic). Cubism's pictorial paradoxes constitute a revelation, then, of visual representation's rhetorical ability to 'conjure' or 'counterfeit' reality. There is an irony, Clark notes, in the versions of recent semiotic and structuralist art history that once again, despite – or is it because of? – their avowed attention to the workings of visual form, institute Cubism heroically as a new 'language' and episteme.[31] But Cubism's materialism is 'base' for Clark in the sense that it really contains no dialectical or transformative power, nor any necessary implication for the development of modern art after it: Cubism, that is, doesn't 'lead' anywhere. Instead, Cubism's complexity and value has three main aspects: (1) as a rebus, riddle, or game of disputable appearances; (2) as 'figured obscurity' – the light/dark tonality in these paintings *literalizing* the metaphor of complexity's 'occluded totality'; and (3) as enigmatic or unintelligible meaning.

Cubism's metaphoric darkness – that is, its sombre meaning – as far as Clark is concerned, consists in the way in which it points ultimately to the contingencies of visual representation and seeing, but not from any kind of visual representation or seeing *outside of* these contingencies. *Woman with Pears (Fernande)* and *Ma Jolie* demonstrate the two sides to this. The former picture figures, through its conventions of hatchings and chiaroscuro facets, the bodily presence of a woman. *Ma Jolie*, on the other hand, reverses this focus: the exploded figural fragments 'of' a woman emphatically indicate, through their dissemination across the picture, the empirical reality of the painted surface. Both pictures, with effort, can be 'seen' – that is, understood – the other way round, which also reinforces our attention to the paintings as what Clark calls 'metaphors of matter': 'paint', 'substance', 'body', 'subject', 'object', 'vision' and 'the visual' itself. But, as with Pollock's drip-paintings, Cubist pictures *simultaneously* metaphorically figure the world and literally figure the devices of visual representation.

To cede priority to either one or the other would be to lapse into either formalism (including its semiotic and structuralist variants) or some crude social history of art position.[32] Great modern art, for Clark, balances on the knife edge between the two. Modernism is ultimately to be judged, he asserts with Cézanne, Picasso, and Pollock particularly in mind, by the passion with which its paintings point to the material and 'social reality ... away from the comforts of narrative and illusionism ... but equally ... of turning the sign back to the bedrock of World/Nature/Sensation/Subjectivity which the to and fro of capitalism had all but destroyed'.[33] Greenberg had offered a strikingly similar verdict in 1948 on the significance of Cubism, at a time when he was thinking about the character and ambitions of abstract painting in the US. Cubism, he states: 'expressed the positivist or empirical state of mind with its refusal to refer to anything outside the concrete experience of the particular discipline, field, or medium in which one worked ... it also expressed the empiricist's faith in the supreme reality of concrete experience.'[34]

Matisse's painting, Greenberg argues in the same essay – though it could not compare with 'classic Cubism's' importance – was by the later 1940s proof that its producer now occupied the position as the 'greatest master of the twentieth century, a position Picasso is further than ever from threatening'.[35] Matisse's painting achieved this, and thus offered a model for American high art, because it retains the qualities that 'classic Cubism' had itself manifested. Though Clark mocks the term ('"classic" Cubism, the commentators call it: as usual pining for something modernism will not give'), Cubism is, he acknowledges, 'the moment when modernism focused on its means and purposes with a special vengeance'.[36]

Look again at Matisse's *Blue Nude. Souvenir of Biskra*, painted the same year as Picasso's *Demoiselles d'Avignon*. Both image a primitivism figured as 'woman' and as ethnic 'Other'. The art-historical literature on these paintings is enormous, and now includes many studies of their relationship to, and implication within, the history of European colonialism and/as the suppression of women.[37] These accounts – along with those linking Picasso's Cubist collages to the Balkan Wars represented in contemporary French newspaper stories – pull modern art decisively into the orbit of social history, and away from modernist criticism's fixations on medium and tradition. Clark's own interpretation of Picasso and Matisse, I suggest, stands awkwardly between these two positions, but would see their concerns, finally, as a quite false antithesis.

Clark's overriding concern is with modern art understood as a worldly practice that wants to position itself *between* visual representation and 'the world', somehow managing to point both ways: to the material and 'social reality of the sign', and to 'the bedrock of World/ Nature/Sensation/Subjectivity'. Modernism, at its best, for Clark, *is* a materialism – that is, a way of knowing – and Picasso's and Matisse's greatest paintings embody this knowledge's 'discipline' and 'concreteness'. But how differently, even oppositely, these qualities may be interpreted and valued! The early critic of modern art, Maurice Denis, wants to see necessity where Clark sees contingency, and idealism where Clark sees materialism:

> particularly in Matisse, is artificiality; not literary artificiality, which follows from the search for expression of ideas; nor decorative artificiality, as the makers of Turkish and Persian carpets conceived it; no, something more abstract still; painting beyond every contingency, painting in itself, the pure act of painting . . . you arrive at ideas, at pure Forms of paintings. You are only happy when all the elements of your work are intelligible to you. Nothing must remain of the conditional and accidental in your universe: you strip it of everything that does not correspond to the possibilities of expression provided by reason. As if you could, inside your own artistic domain, escape from the sum of necessities that always sets limits to what we experience![38]

There goes modernist criticism again: dreaming of absolutes – of absolute Beginnings and Endings. Clark certainly recognizes the power of this recurring dream, the passion with which it gets entertained, and quotes Denis, I think, mostly in admiration of this fervency. Greenberg and Fried generate their own dreams for modernism proposed as an autonomous value. Clark certainly sees the seductiveness of this idea – this is partly what he means by the 're-enchantment' of art – but he refuses it as the daydreaming illusion it is. Cubism's complexities, in fact, for Clark, point to, emblematize, and may even unmask the delusions minds are prey to.

Complexity, mind, and modernism

Clark inherits the sense that Cubism is a 'knowing game' played about the nature of visual representation from a passage in Greenberg's 1940 essay 'Towards a Newer Laocoon'. Consider again *Woman with Pears (Fernande)* and *Ma Jolie* [Plate 5]. 'The destruction of realistic pictorial surface, and with it, that of the object', claims Greenberg:

> was accomplished by means of the *travesty* that was cubism. The cubist painter eliminated color because, consciously or unconsciously, he was *parodying*, in order to destroy, the academic methods of achieving volume and depth, which are shading and perspective, and as such have little to do with color in the common sense of the word. The cubist used these same methods to break the canvas into a multiplicity of subtle recessive planes, which seem to shift and fade into infinite depths and yet insist on returning to the surface of the canvas. As we gaze at a cubist painting of the last phase we witness the birth and death of three-dimensional space.[39] [My italic.]

Note the terms 'travesty' and 'parody'. The *New Shorter Oxford English Dictionary* gives them as synonyms for each other and indicates something of their literary and dramatic origins. Travesty is defined as a 'derisive or ludicrous imitation'; a 'grotesque misrepresentation'. An early meaning derived from French usage pertained to the theatre and meant dressing 'in the attire of the opposite sex'. Parody is defined as a 'prose, verse, or ... other artistic composition in which the characteristic themes and the style of a particular work, author, etc., are exaggerated or applied to an inappropriate subject, especially for the purposes of ridicule'; a 'poor or feeble imitation'. From my discussion so far of modern art's contemporary critical interpretation, it should be clear how much congruency there is between the lexicon of pejoratives associated with initial readings of paintings by Pollock or Cézanne or Manet – 'unintelligible', 'meaningless', 'incompetent', 'flat', etc. – and the judgements implied within the terms 'travesty' and 'parody'. Modernist criticism eventually turns these pejoratives round into terms standing, finally, for value and complexity, though Greenberg's and Fried's stress on 'positivities' and 'tradition' has been opposed continually by Clark's stress on 'negation' and 'situation'. Clark's reading of Cubism continues and elaborates this emphasis, building an account of modernism's complexity and value out of its 'turning over', or travestying, or parodying, of illusionistic pictorial conventions. Greenberg presents Cubism as an apocalyptic moment of revelation in the modernist tradition. This view became art-historical orthodoxy many decades ago. However, for Clark, these paintings are rather to be understood as brilliant absurdist games played in paint on canvas, *leading nowhere*. One aspect of Clark's reading of Cubist pictures stresses the painted surface as an actually mendacious presence. His use of the term 'counterfeit' is designed to suggest this active attempt to confuse or trick the viewer.

In contrast, it is a staple of art history to portray Cubist painting as a coherent 'style' the development of which can be mapped, in paintings by Picasso and Braque, over a period of about ten years. This style is divided, ontogenetically, into phases given names such as 'analytic' and 'synthetic', 'classic' or 'late'. This rhetoric – with its biological overtones – implies that its object is a form of life, or process of evolution, or a special kind of visual representational entity. The latter status Cubism still holds in standard art-historical accounts, which Clark takes to task near the beginning of his essay, quoting this passage from William Rubin, written when he was the Museum of Modern Art's chief curator of painting. Rubin is talking about *Ma Jolie*:

> Such paintings are difficult to read, for while they are articulated with planes, lines, shading, space and other vestiges of the language of illusionistic representation, these constituents have been largely *abstracted* from their former descriptive functions. Thus *disengaged*, they are *reordered* to the expressive purposes of the pictorial configurations as *autonomous* entities.[40] [My italic.]

Such accounts, similar to those produced in later structuralist readings of Cubism, encode the idea that Cubism constitutes a new 'language' in visual form. This notion of 'language', however, is derived from that definition given by the linguist Ferdinand de Saussure in the first decade of the twentieth century.[41] That is, language understood as a set of formal signs ('constitutents') belonging to one system ('reordered'), meaningful *only* in relation to other terms within the system ('autonomous'), and unconnected, as a system of terms, to the world of things ('abstracted', 'disengaged').

Clark's view, in contrast, is that Cubism is no such thing, though it may appear, or 'pretend', to be. 'Cubist painting is not a language; it just has the look of one', he asserts, adding that a language needs at least two 'native speakers', and Braque's role was always subordinate to Picasso's.[42] Neither, he concludes, is 'Classic Cubism'

> a grammar of objects or perceptions; it is a set of painterly procedures, habits, styles, performances, which do not add up to a language game. These are exactly the circumstances in which there

will most likely be one performer who invents the main way of doing things . . . while the other just imitates or reproduces them, not very well. Not very well, because at the deepest level these are not ways of doing things that can be learned [like a language?]. They are not thrown up by any particular descriptive task.[43]

Ma Jolie oscillates, then, between signing elements from the world and reasserting 'itself' as painted surface. The formal manner in which it manages to do this – through evenly distributed configurations of lines and patches of illusionistic painting, these 'respecting' the limit of the canvas support; the narrow range of tones in dark greens, yellows, and browns – certainly achieves an 'effect' of systematicity, or what Clark calls a 'counterfeit'. The painted words 'Ma Jolie', included at the bottom of the painting, could be read as letting the viewer 'in' on the joke ('words point to things', don't they?), at the same time as the viewer is kept from reading 'into' the picture any really consistent or recognizable likeness.

In this sense the painting – and Cubism as a whole, according to Clark – is not so much a mere gamut of mendacious devices as an articulated surface that *points* to mendaciousness in illusionism. 'Illusionism . . . was to be recovered in all its true (enviable) simple-mindedness – as the conjuring trick it once had been', to repeat Clark. Magic tricks are declared as such, aren't they? They happen – get 'performed' to use Clark's word – in contexts where their nature as contrivance is highlighted. It is only the mechanics of the trick that remain mysterious: one knows the trick has been done – that it *is* a trick – but is left to puzzle over how. Paradoxes, undecidables, deadlocks, and face-offs typify the Cubist painted surface. Things can be read one way or the other. In *Woman with Pears (Fernande)* the component elements of this woman's face and upper torso can be read as reversible – concave or convex – pointing the viewer into the picture or outwards, away from it. Clark notes that the 'grid', the systematicity of disseminated markings and tones in *Ma Jolie*, replaces the simply reversible cube: another feint of 'development' or 'progress' for those who want to see it, perhaps?[44]

Clark's argument suggests to me what might be called an implicit attitude of neutrality towards the 'world references' present in Cubist pictures – that is, a downgrading of the significance of *particular* subject matter elements depicted. If Clark's account is taken to reflect a similar neutrality on Picasso's part, then this may go someway to explain the artist's decision to use non-allegorical 'minor' genre subjects, such as portraits, landscape, and still-lifes. The shocking 'history-painting' scale of Picasso's *Demoiselles d'Avignon*, depicting full-length figures – carrying with them the traditional baggage of allegorical and heroicizing intent – puts its authentic 'Cubist' designation into doubt, whatever else one might think about this painting. The significance of Cubist collages including newspaper elements reporting the Balkan Wars raise the same kind of general question. Clark's judgement on Cubism seems similar to his on Pollock's drip-paintings – including his expression of subjective doubts that I shall come to later. Cubist pictures, that is, *do* figure or gesture the tokens of a world beyond art, but in so doing point out, simultaneously, the material nature and mechanics of that act and process of reference.

In this sense Cubism's complexity lies in its own distinctive representation of 'occluded totality', a wholeness figured – 'conjured' – but not, ever, achieved. The double-meaning of 'obscurity' perfectly fits this description. *Woman with Pears (Fernande)* and *Ma Jolie* play their games with light and dark, as well as with line, and therein lies their (un)intelligibility: their not 'adding up' to any identifiable whole, what Greenberg called Cubism's 'difficulty'. It is the obscurity, too, of Manet's *Olympia*, Cézanne's *Mont Sainte-Victoire*, and Van Gogh's *A Pair of Shoes*. What do these pictures really show? [Plates 1, 3, and 2]. Cubism, states Clark,

> does stand in some kind of relation to a world we might recognize and traverse . . . Cubism [has a] deep, wild, irredeemably obscurity . . . Cubism [is a] first move, not [a] final conclusion . . . The problem is to lay and keep hold of Cubism's *ambition* for its obscurity, its seeming certainty about the mad language it used – its great totalizing will . . . [and] coexistence of farce and metaphysics.[45]

Note the congruity of 'farce' with travesty and parody: a 'dramatic work intended only to excite laughter, often by presenting ludicrously improbable events'; anything 'fit only to be laughed at; a hollow pretense, a mockery' (*Oxford English Dictionary*). Cubism is dark and melancholic, then, because it presents, through its travesties of illusionism, the contingencies of seeing and appearances, *but not, to repeat, from any position outside of this contingency*. *Ma Jolie* may put 'illusionism through its paces', but once these visual metaphors of presence and absence – things clearly 'in front of' and 'behind' each other – are set into motion 'they career on to the edge of utter obscurity'.[46]

Clark's stress on negation is a salutary rejoinder to Greenberg's celebration of Picasso's sensitivity-improving 'difficulty' in 'Avant-Garde and Kitsch'. Clark *would* agree, I think, that Cubist paintings form part of what Greenberg calls, in a footnote to his essay, 'Athene': that is, 'formal culture with its infinity of aspects, its luxuriance, its large comprehension'. But Clark stresses that Cubism is *not* an emblem of 'modernist humanism', but rather a sponsor of unsettling ambiguity and incoherence, leading nowhere:

> Look again, the picture says, look beyond the details to the totality! But how, exactly? With what criteria? If the totality does not come out of the details, then where *does* it come from? How is a complex sequence of illusions – imitations of some sort – supposed to generate a non-imitative whole? . . . only Carl Einstein knew how to speak of this side of Cubism with the right apocalyptic snarl – there is darkness and obscurity, a deep shattering of the world of things; but on the other, there are signs of that darkness and obscurity being produced by sheer tenacity of attention *to* the world and its merest flicker of appearance; and a deep fear, not to say loathing, of the picture's totalization looking 'unverifiable' . . .[47]

The stakes here, it should be obvious, are very high: 'darkness', 'shattering', 'apocalyptic', 'fear', 'loathing' are highly emotive – and themselves obscure, that is, metaphoric, terms. Clark is talking about paintings, but about more than that too: avant-garde artists and their art as what he calls a 'not unreasonable response to bourgeois civilization since 1871'. Picasso's *Ma Jolie* and Pollock's *Lavender Mist* (1948) both featured significantly in his acrimonious 1980s exchange with Fried over the questions of tradition versus situation, achievement versus doubt, and positivity versus negation in modern art.

Clark's tone, overall, is much nearer to Greenberg's in 'Avant-Garde and Kitsch' and 'Towards a Newer Laocoon', than it is to Fried the formal art critic. Pollock's and Picasso's paintings might have, or might not have, achieved wholeness, Clark decides, but what should be stressed is the violence with which, in both pictures, 'the normal repertoire of likeness is annihilated and [the question of whether] any other ground for representation had been secured, or could possibly be secured, in the process'.[48] His later answer is, of course, 'no': Cubist paintings may look like a language that could be learned, but they don't constitute one, and don't 'lead' anywhere. 'Why is it,' Clark asks, that 'modernist critics (Fried is typical here), when they encounter a history of modernism in which its masterpieces are not all pictured as triumphant openings on to fullness and positivity, are so ready to characterize that history as merely hostile, telling a story of "futility" and waste?'[49] Negation, Clark restates, is an understandable response by avant-garde artists to the hostile situation of capitalist society.

Cubist pictures, then, have a power to 'contradict experience', and Clark admits that his account doesn't add up to a resolved whole any more than Cubism itself ('better . . . a stream of metonymies than a neat metaphorical mix').[50] Picasso's oval painting *The Architect's Table* (1912) presents a 'great pretense of re-seeing' the world but in practice – in looking at it, that is – the viewer, Clark asserts, is led only back to the surface, 'back to the play of procedures'.[51] But Clark determinedly adds the judgement that if these pictures from 1911 and 1912 revel in their own inconclusiveness, then this is a sign also of their 'failure' – 'their inability to conclude the remaking of representation that was their goal'. Somehow, the acts of illusionism 'work too efficiently, they do not happen enough on the surface. They have lost hold of the metaphor of their own insufficiency'.[52] Clark rhetorically appeals here to a projected subject, conflating and construing, I suggest, both an 'intending agency' responsible for making these paintings and a viewer seen as their 'creator of meanings'. It is to this proposed composite subjectivity – and its literal and metaphorical guises as 'painter', 'painting', and 'interpreting critic' – that I turn now in the final section of this chapter.

Clark's critical subject

Clark's essays on Pollock, Picasso, and Cézanne (the subject, along with Van Gogh, of my next chapter) all declare a self-consciousness and tentativeness of judgement absent in his books on Manet and Courbet. It may be that Clark experienced similar tentativeness when writing those studies, but if so it does not find the recurrent expression evident in *Farewell to an Idea*. Clark, that is, finds it necessary to include these consistent signals of doubts over his analyses and evaluations. Clark's 'attitude towards the paintings' is bound up, he acknowledges, with some unresolved subjective interests. He had declared the inevitability of the existence of such interests *as a general feature of aesthetic experience and judgement*, of course, in earlier essays – particularly in his 1980s argument with Fried, when, whether they liked it or not, both seem to have forced themselves into some unitary position they may not have wished otherwise to occupy.

An explanation of Clark's tentativeness in *Farewell to an Idea* might include discussion of his decision to write relatively short essays about several artists, rather than a full book-length study on one or more of them. For whatever undisclosed reasons and circumstances, then, Clark opts not to produce the kind of extensive ('thick') historical account that characterized his studies of Manet and Courbet – including, in the case of the latter, a companion volume on the wider situation of art in France around 1848.[53] I noted, while discussing his chapter on Abstract Expressionism, the scant attention given to the politics and social history of the Cold War period, in what is, in any case, a short essay. The brevity results in this, and the other essays, often appearing to consist in a series of brilliantly extended stipulations, claims, and qualifications, rather than slower-paced elaborated argument and the subsequent development of nuanced positions. But the factors of length and depth of account will never provide a sufficient answer to the question of tentativeness. In an earlier published version of his essay on Pollock Clark includes several *extending* 'endings' to his account, each making additional points and clarifications. When I first read this I thought I was being introduced to a stylistic device Clark somehow believed was appropriate to the materials under discussion.[54] And anyone who consults the substantial footnotes in *Farewell to an Idea* will see that Clark has intentionally 'buried', or made tertiary, many complicated sub-arguments and elements of analysis that might have entered his main text.

So I think it is the case that his essays on Pollock, Picasso, and Cézanne deliberately foreground – even 'isolate' – his discussion of their paintings as material artefacts of visual analysis. 'Visual analysis' can be a confusing term: it refers both to the activity of looking at, say, a painting, but also to the analytic perspective and protocols that constitute the means of understanding paintings. In this second sense the analysis is never exclusively 'visual', though it includes the actions and processes of literally looking hard and long at the object of study. 'Looking at', however, is a metaphor for 'examining', 'reviewing', or 'engaging with', and many other things besides. Analysis – including literally looking – as Clark himself has been at pains to stress, is inevitably an intellectual, cognitive-linguistic activity: arguably it can have no effective or 'worldly' existence until it becomes an item of discourse communicable to someone else.[55] This could mean, at one level, simply talking to, and arguing with, a companion about what one 'sees' (understands) when looking at, say, *Ma Jolie*, in the Museum of Modern Art in New York; at another, it could mean delivering a lecture, or producing an extensive written study based on examination of a wide variety of materials, along with consideration of the painting itself.

Accounts of the 'direct experience' of paintings in Greenberg's and Fried's own writings have earned the label modernist – since the 1980s often used in a derogatory fashion – because they have stressed, or appeared to stress, a claimed *im*mediate or unmediated engagement with, and understanding of, the artwork. As if this experience was detached in some fundamental way from reflective thinking and all other human social activities, and interests. Yet clarifications of this claimed experience, as I have shown, indicate that both Greenberg and Fried were aware of, and acknowledged, the inevitability of such interests intervening between the painting and the critic's notionally disembodied 'eye'. Greenberg, as it were, nods at one point and states that the sympathetic critics, and others who are sensitive enough, learn to experience modern art *relevantly* – that is, in the 'right' way. But where does the notion of the 'right' way come from? The circularity here is identical to that identified in many critiques of Clive Bell's famous – or infamous – assertion that something called 'aesthetic emotion' is generated *only* by the sufficiently sensitive viewer's recognition that a particular artwork exhibits something called 'significant form'. But how can 'significant form' be sensed except by those capable of experiencing 'aesthetic emotion'? There is, and can be, no 'proof', that is, of the existence of either phenomenon outside of the experience of the other. The 'aesthetic emotion'/'significant form' claim is, then, entirely a matter of subjective belief, rather than rational – that is, falsifiable – argument, and therefore merits the technical philosophical designation of 'ineffable'.[56] Clark makes this point forcibly in his debate with Fried: the claimed modernist aesthetic experience is partly a matter of desire, of *wanting* to have that sense of *im*mediacy, *believing* in the revelation of a painting's value or greatness, *yearning* for a kind of transcendence of normal life (Introduction, p. 32).

But this is completely alien to the kind of engagement with paintings that Clark develops in *Farewell to an Idea*. Clark is concerned with paintings' surfaces as material entities, but also as vehicles for metaphoric meanings that point to the world beyond the material surface. It is not surprising that it is the paintings of Pollock, Picasso, and Cézanne that preoccupy Clark, as he sees them as the most complex, inflected, deliberated, contradictory, and convoluted surfaces in modern art. But as they are not 'resolved' as surfaces, do not achieve this 'irresolvability' through some knowable act of will on the part of their producers, nor exemplify Fried's sense of modernism's 'fullness' and 'positivity', then Clark himself will not claim to have found some conclusive explanatory key to them. Hence he comes to describe some of these paintings as brilliant 'failures' – by which I think he partly means disappointments – and modernism 'itself' as a failure or disappointment. It is so, then, in the sense that its overweening and naive utopian imaginings of new Beginnings or Endings through abstraction, or rediscoveries of Nature or Body or Sensation, will disappointingly turn out to be yet more feints and illusions. We are not living in 'post-modernity', Clark asserts in his Introduction to *Farewell to an Idea*; rather, utopian modernism has come to an end *because* the full actual horrors of modernity have finally arrived.[57]

Greenberg declared in 1946 that although he was a Socialist, 'a work of art has its own ends, which it includes in itself and which have nothing to do with the fate of society'.[58] I do not think Clark could agree with this sentiment as a matter of historical principle – his studies of Courbet and Manet surely demonstrate that – but in the circumstances of the Cold War and the manipulation of art as a vehicle of propaganda throughout the 1930s and the years of the Second World War, the *ideal* Greenberg expressed was very similar to that articulated by contemporary painters such as Pollock and Rothko. And avant-garde artists wanted, on the whole, to separate themselves off from bourgeois society, as much as they were forced into forms of economic or social marginality, though there were notable exceptions, at least for some of the times in their careers – Clark's essay on Kasimir Malevich demonstrates that.[59] Avant-garde art has always been a sign of this social detachment in the context of bourgeois-capitalist re-, and subsequent de-, composition, Clark observes, while ruminating on Greenberg's 1939 essay. That *is* its historical fate and the source of that art's own negating strategies and situation. And that *is* its ambiguous value and meaning.

Clark decides: 'The best I can offer on Cubism is a medley of *pensées detachées sur le peinture* – a set of stabs at description, full of crossings-out and redundancies, a bit like the Cubist grids I am trying to find words for. This disconnected quality seems necessary to me ... because it is the opposite quality I most distrust in the accounts of Picasso's painting ... continuity ... logic ... sequence ... not being broken or interrupted ... not, above all, encountering failure.'[60]

Clark wonders out-loud whether this 'attitude towards the paintings' is itself reliable. Is his 'on the one hand' and 'on the other' a response to 'a dialectic genuinely within Cubism, or just me wanting to have my cake and eat it?'.[61] The literal and metaphorical obscurities within Cubist painting seem to lead Clark to a form of sceptical self-consciousness.

These obscurities of meaning cannot be resolved through recourse to forms of evidence outside of the painting's surface. Obscurity *is* the meaning. *Ma Jolie* is itself a kind of metaphor for this problem of figuratively proposed and obscured subjectivity, be it Picasso's, the identity of the painting as surface, or Clark's own. The picture's

> metaphorizing of its subject, as I see it – and I want to call that subject simply the process of representation – happens in micro-structure: the metaphor, the shifting, is in the relation of procedures to purposes, of describing to totalizing, of 'abstract' to 'illusionism' . . . in the obscurity.

Clark's 'I want to call it' here is exactly the phrase used by Fried who also, in his use of it, inserts a self-declared tentativeness 'into' the picture.[62]

If modern art's 'subject' becomes solipsistic due to the increasing detachment of its producers from broader society, who then occupy various positions against or outside of this society, as Greenberg acknowledges, then the development of 'sympathetic' criticism can surely not remain immune to this process. Some – like Bell (with Cézanne), Greenberg (with Pollock), and Fried (with Stella and Caro) – will come narcissistically to identify themselves with particular modern painters. Greenberg recognizes something of this eventuality in a 1946 book review. 'Rationalism and romantic idealism', he notes:

> holding that the root of all phenomenal reality is the individual consciousness, produced . . . an aesthetic that worshipped the genius, associated beauty exclusively with the fine arts and literature, and identified the work of art with its non-sensory 'idea'. Hitler was in large part a creature of the doctrine of amoral egoism popularized in Germany by romantic-idealist philosophy.[63]

The subject of Chapter 5 will be paintings by Cézanne and Van Gogh, along with their critical interpretation by the philosophers Merleau-Ponty and Heidegger. The political implications of modern art, as far as the 'amoral egotist' Hitler understood them, will also feature. Within these accounts an idealizing – and demonizing – of modern painting's necessarily *material* 'vision' and 'sight' will be particularly evident.

Chapter 5

The materials of seeing

Cézanne and Van Gogh

Art Fiction Two

'Everything he said suggested he was talking about an actual pair of boots, not about a picture of them. That's the point. At no point does he make it clear that he is referring, even indirectly, to a specific representation. He talks about "great works of art" but the idea he has in his head is of a pair of boots, not of a picture of a pair of boots' (statement attributed to Speaker A).

'The mountain is the same, isn't it? It's in Cézanne's head, isn't it? It's not an actual mountain – although the title refers to an actual mountain and everyone thinks it's of an actual mountain. But it's the idea of a mountain, even the "idea of drawing a mountain", but not the drawing of an actual mountain. Doesn't he say somewhere (in French, obviously) that "art – it's in my head"? That proves my point' (questions and statement attributed to Speaker B).

'Same with the flowers. They might be referring to "flowers" but it's the idea of the flowers that matters, not any actual flowers that he might have seen or not seen' (statement attributed to Speaker A).

'And the same with the still-life then? Those apples meant to look as if they've been drawn really carefully, from "life", sort of lying next to the "jug" – it's not a matter of a real jug, or any real apples? Just in his head' (questions and statement attributed to Speaker B).

'Yes. In his head' (statement attributed to Speaker A).

'*When did art get into the head, then?*' *(question attributed to Speaker B).*

'*Well . . . It was always, sort of. But it got into the head in a more obvious way, or a different kind of way, at any rate, at the end of the nineteenth century*' *(statement attributed to Speaker A).*

'*You mean with Cézanne and Van Gogh?*' *(question attributed to Speaker B).*

'*I was thinking more of Manet*' *(statement attributed to Speaker A).*

'*Manet!*' *(exclamation attributed to Speaker B).*

'*What did Fried say – he "was painting consciousness", or something?*' *(question attributed to Speaker A).*

'*Do you mean that was Manet's subject?*' *(question attributed to Speaker B).*

'*Yes*' *(statement attributed to Speaker A).*

'*His own consciousness?*' *(question attributed to Speaker B).*

'*Or maybe it was his "relationship to his consciousness"*' *(statement attributed to Speaker A).*

'*Now that seems obscure!*' *(statement attributed to Speaker B).*

'*I'm afraid it is. Consciousness, I mean, not Fried's sentence – if that was what he did say*' *(statement attributed to Speaker A).*

Courting indescribability

In his review of an exhibition of paintings by Cézanne held at Paul Rosenberg's gallery in New York, in 1942, Greenberg notes what he thinks are the inadequacies he found in two paintings, one of Mont Sainte-Victoire and a still-life. The fact is, he concludes, that

> much of even the best of Cézanne's art seems unconsummated. Pictures filled with superb passages such as would by themselves earn any painter a great reputation *fail* somehow to coagulate, and remain instances of great painting rather than great paintings. Lacking the *simultaneous unity and diversity and the inextricability of part from part of realized wholes*, they miss that final perfection . . .[1] [My italic.]

Consider now Cézanne's *Mont Sainte-Victoire* (1888–1889) [Plate 3], *Still-Life with Water-Jug* (1892–1893), and *The Large Bathers* (1904–1906). In his statement Greenberg implicitly articulates two facets to the concept of complexity in modern art whose elements I have been mapping throughout this study. First, the morceau/tableau distinction – I turn to this fully in my next and final chapter on Manet. Second, the critical motif of 'failure' that Clark mobilizes in his essays in *Farewell to an Idea*. The latter notion, as I have shown, is bound up with the 'negating', 'cancelling' situation of modernism which creates productive incoherence, ambiguities, and unintelligibility in its (complex) objects. In this chapter, through a consideration of paintings by Cézanne and Van Gogh, I shall further examine modernist critical discourse bound up with these notions, and consider their intimate connection to issues of subjective identity and meaning.

Clark sees Cézanne's painting, rather like Picasso's 'classic Cubism', as the source for a general theme within modern art: doubt and indescribability in visual representation – a theme whose significance has been bolstered considerably by the weight and influence of Merleau-Ponty's ruminations on the artist's work. Cézanne's mind, as well as his materials of production, are conflated within these pronouncements. Listen to Clark and Merleau-Ponty:

1   The steadfast gaze [in Manet] rather quickly gave way to uncertainty (in this the case of Cézanne is exemplary). Doubts about vision become doubts about almost everything involved in the act of painting: and in time the uncertainty became a value in its own right; we could almost say it became an aesthetic . . . The courting of failure and indescribability is one main key to what that culture was. [However] Taking indescribability as an invitation not to look, or not to look closely, is truly to get modernism wrong.

(Clark)

2   Cézanne is an example of how precariously expression and communication are achieved. Expression is like a step taken in the fog – no one can say where, if anywhere, it will lead . . . Just as Cézanne wondered whether what came from his hands had any meaning and would be understood, just as a man of good will comes to doubt that lives are compatible with each other when he considers the conflicts of his own particular life, so today's citizen is not sure whether the human world is possible . . . And still . . . [Cézanne] had moments of doubt about this vocation. As

he grew old, he wondered whether the novelty of his painting might not come from trouble with his eyes, whether his whole life had not been based upon an accident of his body.[2]

(Merleau-Ponty)

Evident in both these statements is the implication that, whatever the local 'doubts' and indeterminacies in Cézanne's art, these are, in some way, related to broader social and historical circumstances of which they form a part (Clark's 'culture', Merleau-Ponty's 'human world'). Somehow 'indescribability', 'uncertainty', and expression 'in the fog' are not simply matters of one artist's 'vision' or ability or inability to communicate. Beyond that they are symptoms of a seemingly pervasive if not comprehensive incoherence in human relations – to the extreme extent that, as Merleau-Ponty claims, 'today's citizen is not sure whether the human world is possible'. His essay 'Cézanne's Doubt' was originally published just after the end of the Second World War, in the French journal *Fontaine* – remember, therefore, that the philosopher was clearly making contemporary symbolic philosophical and political use of his account of Cézanne's art. This is *not* to claim, however, that the social and historical conditions under which Cézanne's paintings were produced at the end of the nineteenth century and the beginning of the twentieth had, by 1945, been transcended. Merleau-Ponty, who had allied himself with the French Communist Party during the Nazi occupation, on the contrary, thought the conditions of modern capitalist society had certainly become exacerbated, but not changed fundamentally, since Cézanne's own time.[3] The contexts of Clark's comments are less – or rather, differently – problematic: these extracts are from his 1984 book on Manet and the essay on Cézanne published in *Farewell to an Idea*. Clark, like Merleau-Ponty, though, is pursuing modernism in the visual arts understood as a socio-historical phenomenon of modernity.

Visual 'incoherence' in Cézanne's paintings, then, for Clark and Merleau-Ponty, is evidence of some apparently general state in modern society – though it is bound up, at the same time, with Cézanne's own subjectivity. In addition, Clark believes that Cézanne's paintings have come to typify something of the nature of modernist visual representation. In this lies their value, and complexity, as canonical art objects. 'Certain works of art', Clark asserts, 'show us what it is to "represent" at a particular historical moment – they show us the powers and limits of a practice of knowledge.'[4] For Clark this epistemological significance is 'obscure' (remember the recurrence of this term in his account of Cubism) – he is here thinking particularly of Cézanne's 1875–1877

Bathers at Rest picture – a matter in the painting of what he calls 'inconsistency', 'displacement', the 'whirl of distractions and ambiguities'.[5]

The Large Bathers contains, like *Bathers at Rest*, depiction of human figures (that is, bodies), as well as pictorial 'figuration': the building blocks of visual metaphor in painting. Thirteen depicted human bodies, some rather sexually obscure, are positioned around an apparent clearing in a glade near a pond or lake. The figures seem to be both 'propped up' for the viewer to see them, but some also are posed looking back at the water, or have lines of sight directed somewhere else 'off set'. The painting's scene manages to appear, because of these dual positionings, both 'theatrical' in that the figures are obviously posed, and 'naturalistic' in that the depicted people are shown engaging – admittedly, oddly en masse – in some routine nude bathing and sunbathing. Parallels with Manet's *Le Déjeuner sur l'herbe* (1863) are inescapable – the same kinds of inconsistencies and doubts about place and activities are evident. Are these depictions of *real* people? What are they *really* doing 'there', where ever 'there' is? Cézanne's bodies – all 'nudes' – are both 'there' and 'not there', as one sees when one moves in to look closer at the surface: conjured three-dimensional solidity dissolves into contradictorily placed lines and patches of 'bared' and painted canvas. Are these nudes merely a prop for a great if eccentric performance in painting, the same kind of judgement made, that is, of Manet's hotchpotch scene of scrambled genres – another brilliant *morceau* not adding up to a *tableau*?

In contrast, *Mont Sainte-Victoire* [Plate 3] and *Still-Life with Water Jug* apparently propose visions – 'incoherent' in some ways, perhaps – of objects that this viewer, at any rate, can believe Cézanne might have really 'seen'. That jug clearly sits behind, and to the left, of the plate of apples; scrunched up serviettes have been placed here and there. The scene *is* in danger of 'disintegrating', it's true. The apples are partly invisible, the suggestion of the jug's shadow on the wall threatens to form an unrelated mass of dark green and black paint – but you might still imagine where you could really be standing in real space in order to see this real table in front of you. Similarly, the mountain in Cézanne's picture seems definitely *there* – its salience withering sensibly as it is so far away, and the trees, too, are being blown by the wind a bit into indistinctness. But if Cézanne entertained doubts about how the world looked from moment to moment – and about how these doubts could reasonably be pictured in these latter two paintings, then *The Large Bathers*, in contrast, is like a hulking great fiction, altogether made-up and make-believe. If the landscape and still-life seem to picture actual visual contingencies – how real things are seen and shown in paint on canvas – then in this 'fiction' of bared bodies sitting and moving in nature Cézanne appears to be trying, but failing, to invent what Clark calls a 'new pictorial unity'.[6] (Merleau-Ponty can recover this, though, in good modernist-critical fashion: 'the true meaning of painting . . . is continually to question tradition'.[7] Is that platitude what *The Large Bathers* adds up to, then?)

It seems simply another contingency, or 'accident', that Merleau-Ponty's essay was published for the first time in English alongside Greenberg's 'Modernist Painting' in the Spring 1965 edition of *Art and Literature*.[8] It was around this time, in fact, that Fried recalls encountering Merleau-Ponty's writings for the first time, as part of an intellectual milieu of Marxist and philosophical ideas.[9] Clark, however, in his 1980s exchange with Fried, while denouncing the critic's defence of the paradigmatic modernist aesthetic experience, scathingly discounts this influence: 'In critical practice, isn't *any* account of modern art's engagement with what it is not dismissed as being beside the great ontological point? And when it comes to ontology, all the nods to Merleau-Ponty cannot save Fried's prose from sounding like old-time religion.'[10]

It is, then, this question of 'embodied' vision in Cézanne – and of embodied vision as a kind of metaphor for modern artistic subjectivity – that preoccupies Merleau-Ponty in his writings on the artist and which finds an echo, with a very different resonance, in Clark's own essay. (Fried himself turns to this topic in a footnote on Cézanne in his book on Manet.[11]) In what follows I certainly present no full reading or dissection of Merleau-Ponty's writings on Cézanne; instead I briefly mobilize some ideas, observations, and claims that have a resonance with my own concerns.[12]

For Merleau-Ponty, Cézanne's art is a kind of 'thinking in painting'. For this reason I see the publication of 'Cézanne's Doubt' essay alongside Greenberg's 'Modernist Painting' in *Art and Literature* as a contingency laced with serendipitous significance – both essays present painting as a distinctively material practice which nevertheless has impregnated within it evident philosophical significances. In both cases too – though in markedly different ways – the authors propose that the artists they discuss found themselves somehow locked out of the possibility of knowing what the value of their painting truly was. For Greenberg, as I have shown, 'self-criticism' in painting is always carried on in what he stipulatively calls a 'spontaneous and largely subliminal way', claiming that the 'immediate aims of the Modernists were, and remain, personal before anything else'.[13] For Merleau-Ponty, Cézanne's painting is similarly a matter of immanent meaning:

> What he expresses cannot . . . be the translation of a clearly defined thought, since such clear thoughts are those which have already been uttered by ourselves or by others. 'Conception' cannot precede 'execution' [contrast this with Greenberg's stress on 'conception alone']. There is nothing but a vague fever before the act of artistic expression, and only the work itself, completed and understood, is proof that there was *something* rather than *nothing* to be said.[14]

Somehow 'thought' here has become locked into 'motif', the two made continuous and self-defining: of the painting and its painter, jointly, together as 'embodied subject'. Consider the Sainte-Victoire mountain again [Plate 3]. The task before Cézanne, says Merleau-Ponty, is

> first to forget all he had ever learned from science and second, *through* these sciences to recapture the structure of the landscape as an emerging organism . . . His meditation would suddenly be consummated: 'I have my *motif*', Cézanne would say, and he would explain that the landscape had to be centred neither too high nor too low, caught alive in a net which would let nothing escape . . . 'The landscape thinks itself in me' he said, 'and I am its consciousness.'[15]

Merleau-Ponty's Cézanne, I hope it is clear from this quotation, is pulled two ways. On the one hand, between what might be called a materialism of contingent vision, of seeing by an actual embodied human eye (needing 500 sittings for a portrait, marvels Merleau-Ponty), which then attempts to 'translate' this seeing into a concrete image in paint on canvas.[16] On the other hand, by an idealization of vision: the artist presented as a visionary with special abilities to see and show through painting represented as a primeval and transcendent human practice. This second view isn't too far away from the rhetoric of Barnett Newman's 'The First Man was an Artist' that Clark mocks (see Chapter 3, p. 114) – existentialism of various political and philosophical flavours including Merleau-Ponty's, was current throughout the later 1940s and 1950s in America during the Cold War.

Distinct and opposed, as these two directions surely are in principle, they somehow remain and return bound up together in nearly all of Merleau-Ponty's pronouncements on Cézanne. This is the case, I suspect, because of the philosopher's penchant for abstracting his discussion of Cézanne pictures into what sounds like exemplary, general, or *ideal* terms. For instance, on the integration of body, mind, and pictorial matter [consider Plate 3]:

> What is depth, what is light . . . What are they – not for the mind that cuts itself off from the body but for the mind Descartes says is suffused throughout the body? . . . Yet this philosophy still to be done is that which animates the painter – not when he expresses his opinions about the world but in that instant when his vision becomes gesture, when, in Cézanne's words, he 'thinks in painting'.[17]

Or on the physicality of painting (consider Cézanne's *The Large Bathers* (1904–1906)):

> The painter 'takes his body with him', says Valery. Indeed, we cannot imagine how a *mind* could paint. It is by lending his body to the world that the artist changes the world into paintings. To understand these transubstantiations we must go back to the working, actual body – not the body as a chunk of space or a bundle of functions but that body which is an intertwining of vision and movement.[18]

Note here Merleau-Ponty's explicit reference to Catholic mass ritual and the miracle of bread becoming Christ's flesh and wine His blood! What kind of miraculous visual representation is he proposing here for Cézanne? Finally, on the relations between an artist and his [*sic*] life, the philosopher poses the issue in a clearly, in fact, almost parodically historicist manner:

> Although it is certain that a man's life does not *explain* his work, it is equally certain that the two are connected. The truth is that *this work to be done called for this life.* From the very start, the only equilibrium in Cézanne's life came from the support of his future work. His life was the projection of his future work . . . There is a rapport between Cézanne's schizoid temperament and his work because the work reveals a metaphysical sense of the disease: a way of seeing the world reduced to the totality of frozen appearances, with all expressive values suspended . . . In this sense, to be schizoid and to be Cézanne come to the same thing . . .[19]

Clark, in contradistinction to Merleau-Ponty, as I will show, wishes to reinstate, in biological- and historical-materialist terms, the *psycho-physical* body, *contingent* vision, and *actual* paintings understood as Cézanne's situated response to, and place in the world – including his relation to past and contemporary painting. Clark agrees, though, that 'in' Cézanne 'body'/'vision'/'painting' have developed a kind of locked-in subjectivistic relation to each other. To Merleau-Ponty's idea of 'frozen appearances' Clark counters that a painting such as the 1895–1906 *Large Bathers* has 'a feeling of time here having stopped'.[20] The painting's 'unfinishedness' over such a long time, he claims, '*is* its definitiveness; and it is an unfinish that comes out of forty years spent meditating on what a conclusion in painting could be. This is a conclusion.'[21] Clark concedes, however, in a manner reminiscent of his reflections on his account of Picasso, that his own 'words go round in circles, as I think Cézanne's visualizations do'.[22] It is to these circularities and self-identities of meaning, in Cézanne's paintings and in modernist criticism, that I now turn.

Dreaming, doubting, doubling

For Merleau-Ponty, Cézanne's paintings, understood as 'concretized mind' envelop – or convolute, to use Clark's term as a verb – both actual empirical 'seeing' and idealized, artistic 'vision'. Pictorial composition is, simultaneously, a process of subjective self-composition. Consider *The Large Bathers* and *Still-Life with Water Jug*. 'The painter's vision,' Merleau-Ponty declares:

> is not a view upon the *outside*, a merely 'physical-optical' relation with the world. The world no longer stands before him through representation; rather, it is the painter to whom the things of the world give birth by a sort of concentration or coming-to-itself of the visual. Ultimately the painting relates to nothing at all among experienced things unless it is first of all 'auto-figurative' ... the painting is an analogue or likeness only according to the body; because it does *not* present the *mind* with an occasion to rethink the constitutive relations of things; because, rather, it offers to our *sight*, so that it might join with them, the inward traces of vision, and because it offers to vision its inward tapestries, the imaginary texture of the real.[23]

These 'inward tapestries' suggest something as abstract as what might be called mental events, but they might equally suggest stories. Clark claims that Cézanne wanted to escape from 'narration, and from the dream-space', but *The Large Bathers* and the other big Bathers pictures suggests he couldn't; *Still-Life with Water Jug* may indicate the same, though we are used to seeing these 'minor genre' objects (like the same in Cubist pictures) as basically semantically neutral, or narrative-free.[24] Both Merleau-Ponty and Clark acknowledge that psychoanalysis can take hold of any object, or depicted object, and make meaning from it, and both resort to a psychoanalytically informed consideration of Cézanne's art understood as 'embodied mind'.

Merleau-Ponty's use of the term 'schizoid' to describe the split between the artist's life and work, and their interconnection, becomes the trigger for a broad (rather than narrowly psychoanalytic) account of Cézanne as, on the one hand, agent, subject, and producer, yet, on the other, as 'determined', always already located, and subject*ed*. Merleau-Ponty's idealization of the former condition wins out over the latter – and therefore echoes Heidegger's phenomenology of 'self-making' that I turn to in the second half of this chapter:

> The 'hereditary traits', the 'influences' – the accidents in Cézanne's life – are the text which nature and history gave him to decipher. They gave only the literal meaning of his work. But an artist's creations, like a man's free decisions, impose on this given a figurative sense which did not pre-exist them. If Cézanne's life seems to us to carry the seeds of his work within it, it is because we get to know his work first and see the circumstances of his life through it, charging them with a meaning borrowed from that work. If the givens for Cézanne which we have been enumerating, and which we spoke of as pressing conditions, were to figure in the web of projects which he was, they could have done so only by presenting themselves to him as *what* he had to live, leaving *how* to live it undetermined. An imposed theme at the start [similar to Heidegger's 'thrownness'?], they become, when replaced in the existence of what they are part, the monogram and the symbol of a life which freely interpreted itself.[25]

This existentialist account is a paradigmatic treatise for the autonomous, self-sufficient, transcendent, and 'world-creating' male modern artist-subject.[26]

Clark dourly resists all such idealizations, instead wishing to pursue the materialisms of Cézanne's subjectivity and painting subjects: seeking the 'scientific' and 'positivistic' Freud as a guide to interpretation. This is late nineteenth-century psychology, then, as 'natural science' – with ambitions to reveal the same kind of 'hard truth' as the reality supposedly delivered in neo-Impressionism's systematic dots and dashes of colour – psychical processes understood, that is, as 'quantitively determined states of specifiable material particles' (remember Maynard Keynes: 'Our apprehension of good was exactly the same as our apprehension of green'!).[27] Cézanne owed it to Pissarro's painting, Merleau-Ponty agrees, that he set out to make an 'exact study of appearances'.[28] Cézanne shifts, however, from this 'totalization of matter' to another, claims Clark: the Bathers pictures are 'the final figure of Cézanne's materialism ... his plainest attempt to rewrite phantasy in material terms'.[29] These paintings rework narratives from his earliest pictures in the 1860s and 1870s – 'painted fantasies: a rape, a murder', notes Merleau-Ponty.[30]

But Clark *does not* offer, or seek to offer, a confident or thoroughgoing psychoanalytic interpretation of Cézanne's Bathers paintings. He hedges around this, talking instead of the way Cézanne, as it were intentionally and in control of 'himself', makes his pictures into psychodramas. There is a shifting or conflating of 'subjects' here, to say the least! That is to say, this is the point in *Farewell to An Idea* at which Clark's Marxism ('residual' or otherwise) will *not* surrender critical analysis to the hermeneutic black-hole that psychoanalysis – as a 'symptomization' of everything, as Merleau-Ponty acknowledges – offers.[31] (And of course I have used the figurative metaphor 'black-hole' here deliberately. What of it?) *The Large Bathers* 'irresistibly' brings to mind dreams or nightmares, Clark observes. Is this, then, the meaning of Merleau-Ponty's 'internal tapestry'? Clark, however, makes Cézanne more analyst than analysand. Or, nearer, imitates Mallarmé imitating Manet. Clark, that is, becomes Cézanne:

Let me show you bodies thoroughly subject ... to the play of phantasy; that is, deformed and reconstituted at every point by the powers of mind. But let them appear as they would in a world where all the key terms of our endless debate – imagination, mind, body, phantasy, and so on – would be grasped, by the bodies and imaginations themselves, as descriptions of matter in various states.[32]

The bodies ('figures') in *The Bathers*, Clark states, are like 'paper puppets on a three-inch-deep stage'.[33] That is, they are not 'meant' to be seen as real, but to be seen, obscurely, as representations: Cézanne ('Clark's Cézanne') may have become the analyst, but this will not lead to any evident cure!

Clark himself, that is, is caught between 'real' and 'representation', between pathos and bathos; somewhere where 'cancelling, negating', modernism – at its best! – finds itself. Frozen timelessness, to conflate Merleau-Ponty's and Clark's descriptions of Cézanne's painting, might be another phrase for this modernism. Within the ' "Unhappy Consciousness . . . Everything past is preserved", as Freud put it in *Civilization and its Discontents*', Clark reminds us. 'Hence Pollock's paintings' congestion. Hence their rancor and repetitiveness. A whole history of modernism could be written . . . in terms of the cross-fertilization between Hegel's pessimism and historicism, and that of the Freudians. Pollock would be as much a central instance as Cézanne.'[34]

Clark's own subjectivity forces itself again to the front. He 'admits' his account of Cézanne 'is gross reading-in on my part'. The painting 'invites' or rather, he suggests, 'coerces' it. One kind of abstracted 'seeing' (Cézanne's) demands another (Clark's), you might say.[35] Merleau-Ponty knows this too: 'it is obvious that a [psychoanalytic] doctrine which brings in sexuality everywhere cannot, by the rules of inductive logic, establish its effectiveness anywhere, since, excluding all differential cases beforehand, it deprives itself of any counter-evidence'.[36] The subject's subject is the subject. The object's object is the object. In the end you just have to laugh along with Clark:

> I remember years ago seeing a comic routine about the London *Bathers* in which two idiot visitors to the National Gallery were impressed by Cézanne's ability to make the figures' bottoms 'follow you round the room'. Not bad criticism, I thought at the time.[37]

Some rock-bottom solipsism has indeed been reached.

Clark concedes the power of (obscure) narratives – dreams or nightmares? – in paintings like *The Large Bathers*, but implies, arguably, that these pictures, like Pissarro's paintings of peasants, though 'idealized, or prettified, or sentimentalized . . . may only describe . . . keeping a dream of humanity alive'.[38] This is, then, a part of Cézanne's materialism and his modernism.

Though *not* a 'tradition' in the visual art of the last 150 years, a point on which Clark is adamant, materialism and modernism *have* gone together in the best art.[39] This was the balance of 'full complexity', he notes, that Pissarro wanted and saw in Cézanne's art; a balance 'between peculiar "synthesis" and respect for visual facts, between ornament and awkwardness'.[40] The balance can be seen in *Still Life with Water Jug*: on the one hand, the crude 'thatness' of the apples on the plate; on the other, the vanishing greens and bared white canvas. Somehow, the very 'distortions' (synthesis, ornament?) in Cézanne's drawing, Greenberg similarly notes, in an essay from 1951, were 'provoked by the extremely literal exactness of his *vision*'[41] [my italic]. There's that word again. It seems to suggest empirical, actual seeing, but always connotes, or conflates it with, some overarching, transcending capacity abstractly to 'see' and 'show'. But Greenberg doesn't believe Cézanne usually managed to pull off this unifying task: 'great painting but not great paintings', morceaux but not tableaux. Cézanne, he concludes, was 'even further from the old masters in his means than they: his registration of what he saw was too dense, not in detail but in feeling . . . Think of the effort of abstraction and of eyesight that was necessary in order to analyze every part of every motif into its smallest calculable plane.'[42] Cézanne the mad scientist again, then, or what Clark calls 'long and hard looking and reflection on that looking'.

Listen to the artist, via his 'interpolator-interpreter' Merleau-Ponty, explaining his technique for showing – his 'vision', that is:

'If I paint all the little blues and all the little maroons I capture and convey his glance. Who gives a damn if they want to dispute how one can sadden a mouth or make a cheek smile by wedding a shaded green to a red' . . . The painter who conceptualizes and seeks the expression first misses the mystery – renewed every time we look at someone – of a person's appearance in nature . . . In *La Peau de chagrin* [literally: 'the skin of sorrow'] Balzac describes a 'tablecloth white as a layer of newly fallen snow, upon which the place-settings rise symmetrically, crowned with blond rolls' . . . [Consider here Cézanne's *Still-Life with Water Jug* (1892–1893)] . . . 'All through youth' said Cézanne, 'I wanted to paint that, that tablecloth of new snow . . . Now I know that one must will only to paint the place-settings rising symmetrically and the blond rolls. If I paint 'crowned' I've had it, you understand? But if I really balance and shade my place-settings and rolls as they are in nature, then you can be sure that the crowns, the snow, and all the excitement will be there too.'[43]

Compare and contrast this with the following statement from Heidegger on 'seeing', or 'sensation':

> We never really first perceive a throng of sensations, e.g. tones and noises, in the appearance of things . . . rather we hear the storm whistling in the chimney, we hear the three-motored plane, we hear the Mercedes in immediate distinction from the Volkswagen. Much closer to us than all the sensations are the things themselves. We hear the door shut in the house and never hear acoustical sensations or even mere sounds. In order to hear a bare sound we have to listen away from things, divert our ear from them, i.e. listen abstractly.[44]

Both statements seem to me to be, in their opposed ways, about identity and identification, and equally about objects and objectifications. Van Gogh was after seeing and showing a material truth in his painting of a pair of old shoes. Heidegger saw the subject as a search for an origin [Plate 2]. But was it, after all – like Cézanne – only in his eyes?

'Thinglyness' and peasant leisure

Van Gogh's painting of a pair of shoes [Plate 2], like Cézanne's still-life pictures, has been subject to extensive interpretative debate within both art history and philosophical aesthetics during the twentieth century. I do not intend to review this body of discourse in any detail.[45] In both cases, however, it is striking how the 'smallness' – that is, the apparent lowly significance – of the paintings' subjects has managed to generate an inverse ambitious profundity to the hermeneutic engagement with them. It was modern art's feat, combined with the efforts of its critics, to be able to invest such 'minor genre' materials with a significance and value hitherto reserved for History Painting. Manet's 'scrambling' of the genres in his early 1860s paintings represents a beginning to this process which I shall turn to in my final chapter. Cézanne and Van Gogh – both exemplary modern 'artiste maudit' figures of the late nineteenth and early twentieth centuries – managed to cathect to these paintings ghosts of their expressive natures and 'artistic vision'. 'Modern subjectivism', observes Heidegger, 'immediately misinterprets creation, taking it as the self-sovereign subject's performance of genius.'[46] And once the subject of modern art begins to be thought to be the manifestation of the artist's extraordinary subjectivity *believed to be injected into the artwork* – Abstract Expressionism's ideology of petty-bourgeois individualism writ large in art history – then a picture of anything, or nothing, will be able to take on this expressive significance. Van Gogh's *Sunflowers* (1888), for instance, have come to exemplify this 'symbolic-idealist' substitution of artist-subject for subject-matter, and the artist himself seen, correspondingly, as a 'model of alienated individuality'.[47]

Clark and Heidegger, in contrast, both see Van Gogh as a materialist painter, though in very different ways. Clark's comments on the painter are slight – no essay is devoted to him in *Farewell to an Idea*. But Van Gogh is implicated in discussion numerous times as a modern artist (perhaps like Pissarro?) 'clinging to a dream of martyrdom, or peasant leisure', concerned with depicting the life of the common people, in paintings such as *The Potato Eaters* (1885).[48] Heidegger is equally convinced that Van Gogh is painting, and pointing to, very basic things. His discussion of Van Gogh's picture of shoes in 'The Origin of the Work of Art' (1935) may be interpreted as an early articulation of the 'complexity as value' thesis that has been the focus of my study. My account of this essay will lead into a brief discussion of an infamous parallel contemporary diatribe – that by Adolf Hitler – on the 'corruptions' of modern artistic vision and its socio-historical pathology. Hitler, however monstrous in his proposed 'solutions' to the 'problem' of modern art, actually gets quite a number of things 'right' about its subjectivistic character and solipsistic tendencies. I include this discussion here to indicate that art criticism, philosophy, and art history have had no monopoly in the public examination of modern art: its value and significance has, at times – such as during the 1930s in Nazi Germany – been seen as an urgent and directly social and political matter.

Van Gogh's painting of a pair of shoes, or, at least, of two shoes together, symbolises a question for Heidegger. The picture exemplifies the riddle of the meaning, nature, and value of modern art. The shoes are depicted in no recognizable space, and they have no earth stuck to them as a possible clue to their use. They are, he ponders, simply a 'pair of peasant shoes and nothing more. And yet –.'[49] Heidegger decides to interpret the shoes as belonging to a woman peasant, and proposes their materials and contours as a kind of map of this woman peasant's life. The narrative spins on, evoking a whole world. 'In the shoes', Heidegger claims, 'vibrates the silent call of the earth, its quiet gift of the ripening grain and its unexplained self-refusal in the fallow desolation of the wintry field.'[50] We are far away from the pictorial depiction by now – that is surely Heidegger's point – and the question arises of how any kind of meaning 'read into' this depiction (into modern art in general?) can be grounded, or believed to contain truthfulness. Why are they peasant's shoes? Why a woman's?

Heidegger's interpretation, though subject to much claimed *factual* dispute in many of the subsequent readings of the picture, is most usefully understood as itself a meditation upon interpretation. It points valuably, that is, to the relative groundlessness to modern art's meanings: the relative meaninglessness peculiar to modern art. This is in comparison with the relatively objectified social and conventional meanings given to art *prior* to (1) the abandonment of genres and genre hierarchy, (2) the erosion of the power of state institutions to define the nature of art and the competences of artists, and (3) the decline in the ideological-propagandistic role of art in societies dominated by aristocratic and bourgeois patrons. If no meanings are prescribed, than none can be proscribed: 'meaninglessness' and 'meaningfulness' are thus opposite equivalents. It may be that Heidegger seriously *wanted to believe* certain things to be true about these depicted shoes (as Fried, or Greenberg, or Clark, do about Stella, or Pollock, or Cézanne), but it is the question of the grounding of the truth of these beliefs that most concerns him. These depicted shoes are, it appears, a morceau, a fragment, from which a whole world of meaning and value might be gleaned. How can that be so? How can the 'art work let us know what shoes are in truth?' Mere subjective 'reading-in' can be no answer, Heidegger declares. It must be that 'Van Gogh's painting is the disclosure of what . . . the pair of peasant shoes . . . *is* in truth . . . truth is put into the work. What truth is happening in the work? Can truth happen at all and thus be historical?'[51]

Notice how Heidegger's stipulation here gives way to a set of questions. To any answer there is always another question! There is an inescapable circularity to ascribing meaning and value to the artwork. This is familiar, isn't it? Clark's thoughts 'go round and round', he observes, as do Cézanne's visualizations. All he can offer on Picasso are some 'crossings-out and metonyms', no metaphoric 'fixes'. Part of Pollock is tawdry but not all of it. Abstract Expressionism's vulgarity *is* the truth about petty bourgeois individualism in the US after 1945. Fried and Greenberg might not admit it, but they are dreaming in their readings as much as Clark, who at least admits it! Away, then, with positivities and plenitude and achievement, with modernist *tradition*, rather than negating *situation*! 'Laughing at contingency', Clark says of Picasso's Cubism, but – don't laugh now – not from any position outside of it! Clark's modernism, to repeat, is mordantly anti-historicist and 'theoretically anti-humanist', to revive Louis Althusser's 1960s formulation.[52]

'What art is', puzzles Heidegger,

> should be inferable from the work: What the work of art is we can come to know only from the nature of art. Anyone can easily see that we are moving in a circle ... how are we to be certain that we are indeed basing such an examination on artworks if we do not know beforehand what art is? And the nature of art can no more be arrived at by a derivation from higher concepts than by a collection of characteristics of actual art works ...[53]

No one knows what this 'nature' is! Mallarmé seemed to know when he said that Manet's painting 'shall be steeped again in its cause, and its relation to nature', but it isn't clear for Heidegger.[54] And without knowing its nature it appears that you cannot know its meaning or value. Perhaps 'nature' refers, then, to the artist-subject, the artist as 'origin' of the artwork?:

> As necessarily as the artist is the origin of the work in a different way than the work is the origin of the artist, so it is equally certain that, in a still different way, art is the origin of both artist and work. But how can art be an origin at all? Where and when does art occur? Art – this is nothing more than a word to which nothing real any longer corresponds.[55]

In one sense, declares Heidegger, the only 'real' thing about modern art is its 'thinglyness', which is 'self-evident'. This is the physical quality to the artefacts that the 'shippers' and 'charwomen' operate with – when they have to move them around or dust them down. 'All works have this thingly character', Heidegger observes (does Richard Wilson's *20:50* have it in the same way, though, as Van Gogh's painting?)[56] [Plate 9]. All paintings, we might grant, have their thinglyness in the same way, but this cannot be the basis to their nature as works of art.

In fact, states Heidegger, not all paintings *are* works of art, which are things 'to which something else adheres' – the something else being what he calls at one point 'the much-vaunted aesthetic experience'. Heidegger, to reiterate, is only concerned with, he stresses, 'great art ... [and] only such art is under consideration here'.[57] His answer is that genuine works of art, though they are certainly things that are physically made, stand for something beyond their own 'thinglyness': *allo agoreuei* – they 'speak otherwise'. 'The work makes public something other than itself; it manifests something other; it is an allegory. In the work of art something other is brought together with the thing that is made . . . The work is a symbol.'[58]

Genuine works of art perform a revelation of truth, an 'uncon-cealment' (in Greek, *aletheia*): 'this opening up, i.e., this deconcealing, i.e., the truth of beings, happens in the work . . . Art is truth setting itself to work.'[59] 'Conviction', remember, was Fried's term for this: judgement (of artistic value) turned into fact or truth. Heidegger's notion of value in modern art, then, is also a version of 'good complexity' – a revealed, or 'deconcealed', plenitude of true meaning. It shares much more with Fried's account than with Clark's.

Van Gogh himself had a notion of the world as one 'vast symbol', claim Griselda Pollock and Fred Orton, and saw the universe as 'a great book of hieroglyphs'. Though this led him beyond what they call 'descriptive realism', he remained, they say – agreeing here with Clark's reading of Van Gogh as a materialist – 'deeply rooted in reality, however much he felt free in pictorial terms to heighten or exaggerate in order to convey that reality which was embodied in or clothed by external appearances'.[60] Think of the shoes, here, again – or of those five beings huddled around their table, knobbly faces and fingers on the point of caricature, yet all deadly serious. The people *and* the painting's surface are rough, 'unfinished'. (*The Potato Eaters*.) This picture might stand for Van Gogh's heroic-tragic vision of the 'material world' and his attempt, states Clark, to 'retrieve the shock of it'.[61] How might its means of material making be said to match that material world?

Van Gogh's experiments with technique indicate he searched for that match continually throughout the 1880s.[62] Greenberg, doubting the value of the results, declares that Van Gogh suffered from a 'faulty com-mand not so much of his medium as of his temperament'. Though there was 'much good painting in his bad pictures' – the morceau, but not the tableau again! – Van Gogh, unlike Cézanne, concludes Greenberg, 'could not rejoice in the limitations of his medium'.[63] The artist's sub-jective vision got in the way, Greenberg seems to be saying, of seeing what painting really should be showing. Pollock and Orton dismiss Van Gogh's psychomotor epilepsy condition (a neurological disorder) as any explanation for the way he painted or the meaning of his paint-ings. On the contrary, they argue, quoting Max Lieberman, the 'drama of his life did not embellish but obscure[d] the value of his work'.[64]

Greenberg actually calls Van Gogh, along with Cézanne, a 'mental case' in an essay published in 1946. 'Vision' in Greenberg's argument here ironically amounts to the claim that certain painters – certainly Cézanne, but *not* Van Gogh, who was afflicted by 'madness' – had the 'foresight' to be able to shut their eyes to established examples of art around them and in so doing were able 'to cut through to the ultimate truth of life as it is lived at present'. This is Greenberg's defence of modernism in the visual arts – and contemporary modernity, for that matter – as 'self-criticism': 'concrete sensation, immediate return, tangible datum'.[65] But, once again, the question arises: *whose* vision, and whose 'perspective' and interests, are we discussing here? Heidegger declares that the modern work of art is necessarily released into its own autonomy, let to 'stand on its own for itself alone'. Its producer's 'peculiar intention . . . aims in this direction. The work is to be released by him [*sic*] to its pure self-subsistence'.[66] *Not* Van Gogh's vision or intention, contradict Pollock and Orton: a painting such as *Starry Night* (1889), as well as *The Potato Eaters*, implicated, and was intended by its producer to engender, familiar meanings found – 'inter-textually' – in nineteenth-century novels and poetry extolling the superiority, and what Van Gogh called the 'purer nature', of the countryside over city or suburban life.[67]

What 'purities' or 'impurities' of subjective vision in modern painting did another contemporary critic of avant-garde art, lecturing, virtually at the same time as Heidegger, see?

Vision, value, and the diseased eye

Pollock and Orton concur with Clark that modern artists, by the end of the nineteenth century, had begun to develop a highly self-conscious sense of their own identity, and to think of their working life as a 'career'. They were also considering how they and their work would be seen in the future and thus had a stake – along with dealers, curators, critics, and eventually art historians – in attempting to influence how their artworks and lives could be seen, *retrospectively*, as continuous, developmental, and coherently meaningful. Of course, this self-consciousness wasn't an entirely novel feature of the mid- to late nineteenth century, but it was accelerated by various developments. These included: the growth of a market and dealer-system for contemporary art in Europe and the US; the publication of more journals and newspapers with art review and art news sections; new art museums and galleries fashioning parallel accounts, in exhibitions and catalogues, of the 'lives and careers' of past artists' works in their collections; and the spread of a new genre in fiction writing concerned directly with examining the character and plight of imagined contemporary artists.[68]

Van Gogh's letters and journal entries, then, should not be understood, argue Pollock and Orton, as 'spontaneous outpourings or unselfconscious reflections'. The artist deliberately presented himself as someone who was 'misunderstood and unrecognized'. Through both his writing and this self-presentation: 'he prepared and tailored a picture of himself and a view of his art which has survived, more or less intact, through the complicity of his brother, whose role in this characteristically modernist strategy of self-justification and documentation should not be underestimated'.[69]

His painting of a pair of worker's boots from 1887 (not that painting illustrated here) might have been an oblique 'self-portrait', Pollock and Orton suggest, for, around this time, Van Gogh had rejected bourgeois suits and begun to wear a workman's blue jacket. This putative self-depiction as a 'worker' brings to mind Fried's claim that Courbet had, similarly, portrayed himself *symbolically* as a labourer in his painting *The Stonebreakers* (1848).[70] I consider Fried's additional claim that Manet may have 'allegorized' himself *twice* in the same painting, as 'executioner' and 'executed', in his *The Execution of Maximilian* (1868–1869), in Chapter 6.

To see Van Gogh's painting of boots as a modern kind of self-portrait – inevitably enigmatic and obscure – is to understand it within the framework of the notion of complexity in critical discourse I have established and explored in this study. The painting is also an example of the morceau – that is, the momentary fragment standing for, replacing, intimating, an occluded totality or tableau – for it imitates, or travesties, an example of still-life subject matter while instating, if Pollock and Orton are correct, the artist-subject as the meaning (referent) of the depiction. The depicted boots are, then, *of* Van Gogh in both metonymic and metaphoric terms. Metonymically, as part standing for the whole, they are an element of his attire and desired self-image; metaphorically, they substitute one thing for another, boots for his identity.

In one sense Pollock's and Orton's claim will never be disproved. Such a hypothetical falsification would be dependent upon adducing something like documentary evidence from Van Gogh's writings, or some other source, in which it was stated conclusively that such a symbolic representation was never intended. Even this would not rule out claims – these not possibly falsifiable – that the artist had *unconsciously* wished to have himself represented in this manner in his painting. Throughout this study I have pointed to what I have called the 'dreaming' elements in criticism of modern art by Greenberg, Fried, and Clark: their 'wishing to believe'. Clark, alone, articulates manifest scepticism over some of his *own* claims about twentieth century art, acknowledging that the credence of his accounts of Pollock, or Picasso, or Cézanne, is conditional upon, determined by, the materials under consideration – primarily the intractably enigmatic, obscure, self-cancelling character of these artists' paintings. Conviction of 'truthfulness' in modern painting, and in its critical interpretation and evaluation, has become, to use a Heideggerianism, necessarily 'self-grounding': which is another way of saying that such claims are increasingly recognized to be, at base, subjective – though, of course, all three critics mobilize evidence of various kinds to bolster their assertions. To repeat: what the painting may be said to be 'of' does not tell us what it may be said to 'mean'. Artistic 'vision', for instance, may be interpreted as inspired by genius or corrupted by mental disease.

Listen to Hitler playing the art critic, lecturing in Munich in July 1937 on what the Nazis called 'Degenerate Art' ('*Entartete Kunst*'):

> I have observed among the pictures submitted here, quite a few paintings which make one actually come to the conclusion that the eye shows things differently to certain human beings than the way they really are, that is, that there really are men who see the present population of our nation only as rotten cretins; who, on principle, see meadows blue, skies green, clouds sulphur yellow, and so on, or, as they say, experience them as such. I do not want to enter into an argument here about the question of whether the persons concerned really do or do not see or feel in such a way; but in the name of the German people, I want to forbid these pitiful misfortunates who quite obviously suffer from an eye disease, to try vehemently to foist these products of their misinterpretation upon the age we live in, or even to wish to present them as 'Art'.[71]

Hitler states that modern art has become what he calls an 'international communal experience' and as a result lost any links to particular ethnic (or national) groups. No 'German or French or Japanese or Chinese art exists, but plainly and simply only a "modern art"'. Representation of historical 'times' has also ceased in the creations of 'Impressionism . . . Futurism, Cubism . . . Dadaism'. Instead, what time there is in modern art is only that of the present – 'only an art of the times'. (Fried, as I shall discuss shortly, also stresses both the radical internationalism of Manet's art and the transformed representation of temporalities his paintings manifest.)

The technical 'competence' of modern painters, along with their vaunted 'conception' of artistic purpose (using the term Greenberg will later adopt) is fit only for critical derision, declares Hitler:

> All those catchwords: 'inner experience', 'strong state of mind', 'forceful will', 'emotions pregnant with the future', 'heroic atti-tude', 'meaningful empathy', 'experienced order of the times', 'orig-inal primitivism', etc. – all these dumb, mendacious excuses, this claptrap or jabbering will no longer be accepted as excuses or even recommendations for worthless, integrally unskilled products.

Art and art activities, Hitler claims, have been 'lumped together with the handiwork of our modern tailor shops and fashion industries'. This has been the work of the 'primitive international scribblings' of 'so-called art criticism' that, along with Jewish control over German public opinion, has succeeded 'in confusing the natural concepts about the nature and scope of art as well as its goals'.

If the German nation was not already, by the end of the First World War, an 'already thoroughly diseased body' experiencing 'the total impact of its inner *decomposition*' (remember Clark's use of this term), then modern artists, Hitler declaims, were contributing an addi-tional layer of corruption:

> Either these so-called 'artists' really do see things this way and therefore believe in what they depict; then we would have to examine their eyesight-deformation to see if it is the product of a mechanical failure or of inheritance. In the first case, these unfor-tunates can only be pitied; in the second case, they would be the object of great interest to the Ministry of the Interior of the Reich which would then have to take up the question of whether further inheritance of such gruesome malfunctioning of the eyes cannot at least be checked.

But Hitler intimates that these artists are not necessarily witless or merely ill. They may have formed themselves, and have a sense of themselves, as a kind of opposition (an avant-garde? – 'not an unreasonable response to the events of 1871' states Clark) to mainstream society:

If . . . they themselves do not believe in the reality of such impressions but try to harass the nation with this humbug for other reasons, then such an attempt falls within the jurisdiction of the penal law . . . *For the artist does not create for the artist, but just like every one else he creates for the people* . . . all those cliques of babblers, dilettantes and art crooks which lend support to each other and are therefore able to survive, will be eliminated and abolished . . . We believe that especially today, when in so many realms the highest achievements are being accomplished, that also in the realm of art the highest value of a personality as an individual will make a triumphant reappearance.

Official Soviet Communist art criticism demonstrated, at mid-century, a reassuringly equivalent general literacy in the issues. Ten years after Hitler's pronouncements, on the eve of Pollock's drip-painting phase, the state commissar for culture, Vladimir Kamenov, wrote [consider Plates 3, 5, and 4]:

For all the 'freedom' which artists won after they had driven life from the realm of their formalistic art, they nevertheless tried at the beginning of the [twentieth] century to justify this subjective anarchy by pseudo-scientific, technical, and other subterfuges in their work, writings and declarations . . . to prove its analytical character, and so on. However, very soon even this quasi-scientific terminology was discarded, and in contemporary bourgeois formalistic art the most rampant subjectivism, proclaiming the cult of mysticism and of the subconscious, has triumphed openly, and abnormal mental states are held up as examples of the complete creative freedom of the individual . . .[72]

Might Kamenov also have had in his sights in 1947 the critical defence of abstract art that Merleau-Ponty's existentialist reading of Cézanne promoted, connected as it was at that point to Jean Paul Sartre's own foray into 'voluntarist' or 'Existentialist Marxism'?[73] (Kamenov also, it seems, anticipates Clark's debunking of the standard art-historical interpretation of Cubism as a break-through visual 'science' or 'language'.)

Both Hitler and Kamenov demonstrate the basic insight that avant-garde art can be read – that such art even insists that it *should* be read – as a symptom, morbid or otherwise, of the divisions and antagonisms that infiltrate modern capitalist society. Both also see that modern artists have striven, in their art, to either avoid or 'void' this modernity – or to find new ways of trying to represent their experience of it.[74] Had this not been Cézanne's and Van Gogh's goal: *The Large Bathers* 'back to nature' dream of what Clark calls 'naked intensity in the woods', or the attempt to find fresh expressive means in the unlikely materials of *A Pair of Shoes* [Plate 2] or *The Sunflowers*?[75]

Pollock and Orton argue that Van Gogh's art represented an attempt to 'respond to the change in sensibility, to realize a pictorial equivalent for a world in constant flux, a totality which demanded transformation of the role of colour, the movement and meanings of line, and the conventions for the depiction of space'.[76]

To determine, in fact, as Mallarmé had said of Manet – the producer of 'the first Modernist pictures', according to Greenberg – that ambitious painting 'shall be steeped again in its cause, and its relation to nature', and not limited 'by authority of dogmas'?[77] Greenberg's, Fried's, and Clark's critical accounts of Manet and the Impressionists have become predominant prisms through which the painter's intelligibility, and artistic legacy, has been ordered. In my next and final chapter writing back to modern art I consider their accounts of Manet's use of conventions in the representation of this modern 'world in constant flux'. What kind of 'totality' might this art, in retrospect, be said to have constituted?

Chapter 6

Modernism's Manet

Art Fiction One

In the taxi to the gallery Vicky started to think about whether Olympia was more or less of a flirt than the barmaid. Both were 'in-your-face' girls, there was no doubt about it, and she thought of them both as twenty-first century role models. But Olympia, despite the apparent (superficial?) splendour of her bedroom – or was that a morning room? – definitely had something of the look of a latently hungry, frightened rat about her. Or that was how she remembered it from her last visit, which had been almost ten years before. Thin might be in still but the barmaid, in contrast, looked well-fed, if a little vacant. Her staring eyes (was that what they did?) were still a bit more ambiguously 'come-hither', and not so mocking. Both girls were very sexy it was true – what had Manet done, according to . . . who was it? . . . Mallarmé: 'painted with his semen', or something like that. But there had been something wrong about the language, hadn't there? The original French had been lost so the English had had to be re-translated back into the French. 'Pollen' might have any number of likely (and less likely) synonyms. Anyway, it was quite a sexy idea in any language. Vicky looked out at the Paris night – the museum would be closed soon if the traffic didn't clear. She reflected that her memories of what she had seen were always clouding over and the girls' faces and bodies never appeared quite as she thought they would – they . . . kept changing. Or she kept changing. The two changings were bound up together, perhaps. They both might be Manet's creations – 'Manet's girls!' – but they were real for her: real in the sense that they pushed the right buttons about how she wanted to look and feel now. The ennui and blankness was definitely 2004. Real in the sense that they presented the dream she aspired to. She mostly kept it in her head, of course – seeing the pictures (not just the illustrations) only once or twice in a ten-year period! Maybe that was where the idealization took hold, not when she actually looked. The looking gave her something for her mind to feed on when she was away from the paintings – that was when they were most real and ideal, both somehow at the same time.

The taxi finally drew up. Vicky smoothed her black slit skirt. What would she see this time?

'True? Beautiful? Attractive? No! – what is it, then?'[1]

Manet's paintings change the subject.

Le Déjeuner sur l'herbe (1863), *Olympia* (1863), and *A Bar at the Folies Bergère* (1882) sought materials for art and worked them in such a way that the enterprise of painting, and its relation to criticism, was cast into radical doubt [Plate 1]. The future of painting and the characterization of modernism in the visual arts since Manet's time has been subject to two opposing projections, the contours and directions of which I have examined in this study. I have given these accounts the names 'good complexity' and 'bad complexity'. The former projection, encapsulated in the later ('post-political') criticism of Greenberg and that of Fried writing in the 1960s, erected onto the view of Manet as the 'first modernist painter' a tradition of ever improving positive achievement and absolute conviction that Fried claims reached an apogee in the abstract art of Louis, Stella, Noland, and Olitski [Plates 8 and 6]. Modernist art, Fried believes, evolved with these artists far from its origins in the 1860s. Fried's use of the term 'modernist' was definitive and became conclusive: those 1960s painters had stumbled into a time when painting had 'become' to be principally about aesthetic quality and value, and this had meant a preoccupation with the formal and material conventions of shape, colour, and facture. Those artists, moreover, were aware of the claims Greenberg had made in his essay 'Modernist Painting' articulating and defending his neo-Kantian view of the 'self-critical' aesthetic realm, and had produced their paintings in the light of – *some in concurrence with* – those claims.

'Bad complexity' has been the term I have used to characterize Clark's recalcitrant and sceptical account of modern art in the twentieth century. The achievements of Pollock, Picasso, and Cézanne were real, Clark stresses in *Farewell to an Idea* – these certainly *are* the greatest painters of the century – but their best paintings have installed negativity, obscurity, decomposition, and a sense of almost terminal breakdown at the centre of artistic practice. To call this series of situated 'responses to bourgeois civilization since 1871' a 'tradition', as Greenberg and Fried do, is fundamentally to idealize artworks whose meaning and value lies in, and in a radical sense, *against*, that modern history. Clark's constant stressing of avant-garde art's episodic 'cancelling' or 'effacing' of meaning and questioning of the contemporary terms of critical evaluation is relentlessly anti-historicist. It rejects fundamentally the claims of 'fullness', 'positivity', and 'achievement' that modernist art criticism and art history always wants and dreams that this 'tradition' represents.[2] In this sense, then, Clark, is, as I've stated, a theoretical 'anti-humanist'.

In turning to these critics' accounts of painting in Paris in the 1860–1880s for the putative origins of this set of developments – couched either as 'modernist tradition' or avant-garde 'episodic response' – one encounters a changed and, on the face of it, somewhat disorienting situation. Clark's book on Manet, *The Painting of Modern Life: Paris in the Art of Manet and his Followers*, was published in 1984, and Clark chose *not* to return substantively to the subject fifteen years later when assembling his essays on late nineteenth- and twentieth-century art.[3] He notes, as a kind of half-justification for this, what he calls the 'strangeness' of the nineteenth century and how far away Manet's art is from that of the avant-garde's in the twentieth century. Clark indicates, however, that he thinks Fried's 1997 study, *Manet's Modernism* or, *The Face of Painting in the 1860s* has made a start in coming to understand that strangeness.[4] Fried's book, published nearly thirty years *after* his long essay on 'Manet's Sources: Aspects of his Art, 1859–1865' – an account bound up with his defence *then* of contemporary abstract painting – bears scant resemblance to his 1960s art criticism. *Manet's Modernism* is a social-historical – though clearly in no sense a Marxist – account of painting in France in the mid-decades of the nineteenth century. At the same time, Fried's Introduction to *Manet's Modernism*, his reprinting there of the 'Manet's Sources' essay, and remarks in some footnotes, relate the book to his 1960s writings on much later artists.[5]

Both Clark and Fried, however, whatever their differences, want to understand how the valuable difficulty in Manet's painting – its 'intransigence' or 'illegibility' – is *about* Manet's world and his sense of relationship to it. One signal for this is that they both deploy the critical term I have focused on throughout this book. This is Clark on *Olympia* [Plate 1]: 'this manner of putting on paint ... from passages of open, *complex* brushwork to areas where line and colour had been quite brutally simplified ... should surely be seen as part of a *complex* attempt at meaning ...'.[6] [My italic.]

Now Clark citing the critic Jean Ravenel, who wrote about *Olympia* after its exhibition at the Salon of 1865:

> It is the only Salon entry in 1865 to say anything much – or anything reasonable – about form and content in *Olympia*, and the way one might possibly inflect the other. It seems to accept or produce a measure of *complexity* in its object, and the points of reference it proposes for Manet's picture are not only well chosen, but really explored in the text. This does not mean that Ravenel approves of *Olympia*, or thinks its allusions coherent.[7] [My italic.]

Finally, Fried on Manet's *Le Déjeuner sur l'herbe*:

> The *Déjeuner* ... projects a sense of those conditions [of paint-ing and spectatorship] being features of a world ... with all the largeness and *complexity* of feelings that implies ... All this ... could not be further from ... [the] ... idea that Manet had no more constant purpose than simply to oppose every conceivable structure of pictorial meaning.[8] [My italic.]

Complexity, to reiterate, *means* value and significance; and both Clark and Fried use the term in such a way that it mutually implicates object (painting) and subject (critic). Ravenel's discussion, Clark states, 'accepts' *or* 'produces' this complexity; Fried's (own?) complex 'feel-ings' are generated (in a subject) by the painting (object). The radical work Manet's painting does is to make viewers self-conscious of this subject-object relation, though the experience and meaning of this awareness might be – *was* at the time, and would remain for some – obscure. Manet's depiction of women, in *Olympia* and *A Bar at the Folies Bergère* in particular, draws the viewer's attention to the material fabrication and representation of identity and self-identity; to how other human subjects (and ourselves) might be portrayed, or seen, as objects. For Clark, but *not* Fried, this process in Manet's paintings leads to a kind of cancellation of established meanings, or at least to the threat of such a cancellation.

Clark examines this bad complexity in Manet's paintings using a lexicon of terms by now familiar through their appearance, directly or through a variety of synonyms and cognates, in earlier chapters of this study. These include 'unintelligibility', 'inconsistency', 'enigma', 'lack', and 'decay'. Remembering Clark on Cubism's 'obscurities' (Chapter 4, pp. 133–135), these are some of his remarks on *Olympia*. It is a painting which reveals, he claims, in comparison with other early 1860s paintings of nudes, 'the inconsistencies of its manufacture and breathed a kind of scepticism at the ways that likeness was normally secured'.[9] Remembering Clark on Pollock's 'crossing of metaphors' (Chapter 3, p. 94), Clark claims that Manet's painting, for its contemporary viewers, was '"informe", "inconceivable", "inqualifiable" . . . [Olympia] was "neither true nor living nor beautiful". The negatives multiplied.'[10] Remembering Clark's discussion, in his 1980s exchange with Fried, of the avant-garde oppositional strategy of 'negation', he is prepared – in his book on Manet – to make *Olympia* more or less its archetypal embodiment. This painting of 'prostitute'/'nude'/'model', he claims:

> makes hay with our assumptions as spectators, and may lead us to doubt the existence on canvas of three dimensions, the female body, *and other minds*; but this very negation is pictured as something produced in the social order, happening as part of an ordinary exchange of goods and services.[11] [My italic.]

Fried himself takes up these themes of spectatorship, subjective identity, and the 'depiction of consciousness', claiming, for instance, that Manet's later picture of *The Execution of Maximilian* (1868–1869, Mannheim version) was an attempt by the artist to 'allegorize' his own relationship to painting practice and the psycho-dynamics of spectatorship in the triadic 'painter-painting-viewer' matrix.[12]

Fried's concentration on Manet's self-consciousness and subjectivity, explored through his paintings, is probably the major point of contrast and dispute between his and Clark's accounts. Fried's interest seems to me to be motivated by the same kind of narcissistic identification with Manet that characterized his earlier engagement with the 1960s abstract painters. This is neither intended as a pejorative judgement, nor as a reason to cast doubt on the value of Fried's account of the artist and the socio-historical circumstances of the early 1860s. Fried, indeed, is insistent on the need to place Manet within what he calls 'the generation of 1863' and is at pains to understand Manet as a located, historical agent, active within a structure of social conditions. It is these minimal presuppositions that enable *Manet's Modernism* to qualify as 'social-historical'. Clark's account, however, *radically de-centres* this subjective agency, concentrating instead on the relations between Manet's paintings and their contemporary critical reception. Clark is also clear that the analytical focus of his book is on the relationship between these paintings, others by those he calls Manet's 'followers', and two main socio-historical developments: 'the commercialization of leisure and the beginnings of suburbia'. It is through these linked developments, he observes, that a set of intermediate class groups – the 'nouvelles couches sociales' – set apart from the proletariat, became established.[13] Manet himself certainly *was* a bourgeois artist, Clark stresses, but to make this assertion significant it has to be explained *how* the modernity he and his followers claimed and represented in their artworks was dependent upon their 'being bound more closely than ever before to the interests and economic habits of the bourgeoisie they belonged to'.[14]

As evident also in Clark's accounts of Picasso and Cézanne, the 'bourgeois' quality to Manet's art was present in the form of a *positivism* or *materialism* in his painting: a sharpness of looking and attention to surface detail and density that made modern painting an incisively critical and self-critical practice – 'at least in its first decades', qualifies Clark, adding that any 'present day' (that is, 1984) opposition to modernism had better remember this.[15] I turn to the question of the art of *our* recent past in the Conclusion. The women depicted in *Olympia* and *A Bar at the Folies Bergère* – paintings playing with identities and appearances – are designed specifically to invoke and provoke the bourgeois male, imagined standing in front of the real woman (as image), and in front of the painting artefact as 'image'. *Olympia*'s materialism lies in what Clark calls an 'indeterminacy in the image . . . whose appearance was hard to make out'.[16] 'Art' references to nudes by Titian seemed to 'amount to nothing for most of [*Olympia*'s] viewers . . . The *Venus of Urbino* was painted out or painted over . . . It is as if the work of negation . . . was finally done, but somewhat too well.'[17] The social practice of prostitution in Paris, 'soaked through', Clark notes, with duplicities of appearance finding an objective correlate in *Olympia*: an imagined woman 'spurious, enigmatic, unclassifiable: a sphinx without a riddle . . . Bored chatelaine, misunderstood bourgeoisie, failed actress, corrupt peasant girl . . . blatant and particular, but . . . also unreadable.'[18]

The inconsistencies in *Olympia* and *A Bar at the Folies Bergère* are mirrored in the bulk of the contemporary critical readings they generated – a lack of 'depth' and resistance to interpretation. Critics would claim these pictures were 'unfinished', '*lacking* definition', 'impossible' or 'evasive', with 'incorrectness' of drawing.[19] *A Bar at the Folies Bergère* left the viewer suspended in the air somewhere, not clear of their relationship to the barmaid, to other spectators, or to the picture itself, as what Clark calls 'a possible unity'.[20] These inconsistencies and anomalies prevent the painting from resolving itself as such a 'unity'; as a tableau, that is – a realized whole, the obscure ideal of early and mid-nineteenth century French painting, to which I shall turn in the following section. But this ideal, 'higher' resolution would be incompatible, surely, with what Clark claims is the true aim of Manet's *Olympia*, whose stuffed, decrepitudinous, ugly body confronted Salon crowds, declared the contemporary critic Victor Fournel, as if they were visiting a morgue.[21] This painting, along with *A Bar at the Folies Bergère*

> looks out at the viewer in a way which obliges him [*sic*] to imagine a whole fabric of sociality in which this look might make sense and include him – a fabric of offers, places, payments, particular powers, and status which is still open to negotiation.[22]

The bourgeois man, then – including Manet himself – might both *want and not want* these (images of) woman, *want and not want* the modernity for which these pictures stand. That Manet held 'both sets of beliefs', says Clark, is 'incontestable'. Somehow the tension, the inconsistency, between them gets represented in *A Bar*, 'his last big painting'.[23]

Fried, too, is concerned with what amounts to the comprehension of incomprehension in Manet's paintings. He acknowledges that painting in the 1860s is partly about the control and limiting of expressive meaning and that this has determinants in social modernity. Henri Fantin-Latour, in mock-classical/pastoral paintings such as *La Féerie* (1863) and *Tannhäuser: Venusberg* (1864), Fried states, like Manet, had deliberately painted unintelligible actions and gestures. *La Féerie* is exactly contemporary with *Olympia* and *Le Déjeuner sur l'herbe*. He notes, too, that these sorts of gestures had been represented before, in Renaissance paintings and engravings. Manet's *Le Déjeuner sur l'herbe*, for example, had obscurely deployed Raphael's river gods and water nymphs, 're-thematizing' these motifs in a new pictorial context that Clark believes radically negated the source as meaning of the 'quotation'. Manet's painting technique, Fried concedes, continued to puzzle and even offend his contemporaries.[24]

But Fried's interpretation of the enigmatic quality to Manet's painting extends well beyond, and idealistically above, the material 'fabric of sociality' that concerns Clark. The significance of the poses of figures – singly and in groups – within paintings such as *Le Déjeuner sur l'herbe*, *Olympia*, *The Execution of Maximilian*, or *A Bar at the Folies Bergère* lies in how they pictorially examine the 'beholding' function of painting as an artform: that is, the ways in which these artefacts are both physically and ideationally 'seen' by spectators. Should viewers be metaphorically 'invited into' the picture, via rhetorical techniques of 'theatricality' that interpellate subjects as fictively 'part' of the represented image – such as the eye contact or gesture of a depicted figure signalling directly to the viewer? Or should they be metaphorically 'held on', 'at', or 'beyond' the surface, via devices Fried calls 'absorptive', in which depicted poses and actions signifying pictorial internality 'close off' the painting to the spectator, 'anti-theatrically' preventing illusory identification?

This latter 'absorptive' device, Fried states, was to be set to work extensively in late nineteenth- and twentieth-century modernist painting, giving 'affective "depth"' – by which he means aesthetic feeling and quality – to pictures by Picasso, Paul Gauguin, Toulouse-Lautrec, and Matisse exuding decorative flatness[25] [Plate 5]. But what kinds of morality or politics might be associated with either pole, and why? Such critical terms – 'theatricality' in particular – have persisted as a subtext in my study: they are present, implicitly and explicitly, in Fried's 1960s art criticism in his defence of modernist art against the encroachment of what he calls the productions of a corrupting 'literalism'. The place and role of the spectator, as viewer, *but also as social and moral actor*, is begged by these terms and by Fried's attack on theatricality in art. (Greenberg's 'kitsch' and Clark's 'vulgarity', whatever their own specificities, hover here in a ghostly fashion too – both after-images of sorts in the same debate.)

Morceau and tableau, or alienation and totality

Manet is caught in a double-bind, Fried observes, both wanting to insist on the truth about painting as a material practice, yet also recognizing that there can be no 'entire extinguishing' of the tradition of theatricality – that is, making art to be beheld.[26] This inconsistency is perhaps a kind of parallel case to that which Clark identifies: Manet's holding of 'both sets of beliefs' about modernity. Fried's, however, is pitched at a higher level of abstraction and seems rather remote from the materials of social history. The double-bind manifests itself, Fried says, in Manet's 'courting of unintelligibility, subversion of potentially absorptive motifs, denial of individual psychology, refusal of closure on the plane of technique'.[27] At another level, however, Fried claims his book is specifically about recognizing and clarifying the 'specificity and complexity' of Manet's 'aims' during the 1860s.[28]

These were focused, he claims, on an abstracting use of sources from past art, and Manet may have 'understood his own practice' to be a matter of 'multiple, superimposed quotation'. This decision was Manet's response to seeing that previous European painting had also recycled its imagery 'by selective imitation'.[29] Manet 'must have hoped', Fried asserts, that some contemporary critics would have been able to 'grasp the intentions'.[30] But although the artist had fundamentally wanted to address the 'primordial convention that paintings are made to be beheld'[31] – this, then, is the 'theatricality-absorption' double-bind – 'none did'.[32] Fried presents Manet, in effect, as an abstract painter. 'Abstract' in the sense, that is, of being primarily concerned to examine pictorially the convention of the relations – physical, social, ideological – pertaining between painting as object and spectator as subject. This is also the view, remember, that Fried takes of the significance of paintings by Stella, Noland, and Olitski in the 1960s: theirs' are focused, however, on the 'purely' formal conventions of shape, colour, and facture. However, the moral and political implications – as far as Fried is concerned – of Manet's focus on what might be called the 'convention of relation' remains unclear.

Manet's aims stayed elusive to the critics of the time, too, Fried states, citing Gonzague Privat's claim that his paintings were 'incomprehensible to almost all who viewed them'.[33] Zola's remark that the nude woman in *Le Déjeuner sur l'herbe* 'is undoubtedly only there to give the artist an opportunity of painting flesh' generates more questions than answers.[34] Manet's *Angels at the Tomb of Christ* (1864) had seemed to critics 'incomprehensible, provocative, crudely drawn, hastily painted' and perhaps as 'mere parti pris, understood as a perverse taste for extremity for its own sake or say a desire to attract attention at any price'.[35] It was the critic and proto-art historian Théophile Thoré who came nearest to understanding Manet's involvement with the art of the past, Fried asserts, arguing that Thoré's scholarship became in effect a condition of possibility for Manet's painting: not just an 'interpreter' but a 'collaborator'? I shall return to Fried's account of Thoré's relationship with Manet later, imbricating as it does additional circuits of narcissistic identification.

Critics – Privat for example – declared that Manet's painting never resulted in great paintings; they seemed not to be able to ascend, that is, from the brilliant, if eccentric, morceau, to the realized and complete tableau.[36] The morceau/tableau distinction is central to Fried's account of Manet's painting and exemplifies the notion of complexity as 'occluded totality' that has been at the very centre of my concerns. Versions of the distinction find a form, a metaphoric vehicle, in virtually all the accounts of value in modern painting I have considered. Greenberg's and Fried's 'good complexity' is dependent on the belief that the greatest twentieth-century modernist art *does* achieve the tableau, or full positivity; Clark's 'bad complexity' depends on it being always deferred, or negated. In the case of Manet, however, Fried's account seems more qualified or doubtful. This may be to do with the lack of a clinching argument or proper conclusion in *Manet's Modernism* – Fried never seems to decide what the critique of beholding in Manet's painting finally amounts to, why it is so significant. He acknowledges this.[37] His book itself, then, is rather more a set of precocious, extended morceaux than an achieved tableau.

There is a great irony in Manet's painting remaining seen in its own time as a set of dazzling but unreadable painterly fragments, for the artist, Fried claims, 'aspired to be – and to be recognized as being – a universal artist'.[38] Manet's ambition was evident in the almost full range of genres in which he worked, including the nude (*Olympia*), religious painting (*The Angels at the Tomb of Christ*), and modern history painting (several versions of *The Execution of Maximilian*). Manet also crosses genre – are not *Olympia* and *A Bar at the Folies Bergère* hybrids of modern history painting, too, as well as nude and portrait? [Plate 1]. In 'crossing' genre Manet appears to do away with it – or at least to do away with the meanings conventionally associated with specific genre painting. *Le Déjeuner sur l'herbe* manages to be at once, a large 'fête champêtre', female nude, history painting or allegory' (after Renaissance prototypes), still-life (in left foreground), landscape, and a religious painting, given the depicted bullfinch's allusion (upper-centre) to a dove symbolizing the Holy Ghost.[39] Fried sees this painting as Manet's attempt to transcend the fragmentary nature of art by assembling all genres into a single composition – is this, perhaps, *the* formative example of a proposed Beginning to modern art (and the End of 'past art'), thinking back to Clark's discussions of 'totality' in Pollock and Picasso and Cézanne?

Fried, indeed, calls this Manet's attempt at 'totalization' – the term echoing the connotations relating both to 'tableau' and my own notion of complexity: a painting such as *Le Déjeuner sur l'herbe* operates a 'deliberate marshalling and combining of resources', though if it is all-inclusive, it is also a 'tentative and short-lived' novel conception of painting as an art.[40] These aims were unique, and perhaps limited, Fried suggests, to the paintings he produced in the first half of the 1860s. Manet is no Impressionist, but neither 'a wholly solitary figure'; rather, he is a member of 'a specific generation' (that of '1863') with roots in mid-nineteenth-century French art. He *is* still rightly called a 'modernist', Fried concludes, but the meaning of this term *then* needs to include Manet's ambition to embrace, through deliberate quotation and allusion, past painting from all the major national schools – French, Italian, Spanish, Dutch, and Flemish. Most conspicuous in his choice of 'subject-matter' (unstable notion, that!), Fried states, is his desire to manifest connections to the art of the Old Masters.[41] Yet Manet's appropriation of these 'sources' in paintings by Velásquez, Le Nain, Watteau, Chardin, and Courbet is designed, Fried claims – apparently paradoxically – to secure the very Frenchness of his own painting as the basis for a new kind of artistic universalism, or what Fried had described in his Ph.D. dissertation (the basis for his 1969 'Manet's Sources' essay) a 'comprehensive totalization' of the resources of painting.[42]

Manet's painting, then, *cannot* be understood in isolation from what Fried calls 'some of the most important intellectual and spiritual currents in nineteenth-century France'.[43] Questions about the 'nature and destiny of French art' become bound up with the future of modern art 'as such'.[44] Fried agrees with Meyer Schapiro that Manet chose subjects for paintings because 'they were his world in an overt or symbolic sense and related intimately to his person or outlook'.[45] But Manet's references, for instance to Le Nain, in the paintings *Portrait of the Artist's Parents* (1860) and *The Old Musician* (1862), and in the etching *The Gypsies* (1862) indicate that he saw his (Le Nain's) work as 'essentially realist in intent' and thus as an invitation to compare his painting with that by the great artist of the previous generation, Courbet.[46] Does Manet's use of Le Nain's paintings implicate Manet himself in a 'realist' project of some sort? If the answer is yes, then what kind of a 'realism' might this be, given Fried's equal stress on Manet's desire to 'universalize' through the abstracting and referencing of motifs from diverse past art, and to 'quote' – as it were, in opposition to Le Nain – the hyper-theatrical 'fantastic, aristocratic, frivolous, contrived, and dissolute art of Watteau', scourge of Champfleury, Courbet's own critical champion?[47]

Fried's answer, however – sidestepping the problem of 'realism' altogether – is that Manet's hyper-ambitious goal was no less than 'the accomplishment of access to the art of painting *in its entirety*'.[48] Thoré's historical labours, contemporaneous with Manet's painting in the 1860s, had similarly aspired, Fried claims, to 'a universal history of art'.[49] Manet's *Olympia*, *Le Déjeuner sur l'herbe*, *Dead Torero* (1864), *The Angels at the Tomb of Christ*, *The Luncheon* (1868), and *The Balcony* (1868–1869), among others, figured this 'universal history of art' in paint. Manet's art, Fried declares:

> the pursuit of a new form of *tableau* or portrait-*tableau* was linked ... with both the impulse toward totalization and the concerns with facingness, instantaneousness, strikingness: as if only a *tableau*, not a *morceau*, were capable of responding to those concerns with sufficient focus and force, and as though a substitute had partly to be supplied from 'outside' (via national schools, and in the *Déjeuner*, genres) for the absorptive/dramatic unity that had always been the essence of the tableau and that his eschewal of absorption prevented him from mobilizing.[50]

Yet Manet's pictures, as Fried and Clark both show, were read recurrently by contemporary critics as significantly 'unfinished' or as mere 'fragments'.

Le Déjeuner sur l'herbe, for example, was admitted by the connoisseurs, says the critic Carle Desnoyers, to show Manet's 'exceptional qualities' as an 'admirable' *ebaucheur* (sketcher).[51] But the artist's execution was not 'pushed to a sufficiently resolved point, his modelling lacks firmness', judged Théodore Duret in 1867.[52] Théodore Pelloquet, in turn, thought *Le Déjeuner sur l'herbe* was a 'rebus', an enigma.[53] If the exact definition of a successful tableau was never clearly agreed – though the term's use by critics such as Thoré, Jules-Antoine Castagnary, Zacharie Astruc, Pelloquet, and Ernest Chesneau implied the ideal of a 'portable, self-sufficient, esthetically autonomous easel picture' – Manet, claims Fried, along with others in the generation of 1863 such as Fantin-Latour, accepted the morceau/tableau distinction.[54] But the achievement of a tableau, or, for shorthand, what Fried calls 'compositional and coloristic unity ... [able] to produce a powerful and instantaneous effect of formal and expressive *closure*' appeared to be somehow basically incompatible with Manet's aim – which Fried, Schapiro, and Clark are all agreed upon – of engaging with his own contemporary world through his painting.[55] Such an aim merits the adjective 'realist'. Hadn't it also been said, for example, that Courbet's self-avowedly realist paintings, such as *Burial at Ornans* (1848), though 'superbly painted' had failed 'to conform to traditional notions of compositional unity' and, whatever their literal size, had remained in some important, determining sense fragments, or mere morceaux?[56]

This is Pelloquet on Manet's painting *Le Déjeuner sur l'herbe* submitted to the 1863 'Salon des Refusés':

> Manet doesn't know how to compose a *tableau*, or rather, he's not aware of what one understands by a *tableau*. I don't say that one learns that like a recipe, but finally it's necessary to come to know it. If one knows it in a different fashion from others, all the better; that's the privilege of great painters. But when he places two or three nude figures on a large canvas alongside two or three dressed in overcoats, in the middle of a landscape, brushed in indifferently, I would like him to enable me to understand his intention. I'm not asking for a philosophical lesson but the visible translation of some sort of impression. I seek his and don't find it; the picture is a rebus of exaggerated dimensions that defies understanding.[57]

Fried's response to this is, in one sense, that one *does* need a philosophical lesson to make sense of Manet's painting. Manet's flat, 'indifferently' brushed in landscape, containing enigmatic dressed and undressed figures, is an attempt to 'acknowledge, not negate or neutralize, the presence of the beholder'. The 'notorious "flatness"' of this picture is an effect created in order to attempt to make the painting 'in its entirety – the painting as a painting, that is, as a [physically real] *tableau* – *face* the beholder as never before'.[58] This is how Manet, through his paintings, attempts to engage with his own contemporary world: by addressing and examining the conventions of modern spectatorship and the real *physical, social, and ideological* relations between painting and viewer.

Fried agrees with Clark that Manet's painting achieved a kind of initial critical 'essential *un*intelligibility', but their explanations of this phenomenon, *though not logically or social-historically incompatible*, are couched very differently.[59] If Clark's explanation centres, for instance, on *Olympia*'s deliberate confusion or convolution of meanings around the pictorial conventions of representing 'woman' as idealized nude or courtesan, using the surface of the painting as a multivalent metaphoric vehicle, then Fried will claim, in a much more abstract register, that Manet is primarily concerned, through his deployment of enigmatic poses or emphasis of the flatness of *Le Déjeuner sur l'herbe*'s surface, to attempt to 'establish a new type of connection with the beholder'[60] [Plate 1]. These are *not* exclusive, or even necessarily different, effects. Both Fried's and Clark's accounts agree that Manet's paintings were intended to confront their beholders, to make them think critically, and to become 'self-conscious' about such questions as: *who* is looking; *what* one is looking at, and *why*; and *how* visual representations such as paintings might make one reflect on the nature of the world which includes such representations.

These issues, for Fried, are unavoidably philosophical because they raise very basic questions about the nature, or ontology, of objects – specifically paintings – in the world. He believes that Manet, as one of the painters of the 'generation of 1863' has a particular interest, a 'shared engagement', in this question of painting's ontology *then*, in that moment of 'historical singularity'.[61] The oddities in paintings such as *Olympia* and *Le Déjeuner sur l'herbe* – for instance, the 'hostile, almost schematic cat' in the former, and the 'unintelligible gesture of the man on the right' in the latter – are 'estranging' devices, intended to dramatize, draw attention to, the beholder's alienation, or 'outsideness', from that which the painting depicts.[62] For more than a century before the 1860s 'anti-theatrical' painting had sought to establish the 'ontological illusion ... that the beholder did not exist'. This had reached an apogee in Millet's paintings, such as *Woman Sewing By Her Sleeping Child* (1854–1856), which exhibits, Fried claims, an 'excess of absorption'. The later 'generation of 1863' – Fantin-Latour, James McNeill Whistler, Alphonse Legros, but Manet in particular – had then attempted radically to re-conceptualize painting through the devices of 'intensity, instantaneousness, facingness, and strikingness' embodied, for example, in model Victorine Meurent's 'distancing calm stare' out of *Olympia* and the *Déjeuner*.[63] These devices were an attempt, Fried claims, perhaps with a nod to Clark, to 'recapture an original *resistance* to available modes of pictorial understanding'[64] [my italic].

Manet, that is, by the use of such devices refuses what Fried calls 'hermeneutic penetration': his pictures produce an 'obduracy ... (or "blankness" or "indifference")', such as the look of the barmaid in *A Bar at the Folies Bergère*.[65] Such an attack on absorptive closure in Manet's paintings, goading or forcing the viewer to confront the nature of spectatorship was, at the time, 'literally indescribable except in negative terms, as faults, ineptitudes, violences ...'.[66] This sounds rather like Clark on 'negations' in the paintings of Pollock and Picasso: parodic assaults on, or travesties of, the conventions of pictorial representation which nevertheless end up acknowledging their indispensability. 'To liquidate the past and so enter a new world', states Fried, musing on what Manet might have thought his task as a modern painter was, again sounding a bit like Clark. All the resources and motifs of past art might be marshalled and assigned a role in that absurdly ambitious task, as Manet's pictures from the first half of the 1860s suggested.[67] What kind of 'subject' could this 'spectator' or 'beholder' of Manet's art – seat of what Fried calls painting's 'primordial convention' – be, or become?[68]

Subjectivity and surface

The 'true strangeness' of the nineteenth century, as Clark puts it, has found its way into Manet's paintings: some fundamental troubling and unsettling of identity, place, and role – of the artist himself; of the nature of his paintings; and of the paintings' viewers too. The troubling and unsettling of these identities and of the relations between them – the matrix they constitute – *is* modernism's complexity. Clark and Fried both see it in Manet, but only Clark truly goes on to emphasize it, to harp on its negations – its 'bad complexity' – in his accounts of later artists, such as Picasso and Pollock. Baudelaire had also seen it in Manet when he observed that the artist, his friend, was 'the first in the decrepitude of your art': performing, I think he means, some erosion of inherited conventions, procedures, attitudes, and values.[69] But in order to produce what?

Listen to Clark on *A Bar at the Folies Bergère*. He is pondering the notional place of the viewer of the picture, given that the man at the far right, shown in what appears to be a mirror, is facing opposite the barmaid, who faces *out* at where the actual viewer stands:

> *We* must be where *he* [the mirrored man at the far right] is. But we cannot be; not, anyway, if we are to remain what the easy 'we' implies, in the discourse of looking – the single viewer of the painting in question; ourselves, myself; the subject for whom the picture exists and makes sense, who stands and sees a determinate world. 'We' are at the centre; he is squeezed out to the edge of things, cut off by the picture frame. His transaction with the barmaid cannot, surely, set the tone for ours.[70]

The painting confounds the viewer's sense of place in relation to what the picture *appears* to show, thereby provoking doubts in the viewer as to the nature and meaning of that which is shown and how the viewer *might* enter into relation to it.

In this sense the painting might be said to be 'about', and to 'depict', social relationships: those with meaningful *visible* components (indicating propriety of dress, signs of sexuality, status, and class, etc.) and those that are *ideational*, or mental. Thus Fried says that Manet, though starting out to paint an 'objective transcription of reality' – and mobilizing models of this in the art of Velásquez and Frans Hals – becomes 'sharply conscious that his own relation to reality is . . . problematic'. He must paint, then, not only 'his world'

> but his problematic relation to it: his own awareness of himself as *in* and yet *not of* the world. In this sense Manet is the first post-Kantian painter: the first painter whose awareness of himself raises problems of extreme difficulty that cannot be ignored, the first painter for whom consciousness itself is the great subject of his art.[71]

However, this is Fried, remember, not in *Manet's Modernism*, nor in 'Manet's Sources', but in a long footnote to 'Three American Painters', and one can see how he is gearing up with it in order to make Stella's, Noland's, and Olitski's abstract paintings the heirs of this putative originary modernism of 'mental abstraction', in similar fashion to the way he delivers the 'optical' Pollock in the same essay. Fried, writing thirty years later, recognizes problems and inadequacies in his claim – what he calls its 'crude' and 'untenable basis' – but notes that it bears some comparison with accounts of social alienation in the social art-historical readings of Manet, including Clark's.[72]

It simply could never be proved, or disproved, that Manet's 'subject' is the painting of consciousness. One can argue, until the cows come home, over what Fried might have meant at the time of writing by saying that Manet was *in* but not *of* the world: I think his own retrospective interpretation is meant sharply to relativize his earlier claim. Fried takes it to mean Manet is an avant-garde painter, *mentally* separated, and separating himself, from the bourgeois class of which he is still, emphatically, economically speaking, a member.[73] Fried makes claims in *Manet's Modernism* that remain equally ineffable, however. These claims are Fried, the critic, dreaming, conflating subjects and consciousnesses, intentions and interpretations – including his own.

Manet's embodied 'subject' and 'consciousness' get into his paintings in a variety of ways. For instance, Fried claims that the artist's depictions of the bullfinch and frog in *Déjeuner sur l'herbe* are a painterly meditation on the acts of looking and rendering. The bullfinch (top middle in the painting) though depicted in flight, possibly hovering, is painted meticulously, in a 'slowness' of technique that contrasts with the thing as seen. The frog (lower left in the painting), though immobile, is depicted rapidly, again in contrast to how it is seen, in an Impressionistic manner Fried describes as 'loosely brushed'. This is an example of what Fried calls 'cognitive dissonance', and indicates Manet's self-conscious sense of the 'mutual *entanglement* of eye and hand, seeing and rendering'.[74] (Baudelaire, in 1859, had remarked on the meditative, 'dreaming' quality of modern painting, in the face of the rise of photography: 'Each day art further diminishes its self-respect by bowing down before external reality; each day the painter becomes more and more given to painting not what he dreams but what he sees. Nevertheless *it is a happiness to dream*, and it used to be a glory to express what one dreamt. But I ask you! does the painter still know this happiness?'.[75])

The issue of experienced and visually represented temporality, divided between the poles of what Fried calls 'sheer duration' and 'instantaneousness', connects to the tableau/morceau hierarchical distinction, and to the problematic of theatricality and absorption.[76] It also links back importantly to my earlier discussion of 'at onceness' and *im*mediacy in modernist-critical accounts of aesthetic experience and judgement. Manet's *Le Déjeuner sur l'herbe*, Fried argues, *is* a radical and ambitious attempt to create a modern tableau – that is, a unified, aesthetically autonomous, pictorial composition, but its figural elements and facture are oriented to the pole of 'instantaneousness' of viewer-engagement, *not* to that of 'sheer duration', which had traditionally been the effect, Fried claims, of absorptive compositional devices in paintings.

In traditional painting the belief in the successfulness of the work, that is, the

> achieved unity of the absorptive *tableau* was meant to facilitate that ... conviction [of the painting's successfulness – remember 'conviction' from Fried's 1960s criticism] even as absorptive effects conduced to the temporal effect of duration, which is to say that the absorptive *tableau* was designed to offer the viewer immediate imaginative access to the depicted scene and then to hold the viewer indefinitely before a composition.[77]

Manet's *Le Déjeuner sur l'herbe*, however, tries to accomplish the tableau via a barrage of compositional figures and facture effects oriented to theatricality (or what Fried also calls 'facingness' or 'strikingness') and instantaneousness, *rather than* to absorption and sheer duration.[78] On the painting's sketchiness or unfinishedness, for instance, Fried claims:

> It has usually been viewed as an assertion of flatness, which in a sense it was . . . what has not been sufficiently remarked is that it was also a means of enforcing a certain rapidity of perception with respect to both the depicted figures and, beyond them, the painting as a whole; as if the traditional exploitation of half-tones to evoke solid forms in space had always tacitly invoked an awareness [consciousness and self-consciousness?] of the time that would be needed to explore so densely and minutely tactile a world.[79]

On the oddities of the human figures, their demeanour, grouping, and interactions depicted in this sketchy landscape Fried states that these are part of a strategy chosen by Manet in order to 'evoke the instantaneousness of seeing, of visual perception, itself', as his subject. By *not* depicting a meaningful moment in a narrative (such as, for example, one would find in a dramatic composition by David), by 'blatantly *violating* the demand for narrative and dramatic intelligibility', by *avoiding* absorptive effects and forestalling the possibility of 'compositional closure', Manet wishes to draw attention to the beholder's consciousness – of objects (paintings), and of subjects (both those depicted and those doing the looking, and painting).[80]

Notice all the italicized negatives in these last few exegetical sentences. Yet Fried, finally, wants to see these as moments in modern art's dialectic of positivity and achievement – remember his accounts of convention challenging and convention focusing in later modernist art: his 'optical' Pollock and the 1960s abstract painters. Clark, to the contrary, understands negation as a punctual situated and contradictory response to, and refusal, not only of what art had been, but of what bourgeois society after 1871, had become. Manet's painting embodies both this negativity and contradictoriness, not just, for example, in his attitude towards the subject of *A Bar at the Folies Bergère*, but toward modern life in Paris. To repeat what Clark claims, Manet's painting of that place manifests evidence:

> that a degree of conflict exists between that attitude [towards the *Folies Bergère* and modern life] and the beliefs about painting and vision – the metaphysics of plainness and immediacy . . . That Manet held both sets of beliefs is incontestable, and the tensions between them was never more visible than in his last big painting.[81]

Olympia – though I think also of Clark's account of Pollock's drip-paintings at this point – was equally divided: 'not quite creature of fantasy and not quite social fact, neither metaphor nor violation of one, neither real nor allegorical'[82] [Plates 1 and 4, think also of Pollock's *Untitled (Cut-Out)* 1948–1956]. Society after 1871 encounters, creates, then, a new kind of polarity: between the conscious and unconscious mind and has to grapple with how the insides of minds can be read – or 'hermeneutically penetrated' to use Fried's Freudian phrase – or not read from public signals and signs, in Manet's paintings, as much as anywhere else.[83]

Manet's use of the model Victoria Meurent, the 'nude' depicted in *Olympia* and in *Le Déjeuner sur l'herbe*, as well as in several other paintings, such as *Mlle V . . . in the Costume of an Espada* (1862), in which she is posed as a Spanish bullfighter, is one further vehicle for the artist's pursuit of this question of the pictorial en-codification of subjective identity and inter-relationship [Plate 1]. Meurent's challenging stare out of these pictures straight at the beholder – examples of what Fried calls the device of 'facingness' or 'strikingness' – is part of Manet's confrontation with the 'primordial convention' that paintings are made in order to be beheld. These poses, then, are part of the way in which the pictures as a whole might be said to 'stare' challengingly back at, even 'face down', the beholder. In fact, in these pictures through the use of Meurent's stare – and front-on position, particularly in *Olympia* – Fried claims that Manet is dramatizing, figuratively, the triadic relation 'painter-painting-model' as a means to examine or test the dyadic 'painting-beholder' convention.[84]

Downgrading the significance of the ostensible 'subject matter' of Manet's *The Execution of Maximilian* – the fate of the French-imposed emperor of Mexico shot by nationalists in 1867, an event photographed and printed in newspapers in Paris soon afterwards – Fried makes the startling, though ineffable, claim that Manet 'allegorizes' himself as 'executioner' and 'executed' figures depicted in this painting. The executioner, in this interpretation, stands for 'Manet the painter', and the executed represents 'Manet as his painting'; the event takes place in front of the firing squad re-interpreted as 'Salon viewers'.[85] Through this allegorical scene Manet, Fried suggests, 'externalizes' his conflicted sense of self as an artist and his public representation in criticism and cartoons as eccentric genius, madman, or fool. Manet, remember, chose to dress himself in conventional bourgeois attire: one further way of encoding, or obscuring, his own identity as an artist. In doing this he respected his friend Baudelaire's judgement, made in 1846, that the 'time is past when every little artist dressed up as a grand panjandrum and smoked pipes as long as duck-rifles'.[86] Representation and self-representation, consciousness and self-consciousness, painting's appearances and surfaces, fold into each other with Manet and his pictures, in an intricate network of coeval signs and meanings.

The 'generation of 1863' artists proposed, claims Fried, a 'seemingly uncompromising realism' of representation.[87] Yet the contemporary process of self-portraiture, based on depicting one's own face and upper body as seen through a mirror – in, for instance, Manet's *Self-Portrait with a Palette* (1878–1879), or in Fantin-Latour's three *Self-Portrait* drawings from 1860 – often elided the presence of the mirror and exactly reversed the facts of the face's visual appearance. The self-portrait then, might itself stand as an allegory for the subject of painting, symbolizing the *fiction*, then, of an 'uncompromising realism' or 'complete seeing'. Imagination, that is, necessarily plays a part in what Fried calls the 'ocular realist' double-bind – the 'realism of eyesight, of visual perception'.[88] Fried contrasts this with what he calls 'corporeal realism', traceable back to Courbet, which managed to include pictorial traces of the artist's own 'bodiliness'. James Whistler's etching *La Vieille aux loques* (1858), for example, contains visual traces of his fingerprints and palm prints – products of the so-called 'foul biting' phenomenon that occurs when the coated metal plate used in the process has been touched too much by the artist, leading to indices of the artist's digits appearing on the print.

Fried, however, implies these are deliberately created marks or signs – a way in which Whistler can get himself – that is, incorporate or 'prolong' his own bodiliness – in the etching; as if *La Vieille aux loques* were 'a body part in its own right, *un morceau de Whistler*'.[89] The 'generation of 1863', including Manet, is caught, Fried decides, between such 'bodily' and 'ocular' realisms, 'between Courbet's Realism and the realism of the Impressionists (or at least of early Impressionism)'. Or, rather, that a 'crossing of borders' *between* these two realisms fell to Manet and other painters in this generation.[90] Both realisms, though, acknowledge the conventions of visual representation, attempt to rework those conventions, but admit that such conventions – of depiction and composition, and of beholding and spectatorship – remain indispensable.

Modernism, criticism, and self-criticism

The surface of a painting, then, is both a literal and a metaphorical border – between what is 'in' the painting and what is 'in the world' outside of it; between the work of representation that the painting does, and the things that are represented. The surface understood as border is also a potential barrier or crossing-point. It can invite the viewer 'in' and it can confront, hold, the viewer on the outside; or manage, somehow, to do both at the same time. Fried's and Clark's accounts of Manet's paintings' surfaces concur that they *do* do both, but for different, or differently stressed – but, I would judge, *not* on the whole, contradictory – reasons. The border between Fried's and Clark's accounts of Manet's painting might equally be seen as both a barrier and a point of access, the limits to which remain somewhat uncertain. This *cannot* be said, however, of Fried's and Clark's accounts of twentieth-century modern art, for all the reasons I have provided in this study: their 'critical modernisms', their versions, that is, of modernist complexity, seem to me to be simply and radically incompatible – experientially, historically, politically, and ideologically.

Manet has become an arch-symbol of modernism: the 'first Modernist painter', declaimed Greenberg. But the meanings of modernism, with or without a capital 'm', remain disputed. Fried *himself* produces different, if not necessarily or clearly contradictory accounts of it, if one compares, for example, his 1997 study of Manet with his 1960s art criticism. One way to make sense of this is to agree with him that modernist art 'literally' historically *changed* and became, by the 1960s, to be solely – formally – about something called 'aesthetic quality'. Though there are points of overlap, which Fried identifies, and is at pains to stress in *Manet's Modernism*, the difference is that Manet's painting, unlike, say Stella's, seems only explicable, for Fried, if a complex account of his times and the critical reception of his art is made part of the analysis. Though in no sense 'Marxist' in its assumptions, aims, methods, or values, Fried's 'Manet' is a recognizable flesh-and-blood socio-historical creature, akin to Clark's 'Courbet' and 'Manet'. And Manet's 'self-criticism', for both Fried and Clark, is animatedly multifaceted – Manet reflects on art, but also explicitly on himself as an acting male bourgeois subject, and on the world at large. This 'self-criticism' bears no relation to reductive formalist notions – merely vacuous ideologies – of self-criticism understood simply as another name for 'art for art's sake'.[91] Self-criticism, in its full sense, means hard attention to, and reflection upon, the whole nexus of conditions and circumstances – material, aesthetic, subjective, social, historical, *art-historical*, and ideological – within which modern art-making occurs.

The scope and significance of this self-critical attention and reflection is implied in Mallarmé's epigrammatic, though also enigmatic, statement in 1876 that Manet's painting 'shall be steeped again in its cause'. Clark suggests this is very close in sentiment to Greenberg's formulation that 'each art in the new age is . . . obliged "to determine, through the operations peculiar to itself, the effects peculiar and exclusive to itself"'.[92] Fried remarks in *Manet's Modernism*, however, that it was Greenberg's account of Manet (whom Greenberg, he claims, conflated tout court with the Impressionists) that had added – perhaps even led – to the pernicious influence of what he calls the 'standard formalist-modernist accounts'.[93] For Greenberg to understand Manet's paintings simply in terms of 'flatness and opticality', Fried declares, was to read them through a highly reductive analytic filter that was largely what he called 'an artifact of Impressionism'.[94] [Plate 1]

Greenberg in 1940, for instance, had written in 'Towards a Newer Laocoon':

> Manet . . . closer to Courbet, was attacking subject matter on its own terrain by including it in his pictures and exterminating it there and then. His insolent indifference to his subject [contrast this claim with what Fried, agreeing with Schapiro, says about the personal significance of the subjects Manet chose to paint], which in itself was often striking, and his flat color-modeling were as revolutionary as Impressionist technique proper. Like the Impressionists he saw the problems of painting as first and foremost problems of the medium, and he called the spectator's attention to this . . . Impressionism, reasoning beyond Courbet in its pursuit of materialist objectivity abandoned common sense experience and sought to emulate the detachment of science, imagining that thereby it would get at the very essence of painting as well as visual experience.[95]

Terms here such as 'medium', 'spectator', and 'essence' receive, of course, very different definitions, as I have shown, in Fried's and Clark's socio-historical accounts of Manet's painting! Fried points out, too, that Greenberg in 1965 excised a key sentence (referring to contemporary painting) from the first published version of 'Modernist Painting', the removal of which had the effect of implying that modern art *retained* throughout the late nineteenth and twentieth centuries what Fried calls 'a consistent optical bias from Manet and Impressionism through Mondrian to the present'.[96] This supposed 'optical' bias, Greenberg had claimed – for instance, in his statement quoted above – had developed as an acknowledgement of the modernist 'discovery' of painting's ontological 'essence' as an autonomous practice of mark-making upon a limited and shaped support. Later notions of 'opticality', the 'sheerly or purely visual', etc. – all the claims pejoratively called 'formalist', in fact – might be said potentially to subsist in this dropped statement: 'The latest abstract painting tries to fulfil the Impressionist insistence on the optical as the only sense that a completely and quintessentially pictorial art can evoke.' Though Fried proposes, as I've discussed, his *own* criticisms of elements of Greenberg's conceptual apparatus – particularly, and most fundamentally, the idea of painting's 'essence' – it is obvious that Fried's own claim in 1965 that the history of modernist painting evinces 'an increasing preoccupation with problems and issues intrinsic to painting itself' might be said to have genetic links *itself* to Greenberg's notion of Impressionist painting's 'optical bias'.[97]

If the idea of modernist self-criticism can entertain reductive as well as sophisticated definitions, then so can the notion of painting's 'surface'. Greenberg claims that Manet's paintings' surfaces are such that the viewer sees them as pictures *first*, and *then* as painted surfaces containing imagery – that this is so, Greenberg concludes, indeed indicates that modernist painting is 'a success of self-criticism'.[98] Clark observes, however, that the critics who first wrote about Manet's paintings 'kept the surface present almost too vividly' in their accounts. It was on the surface that imagination could do its work, where Manet's 'exaggerated play with normal identities', his altering of worldly appearances, happened.[99]

The surface of the face of the depicted woman – 'barmaid' and 'prostitute'? – in *A Bar at the Folies Bergère*, for instance, is both 'the face of the popular', claims Clark, but also 'a fierce, imperfect resistance to any such ascription . . . It is a face whose character derives from it not being bourgeois, and having that fact almost be hidden.'[100] (Mallarmé, writing in 1876, had talked of the painting of what he called, enigmatically, the 'flesh-pollen' of the surface of a woman's face.[101]) Fried observes that, although Manet's surfaces, along with those by the Impressionists, *were* stressed, they certainly shared this with Courbet's – 'frankly and massively declared' – such as the *Burial at Ornans*. He qualifies this, rather obscurely, though, saying that in Courbet's case it wasn't so much a matter of declaring the surface of the canvas upon which the paint was put, rather it was 'their status as surfaces made of paint'.[102] No clear distinction should be drawn, he adds – sounding here a bit like Clark – between Courbet's 'realism' and Manet's 'modernism', given the centrality of surface to both artists. The larger story of painting in the later-nineteenth and twentieth centuries is that of what Fried calls a 'plurality of modernisms or say of modernist adventures'.[103]

To reiterate, neither should Manet's own 'modernism' be understood through what Fried calls 'an "Impressionist" reading' – one, that is, like Greenberg's, which claims for that art an essentialist simplification based on 'the dual thematics of flatness and visuality'.[104] 'Impressionist' here, somewhat confusingly, seems to be simply a synonym for 'formalist-modernist'. Whatever the complexities of Manet's relation to the Impressionist painters, and given Fried's own partial and mostly unelaborated reading of Impressionism as a form of what he calls 'ocular realism', he is adamant that the artist's concerns (his Mallarméan 'cause') as a painter were much broader.[105] Manet's 'profound involvement with instantaneousness – also with strikingness – as a marker of the primordial encounter', Fried asserts, 'the inescapable or quasi-transcendental relation of mutual facing, between painting and beholder was a decisive feature of his work from the beginning'.[106] This summary is perhaps the closest Fried gets to defining the aim and nature of Manet's 'realism'.

What else has Fried's *own* encounter with 1960s abstract painting been, if not an involvement with – the experience of, belief in, desire for – such 'instantaneousness' understood by him as a condition and guarantee of true aesthetic value? When Fried speaks of 'the beholder', his *own* beholding must be an experience his memory and understanding of which informs his sense of what that beholding fundamentally, 'primordially' *is*. Manet's and Stella's paintings changed Fried's subject.

Clark's *The Painting of Modern Life*, Fried explains in the preface to *Manet's Modernism*, 'transformed' studies of that artist, and its author became Fried's 'chief interlocutor' and friend after they spent two days together looking at Manet's paintings at the 1983 retrospective exhibition at the Grand Palais in Paris.[107] Great art's 'instantaneousness' of affect, then, is best conjoined with review and debate – as much for critics as for artists – 'not just interpreters, collaborators . . .' states Clark, apropos of Pollock. Baudelaire and Manet had been similarly entwined over the ways in which past art, the art of the museums, might have a presence, open and subliminal, in modern painting.[108]

Manet's *Execution of Maximilian* articulated its producer's relation to such past art (Goya's, above all) with what Fried calls a dramatic 'literalizing of strikingness', a dramatizing, that is, of the confrontation between painting and beholder: 'a field of multiple, labile, and conflictual identifications and counteridentifications, with Manet himself – Manet as painter-beholder – at once everywhere and nowhere'.[109] Greenberg's,

Fried's, and Clark's accounts of modern painting – their shifting, some-times overlapping, but also radically diverging critical modernisms, split between accounts of its 'good' and 'bad' complexities, 'positive achieve-ments' and 'negations', tradition and situation – might equally be said to be full of such 'identifications' and 'counteridentifications'; to contain allegories of themselves as simultaneously reasoning, feeling, and dreaming subjects.

Having written back, then, to modern art, it is now time to ask, in conclusion, what became of what was supposed to have been its successor – *post*modernism.

Conclusion

'Post' script

Medium as mediation

There she stands, with bloodied knife in hand (palm opening towards us). Fixing us with a glance – a weary stare? In her other hand's grip is the severed head of an old, startled man. She is in costume: 'art' robes, in front of stage curtains, on a stage. Pastiche or parody of 'Judith and Holofernes'? Image filtered through Hollywood and television mediations? One of many: many of one?

*Cindy Sh*erman's *No. 228* (1990) is a chromogenic colour print, nearly 7 ft by 4 ft: a portrait-painting size photograph, facing us down, with her head cropped and the toes of her right foot out of frame [Plate 10]. Her body *is* the photograph: it fills the space. Sherman is 'there' in the picture – in all the photographs she has taken of herself in character, since the 1970s. Whoever else she has posed as – types rather than individuals – 'her' 'own' 'self' has appeared 'there' too. Sherman's *No. 228* is 'theatrical' in the sense that it exaggerates and shows, in a showy way. Her gaze is certainly intended to draw the beholder in. Sexual connotations are never too far away in these photographs: in her posings as starlets or students in photographs such as *No. 6* (1977) and *No. 13* (1978). Unlike Richard Wilson's *20:50* (the media-*mixed* installation, not the photograph of it: Plate 9) however, Sherman's art-form is medium-*specific*; her form of 'theatricality' – one inherently reproducible – lies 'on the surface'. It is a matter of photographic dramas and photographed-images-as-dramas.

Greenberg, Fried, and Clark all talked, at various points and places in their lives and criticism, about reproducible technologies of visual representation that in some ways engaged them but that they were not able or willing – for whatever reasons – to write about at length. Sherman's photographs encapsulate a range of questions and issues that have been identified as characteristically 'postmodernist', and I shall come to these shortly as a way, finally, of considering art, culture, and society in the last thirty years or so. But before that I want to prepare the ground for seeing some connections, directly, between my three proponents of 'critical complexity' and the world of art and art-writing after the 'end of modernism'.

Fried, for example, writing in 1967 in 'Art and Objecthood', includes an aside – significantly *not* relegated to a footnote – on the status of the movies in contemporary culture. If great modernist painting has been able to overcome (in Fried's specific sense) 'theatre' – because, that is, it is medium-specific, and draws our attention to conventions, stressed anew, in representation, neither exploits our bodilyness nor objectifies itself in the process, and manages to contain and compel feeling and commitment of the highest order – then the movies, he states, 'by its very nature, escapes theatre altogether'. In a note Fried speculates on why this might be the case. This discussion, *like Sherman's photographs*, is also general: Fried is talking about the 'movies' as a form, as a system or repository of images and narratives. Obviously, he decides, the movies share something with literal theatre meaning 'stage drama'. But the movies, as a form, requires a different 'phenomenology'. In them, for instance, he observes, the actors 'are not physically present'. The film, he notes, is 'projected *away* from us'. The screen upon which the movie is projected somehow is, he decides, 'not experienced as a kind of object existing in a specific physical relation to us'. Now you or I may dispute this latter observation – in the same way, of course, that all of Fried's judgements have remained open to dispute. But whatever the reasons, Fried claims that movies:

> including frankly appalling ones, are acceptable to modernist sensibility whereas all but the most successful painting, sculpture, music, and poetry is not. Because cinema escapes theater – automatically as it were – it provides a welcome and absorbing refuge to sensibilities at war with theatre and theatricality. At the same time, the automatic, guaranteed character of the refuge – more accurately, the fact that what is provided is a refuge from theatre and not a triumph over it, absorption not conviction – means that that the cinema, even at its most experimental, is not a modernist art.[1]

Fried is talking about himself here, let's be clear. He *likes* going to the movies. It's a form of 'refuge' from 'theatricality'. He doesn't go into what are, for him, its 'acceptable' pleasures. Whatever the movies *do* offer, however, it is not the possibility of 'high art'. Contrary to this heterodox claim, decades of making and theorizing film conclude that it *is* a modernist art.[2] Different, and opposed, notions of modernism, then – unrelated in most respects to the concerns of Greenberg and Fried (but *not* Clark) – need to be brought alongside and compared with the models I've focused on in this study.

Greenberg, in contrast with Fried, commented in a 1978 interview that he took photography 'very seriously'. It had in fact, he claims, 'as much status as any of the other arts'. Greenberg, unlike Fried on film, does not implicitly dismiss photography or its study. *Like Sherman, he is interested in its 'iterative' qualities and meanings.* 'I realized', he states,

> that the criticism of photography was tough, tough, tough. There are so many contradictions. There are photographs that will reproduce anywhere and remain great – reproduce in a newspaper. There are others, like Paul Strand's, where if you don't see the original print, you'll miss it.

Greenberg comments that photography has been best when it has been 'literary, when it tells a story; and storytelling in photography is a new kind of storytelling'. Contrast that with Greenberg's aversion to 'literariness' in modernist painting! Greenberg registers that photography is alien to painting, and *cannot*, therefore, be judged by the same standards or values. Neither is it, like the movies appear to be for Fried, somewhere you 'go' for a lesser, if still benign, form of aesthetic experience. Greenberg had considered writing about photography in the mid-1960s, when he believed he might be able 'to wrap up the question of realism and photography'.[3]

Clark chooses to end *Farewell to an Idea* with a short discussion of Italian 'neo-realist' film from the period after the Second World War. This is one way in which he shows – acknowledges – a different kind of modernism: meaning a different kind of art and a different kind of criticism and history. His tone is, as in earlier parts of his book, somewhat confessional. Italian film, he explains, was the 'modernism that mattered most' to him when he was young: 'for years I had a blow-up from Roberto Rossellini's *Paisà* on my wall'. Films like Italo Calvino's *The Path to the Nest of Spiders* (1947), Michelangelo Antonioni's *The Cry* (1957), and *L'Avventura* (1960) were important to him. Like

Pollock's and Picasso's paintings, one might conclude, these films offered to Clark image-dramas of beginnings and ends, utopias and hells. Luchino Visconti's *Rocco and his Brothers* (1960) – which Clark illustrates with a shot from its closing sequence – pictured modernity; meaning:

> a wilderness of building sites, skeletons of factories and tenements, dirt roads waiting for asphalt, billboards for candidates and hair cream. Bland promises, great collective dreams. The shot reaches back to a world of nineteenth- and early twentieth-century longing . . . passion and history . . . the myth of socialism.[4]

Clark's conclusion indicates, I suggest, that a defence, celebration perhaps – a canon even – of one kind of art does *not* necessarily have to be conditional on the derogation, or demonization, of others. Greenberg, Clark, and Fried, however, as I've shown, *have* conjured up their own demons: theatricality, kitsch, vulgarity. With all three terms one is required to do a lot of thinking 'between the lines' about the unsaids in their explanations of these conceits and their proposed anti-thetical relation to modernism: attitudes subtend, in all three concepts, towards (1) popular or mass culture in capitalist society; (2) judgements on the wider contemporary social order; and (3) the possibilities within it for art and culture.

The Minimalists in the mid-1960s formulated, articulated, and orchestrated ideas and values in a combative philosophically challenging way: they did their own 'writing back', that is, to critics such as Greenberg and Fried. And Greenberg and Fried took this challenge seriously.[5] In the late 1960s the emergence of 'Conceptualism' in art – in its broader sense – indicated that the earlier development was not a flash in the pan. The binding together at this time of diverse artistic practices with philo-sophical, political, and social analyses of a wide variety of kinds – many 'counter-cultural', connected to socialist, feminist, 'postcolonial', and eco-logical currents – pushed art *and* criticism into a new phase of existence and led to these central terms themselves coming under serious and continuous strain. Could 'art' and 'criticism' adequately describe the new practices of making and thinking, representing and analysing?

In Chapter 2 I mentioned that Fried was wrong to attack what criticism 'came to be about' by the end of the 1960s and the 1970s: what he calls, highly selectively and reductively, 'cultural commentary, "oppositional" position taking, exercises in recycled French theory, and so on'.[6] His slur forms no part of any serious consideration of writing about art in the last third of the twentieth century. It is as 'throw-away' rhetorically, one might say, as his account of 'theatricality' was in his

mid-1960s essays: mostly designed, that is, to let you know his preju-
dices, but never offered as substantive social or historical analysis.
However, while 'theatricality', I think, actually *is* an important notion
– and seriously pursued historically by Fried in his books on French art
in the eighteenth and nineteenth centuries and significantly related to
Clark's situationist-influenced critique of capitalism – Fried's judgement
on the nature and purpose of art writing 'after modernism' is wholly
misleading. It *did not* represent the end of what Fried calls 'evaluative
criticism', by which he means deciding what is good and bad in art,
and why.[7] In its myriad forms, defeating any adequate generalization
here, art writing since 1970 has been nothing less than a comprehensive
re-evaluation of art, the meanings of 'aesthetic', and criticism (including
modernist criticism), connected directly to a criticism taking place imma-
nently in many of the novel art practices that evolved in the wake
of those artefacts produced by the Minimalists. Both these practices
and the forms of art writing that developed after 1970 have effectively
redefined the criteria for undertaking any such description, analysis,
and evaluation. It is hardly surprising that Fried and Greenberg felt
undermined by this development. Their statuses as authority figures
were undermined. The art and type of criticism they valued *lost value*
in this period.[8]

As Sherman's photographs suggest, artists 'after modernism' *continued*, using traditional, new, and combined media, an investigation
into the conventions of visual representation that Greenberg, Fried, and
Clark all see as a core element of the enterprise of modernist painting.
Art writing, too, began a systematic review of its procedures of composition, in so wide a variety of contexts and with aims so diverse that
'criticism', in any unitary or narrow sense, simply became an inadequate
term for the activity. But evaluation in Fried's sense *remained* a key concern: what changed were the objects evaluated, the criteria of evaluation, and the purposes of judgement.[9] Think of Sherman's photograph,
then, as an attempt to encourage you to deliberate on conventions: in
art (that is, in the history of painting and photography), in film and in
film's relation to painting and photography in contemporary society,
and in society as a whole. Images, narratives, and conventions-as-
rituals have come to constitute, one might conclude, a large part now
of 'spectacularized' social and political life. They are the mobile and
ubiquitous components of 'drama', as Raymond Williams once put, 'in
a dramatized society' [think here, though, of Manet, Cézanne, Picasso,
Pollock, Stella, as well as Sherman: Plates 1, 3, 5, 4, and 6]. Such images
and dramas, Williams observed,

challenge and engage us, for . . . they *were* images of dissent, of conscious dissent from fixed forms. But that other miming, the public dramatization, is so continuous, so insistent, that dissent, alone, has proved quite powerless against it . . . A man I knew from France, a man who had learned, none better, the modes of perception that are critical dissent, said to me once, rather happily: 'France, you know, is a bad bourgeois novel.' I could see how far he was right: the modes of dramatization, of fictionalization, which are active as social and cultural conventions, as ways not only of seeing but of organizing reality, are as he said: a bourgeois novel, its human types still fixed but losing some of their conviction; its human actions, its struggles for property and position, for careers and careering relationships, still as limited as ever but still bitterly holding the field, in an interactive public reality and public consciousness. 'Well, yes,' I said politely, 'England's a bad bourgeois novel too. And New York is a bad metropolitan novel. But there's one difficulty, at least I find it's a difficulty. You can't send them back to the library. You're stuck with them. You have to read them over and over.' 'But critically,' he said, with an engaging alertness. 'Still reading them', I said.[10] [My italic.]

I hope you might now see part of my purpose in including the short 'art fictions' at the beginnings of Chapters 2–6, and bleeding the italic I used to denote their 'fictional' status into the beginning of this Conclusion. These were intended to draw attention to the narrative conventions always active in art criticism and art history, and to suggest imagined worlds beyond these fixed discursive forms that attain authority – sometimes against the wishes of the authors themselves – in institutions such as universities and museums. The best of contemporary art and the best of contemporary art writing continues to point to conventions and examines their predominance: Sherman continues this practice, then, across the divide that supposedly separates modernism from that which came after it. I now turn to the question of how that 'afterlife' has been understood.

Modern to postmodern

[Cindy Sherman's] . . . photographs depict seemingly different women drawn from many walks of life. It takes a little while to realize, with a certain shock, that these are portraits of the same woman in different guises . . . The . . . insistence upon the plasticity of human personality through the malleability of appearances and surfaces is striking, as is the self-referential positioning of the author . . . as subject . . . Cindy Sherman is considered a major figure now in the postmodern movement.[11]

The most viable sections of the Fontana [steel] plant were . . . sold off . . . to a consortium that included a Long Island businessman, Japan's giant Kawasaki Steel, and Brazil's Campanhia Vale Rio Doce Ltd. In a mind-bending demonstration of how the new globalized economy works, California Steel Industries (as the consortium calls itself) employs a deunionized remnant of the Kaiser workforce under Japanese and British supervision to roll and fabricate steel slabs imported from Brazil to compete in the local market against Korean imports. Derelict Eagle Mountain, whose iron ores are 5,000 miles closer to Fontana than Brazil's, has meanwhile been proposed as a giant dump for the non-degradable solid waste being produced by the burgeoning suburbia of the inland empire.[12]

Over the past twenty years, since the term 'postmodernism' achieved a relatively wide currency – though mainly still inside academic debate and the publishing industry – it has been used rather more to refer to cultural and artistic artefacts, practices, events, and developments than to explain the character of broader contemporary economic and social structures or transformations. Since the mid-1990s, however, the term has had to compete with at least two others – 'globalization' and 'the postcolonial' – that *have* been used to designate wholesale change within the organization of societies and relations between nation-states, regions, and continents.[13] On the whole, changes in artistic forms and practices deemed to be 'postmodernist' were welcomed and celebrated as evidence of release from previously constraining 'modernist' codes and conventions, and held to be demonstrative of continuing innovation and creativity in the cultural sphere. This contrasts sharply with the connotations of both 'globalization' and 'postcolonial' which, although still suggesting liberation from inherited forms of social order and political oppression – restrictive or imposed national identities and direct forms of imperial domination – now also imply a generalization across the world of new insecurities based on, for example, the threat of terrorist attack and subtler, more insidious forms of economic and cultural subordination to predominant international forces and organizations.

Conventionally understood, postmodernism has become the name for forms of expression and representation in culture – literary and philosophical, as well as visual arts-based – which draw their resources eclectically from a wide range of contemporary as well as historical sources, using narrative and allegorical forms, mobilizing and mixing motifs and media from virtually any pre-existing artistic or discursive forms. Wilson's *20:50*, then, inheritor of the Minimalist focus on situation and the body in relation to installation-artefact, would thus qualify as 'postmodernist' [Plate 9]. Photographs such as those by Sherman have been taken as exemplary of this artistic rule-breaking. Her evocation of types from, for example, Hollywood film or figures in 'high art' paintings, as in *No. 228*, 'recreate', however, as I've said, generic and allusive, rather than specific, references [Plate 10]. It may be that the imaginative power of these images lies precisely in the suggestive 'vagueness' of this kind of appropriation.

Yet it is arguable that conceiving postmodernism in cultural or artistic terms, within a broadly sanguine perspective on perceived transformations and reorientations, usually went hand in hand with an ignorance of, or failure to acknowledge, decisive reorganizations in human economic, social, political, and international life which have taken place locally, but which are, ultimately, part of a global process. Mike Davis's account, at the beginning of this section, of the 'plasticity' and 'malleability' of the Fontana Steel company in California in the 1980s serves as an indication of basic economic, social, and political conditions of life in contemporary Western societies. Whether the term postmodernism has any explanatory power in this broader context of analysis remains an open question. My pairing of the Davis statement with David Harvey's remarks on Sherman's photographs is intended to indicate that the economic, social, political, and cultural issues bearing on contemporary life are conjoined and interdependent.

To make progress with the idea of the 'postmodern' its relations to 'modern' and modernism need examination. Postmodernism, like modernism, has both a utopian and a dystopic face: a side embraced and celebrated, and a side rejected and mourned. What I've called Greenberg's and Fried's *good* critical complexity represents an exemplification of the former position in relation to modernism; Clark's *bad* critical complexity the latter – though his judgements remain, in their detail, shot through with an almost wilting ambivalence and recalcitrance. The modernist paintings of Picasso and Pollock *are*, Clark agrees, great, extraordinary achievements; but they are, at the same time, dark: 'annihilation' and 'totality', as Clark puts it, jostling side by side

[Plates 5 and 4]. Both modernism and postmodernism have had their advocates and their detractors. On the face of it, only a 'post' separates the modern from the *after*-modern. Both terms also share the same modifying suffixes: modern*ism*/postmodern*ism*, modern*ist*/postmodern*ist*, modern*ity*/postmodern*ity*, modern*ization*/postmodern*ization*. 'After' or 'post' implies both a difference from that which came before *and yet* a continuance of traits previously present. To describe a painting, for instance, as 'after' Velásquez means both these things – consider Robert Rauschenberg's 1964 silk-screen on canvas *Persimmon*. Although Rauschenberg clearly includes an image of Velásquez's *Venus* in this work, it is equally clear that this is a 'processed' reference – or quotation – using photographic sources within a print and paint artefact which re-situates the *Venus* reference in a new aesthetic and semantic configuration.

'Modern' society is usually dated from the mid-nineteenth century and understood as synonymous with the development of urban, industrial, and capitalist social life. Sometimes the date is pushed further back to include the French Revolution in 1789 and a more opaque historical event called the Enlightenment. The intention here is to bring secular philosophical rationalism into the definition of the 'modern' and, together with the (as it turned out, temporary) abolition of the monarchy in France, to indicate that the state of modernity characteristically is urban, industrial, capitalist, and democratic. It is highly significant that, as the great nation-states of western and central Europe acquired empires through military and economic colonization, modernity became synonymous also with *western* and *northern* power in the world, although conquered peoples and territories came to occupy a specific subordinate place within the geography and political economy of modernization.

If modern*ism* in the visual arts can be given, for the sake of argument here, a general definition and accounted for in terms temporarily set apart from the specific critical complexities of Greenberg's, Fried's, and Clark's explored in this book, it is that the term refers to artists, from the mid-nineteenth century onwards, who had an intense concern with, and desire to represent, these new components of social life. This centrally included representation of urban – and, with the growth of Paris, Berlin, and then New York – metropolitan society. The depiction of modern economic and social relations between town and country became an important theme in works by, for example, Manet, Cézanne, and Van Gogh [Plates 1, 3, and 2]. Artists chose to represent developments at the very heart of modern life, changes propelling the development and transformation of human relations and consciousness – themes, as I've shown, at the centre of both Fried's and Clark's concerns. Early modern*ist* artists, forming 'avant-gardes' – significantly a military term – also opposed the forms, conventions, and institutions of academic art, though Manet's relations to these were, as shown in Chapter 6, extremely complicated. The term 'realist' was applied to *some* of these militant artists who developed pictorial aims with directly political and ideological allegiances – for instance, the Communist artists John Heartfield and Georg Grosz who were active in Germany in the 1920s and early 1930s. Self-exile and bohemian marginality rather than avant-garde political engagement were, however, as Greenberg suggests, the majority forms of dissent for modern artists.

Modernism in the visual arts, then, has had a long and multi-faceted history, only one significant current of which I've focused on in this book. Three prevalent formations, overall, may be distinguished. First, those who might be called the *avant-garde modernists,* committed, within their art, to a direct social and political engagement. This would include, for instance, Courbet, involved with the uprisings in France in 1848 and again in 1870–1871; the activities of the Dadaists and some of the Surrealists in the inter-war period; and the Constructivists and other groups who supported the Bolshevik uprising in Russia in 1917. Artistic practice, within such engagement, exhibited pictorial, as well as social, radicalism though it included the use of both 'realist' (e.g. Courbet) and 'abstract' (e.g. El Lizzitsky, Malevich) conventions and devices.

Second, *modernism understood as a form of psychological human-ism* was the search – usually instigated by individuals, not groups – to find novel ways to express or represent personal and subjective states or crises, though these were typically related to social and historical traumas such as alienation, war, and loss of belief in political or religious belief systems. Generally uninterested in class and ideologies – though Clark sees the Abstract Expressionists as wholly the creatures of US petty bourgeois individualism after 1945 – artists such as Rothko, Newman, and Hofmann, for example, believed they were developing formal, abstract, means in painting through which to picture subjective somatic, psychological, and spiritual states.

Third, the notion of *modernism as aesthetic autonomy* is associated particularly, as my book has shown, with the criticism of Greenberg and Fried produced after the Second World War. While Greenberg's 'Modernist Painting' came to exemplify and codify this position during the 1960s, he had inherited informing notions from earlier critics, such as Clive Bell and Roger Fry, whose disinterest in the intentions of artists and in the social circumstances within which they produced their paintings, prefigured aspects of Greenberg's – and Fried's – later theorizations of twentieth-century abstract modernist art. Clark's own critical complexity, in contrast to Greenberg's and Fried's – notwithstanding their own provisos and qualifications on aesthetic autonomy – might be said to lie in his distinctive creative integration of aspects of avant-garde modernism with the attention to formal analysis and sophisticated self-criticism characteristic of Greenberg and Fried at their most rigorous and searching.

Given modernism's difficult, contested history, it is not surprising that the concept of postmodernism has brought with it an equally tangled set of positions, values, and interests. Just as vast an array of artefacts, texts and visual representations have been designated postmodernist as those previously called modernist: along with Sherman's *No. 288* and Wilson's *20:50* would stand, for instance, John Portman's Westin Bonaventure Hotel in Los Angeles (1977), paintings by Andy Warhol and David Salle, videos produced by Nam June Paik and films such as David Lynch's *Blue Velvet* (1986), and 'photo-text' pieces by Barbara Kruger and Martha Rosler. From observation of these artefacts and images it is possible to identify a number of features associated with postmodernist ways of using materials and representing the world.

Fredric Jameson has argued, for example, that Portman's Bonaventure Hotel contains many allegorical devices, including escalators and elevators – 'giant kinetic sculptures' – and a greenhouse on the sixth floor. This is related to his claim that the hotel offers a 'postmodern hyperspace', not part of the city, 'but rather its equivalent and replacement or substitute'.[14] Warhol's painting and silkscreen *Marilyn Diptych* (1962) contains references to mass culture images and uses devices of multiple representation drawn from commercial art and design practices. Along with David Salle, whose allegorical painting *Wild Locust Ride* (1985) juxtaposes three different forms of figurative art representing a Santa Claus, a girl sitting in a chair, and a 'Socialist Realist' crowd, Warhol has been credited with a return to figuration, to naturalist conventions, which yet contain within the picture frame a 'practice of fragmentation . . . diptych framing, sequential collage, scissored images . . . screen segmentation'.[15]

Nam June Paik's multiple video presentations of objects of electronic technology (such as television sets) interspersed with vegetation in an installation such as *TV Garden* (1982) promotes, it has been claimed, concepts of difference and striking association. According to commentators, Lynch's thriller-genre film *Blue Velvet*, set in the US in the 1950s, both mobilizes the theme of the sado-masochistic body and invokes nostalgia for a lost – or perhaps only ever imagined – America. Kruger's photo-text images, such as *Your Gaze Hits the Side of My Face* (1981) and Rosler's *The Bowery in Two Inadequate Descriptive Systems* (1974–1975) have both directed attention to systems and means of representation, and reintroduced explicit politically interventionist art, drawing on feminist and anti-capitalist themes. Kruger's photomontage shows the profile of a neo-classical sculpture of a woman's face. Down the side of the photograph are printed the words 'your gaze hits the side of my face'. Kruger uses a bust of a face, rather than simply a photograph of a woman, to emphasize further the issues of representation, mediation, and their relation to reference and meaning. Rosler's work consists of two panels. One is a photograph of the edge of a building in the financial district of Manhattan in New York. Below a sign reading 'First National City Bank' two beer bottles sit on a stone ledge. On the second panel Rosler has simply typed the words 'plastered – stuccoed – rosined – shellacked – vulcanized – inebriated – polluted'. The terms refer both to literal drunkenness and to the façade of the bank, implying a critique of financial institutions and a capitalist social order devoted to seeking profit. The use of image and text by both artists is a characteristic postmodernist convention.

Drawing general features or tropes out of these specific examples of postmodernist art, it is possible to identify: (1) an appropriation and/or *pastiche* of conventions from past art (remember, in comparison, earlier discussions of Manet's use of sources); (2) the making of allegories; (3) reference to, or use of, mass culture elements; (4) a use of figurative and naturalistic conventions – though in new contexts sometimes including a fragmentation or multiplication of imagery; (5) a promotion of differences and the creation of striking associations; (6) an invocation of nostalgia; (7) depiction of the human body as a site of, or agent in, sexual and/or violent actions; (8) a foregrounding of representational practices and conventions ('self-criticism' or 'self-referentiality'); and (9) a return to politically interventionist art.

How might it be possible or valuable, then, to relate this artistic postmodern*ism* to a state of postmodern*ity*, to a world and set of conditions in contemporary social life? In the light of the examples set out by Davis and Harvey above, how might the 'malleability' and 'plasticity' of represented appearances in Sherman's photographs be mapped onto the 'malleability' and 'plasticity' of human economic and social relations of work at Fontana Steel? Once again, to proceed to examine the 'postmodern' requires a re-examination of the 'modern' before it.

Postmodernity: when the modern finally arrives

The nineteenth-century modern Western world was one of rapid urbanization, fuelled by the increasing predominance of capitalist economic and social relationships, bound up with industrial work practices exemplified by the factory system, and the haphazard movement towards electoral politics based on a slowly increasing suffrage. All the great philosophers and commentators of that century were, in equal measure, exhilarated and repulsed by the scale and degree of transformation occurring in the reorganization of social life. It is not surprising then that the modern social order developing in western European countries in that century provoked many individuals and groups to make images of, and plans for creating, alternative and better ways of life: utopias. These constituted 'visions' of a different, new world, magically freed from the realities of urban industrial capitalism. Much of that actual world – its preponderant part – was seen to constitute the opposite: a dystopia. As Marx understood it, the modern world which promised so much at the same time rendered itself unlivable; society had become a hideous composite of vertiginous innovations and social debasements.[16] As I've shown, Clark, in particular, and Fried and Greenberg to a much lesser degree, identifies modernist painting's utopian yearnings (however convoluted these are with dark things). Consider, for example, Cézanne's 'naked intensities' in *The Large Bathers*, or Pollock's willing of his own carnal and unconscious nature onto the surface of *Number 1A, 1948*. If the imbrication of utopic and dystopian elements may be said to be a characteristic of modernism, and modernity itself seen to constitute a precariously tilting balance of such nightmares and dreams – 'annihilations' and 'totalities', as Clark has it – then is it not likely that a similar state of affairs exists within contemporary art, forming not a break, but rather an extension and exacerbation of this longer history?

It has often been claimed that postmodernist art is constituted out of a pluralism – or 'radical heterogeneity' – of activities, values, and interests.[17] Sometimes such pluralism in postmodernism has been claimed to have replaced, or displaced, a prior, *unitary* modernism. My brief characterization of modernism's three dominant current outlined above, however, should indicate that, although a particular account might claim to identity a mainstream or centre to definitions of, and developments in, modernist art – and Greenberg's and Fried's 1960s theorizations certainly offered that – the actual history always included several different, even opposed, selections, stresses, and interpretations. The identification and stressing of *one* kind of postmodernism may be subject to the same criticism: different artists, critics, and commentators typically select one feature in preference to another, and contrast it (favourably or not) with a selected feature from one account of modernism.

Rosalind Krauss, for example – closely associated with Greenberg and Fried's interpretation of modernism in the mid-1960s – broke from that position to make the claim that sculpture 'after modernism' had entered, or created, an 'expanded field' of possibilities. By this she meant that the previous received understanding of 'sculpture as a "universal category", used to authenticate a group of particular . . . [objects] had collapsed'; the 'logic' of sculptural form could now be separated from the construction of monuments.[18] The resulting 'expanded field' now enabled artists to work with a wide variety of materials, and combination of materials, never used before in traditional sculptural practices. For example, Robert Smithson's *Spiral Jetty* (1970) was constructed out of salt crystals, rocks, and mud arranged in a coil shape in a lake in Utah. Wilson's *20:50* is another example of an installation-artefact whose materials and purpose evades the traditional definition of 'sculpture' [Plate 9]. The enlargement and reorientation of the concept of sculpture brought about by the Minimalists made it possible for its producers to both fabricate and situate their works in sites not previously designated for sculpture, making this artistic practice both 'post-studio' and 'post-gallery'-based. Krauss clearly welcomed this new, heterogeneous array of artefacts created for an expanded range of aesthetic, social, and intellectual purposes.

Yet this celebration of 'pluralism' in postmodernist sculpture was recast as a deadening *fragmentation* in other contexts of criticism. For example, the British critic Peter Fuller attacked the 'new figurative' paintings of artists such as Anselm Keifer, Julian Schnabel, and Bruce McLean (involved in the 1981 exhibition 'The New Spirit in Painting' held at the Royal Academy in London) as evidence of what happened to art in what he called the 'absence of a shared symbolic order', by which he meant belief in God and humanist values.[19] Although Kiefer and Schnabel made their paintings using traditional and non-traditional materials (Schnabel infamously including smashed plates), thereby challenging Fried's dictum that art is necessarily medium-specific, their resort to narrative, naturalistic painting and concern with representing the human body *did not* constitute – as far as Fuller was concerned anyway – an artistic renovation. Unlike Harvey's admiring description of the attention to surfaces and malleability of appearances in Sherman's photographs, which he takes to be an index of creativity and 'critical self-authorship', Fuller saw in 'new figuration' only an emptiness and banal flatness in the use of painting's conventions. For him it was an instance – one of many – of the rootlessness of contemporary culture and society, disconnected from any sustaining collective belief system. Fuller's views, however, right or wrong, indicate that writing about art after modernism certainly *did not* see the end of what Fried called 'evaluative criticism'.

Just considering the examples of Krauss and Fuller it is clear that a wide stratification of definitions, analyses, and evaluations fall within the rubric of postmodernism. Different senses of 'modern' and 'modernism' are also implied in their accounts – although in both these cases the critics may be said to be occupying 'anti-modernist' positions. This, however, guarantees nothing in terms of what critics conclude on the merits of items of postmodernist art. How might the value and meaning of these contrasting judgements be explained? The introduction of a broader analytic framework at this point may offer a way forward. Consider the following statement from Clark and compare it with that by Hilary Wainwright, a British feminist and socialist, both writing in the 1970s:

> I'm not interested in the social history of art as part of a cheerful diversification of the subject, taking its place alongside the other varieties – formalist, 'modernist', sub-Freudian, filmic, feminist, 'radical', all of them hotfoot in pursuit of the new. For diversification, read disintegration.[20]
>
> (Clark)

> We are now faced with creating a socialist organization not primarily through debates, struggles and splits within existing parties . . . but through the coming together of socialists based in the various 'sectoral' movements [feminist, ecological, anti-colonialist, anti-militarist, etc.], the majority of whom are not members of any political party . . . the possibilities in the localities, of going beyond the fragments of creating the foundations of a revolutionary movement, will be far greater than on a national level.[21]
>
> (Wainwright)

The continuities that could be identified between postmodernist art and the organization of intellectual and political life characterized above are striking. The terms 'fragmentation', 'integration', and 'disintegration' take on meanings that may in different contexts, be: (1) artistic; (2) broadly cultural; (3) intellectual; and (4) directly political. In artistic terms Krauss and Fuller both see conventions in sculpture and painting as analogous – in complex ways, no doubt – to norms and values in social life (this was also true, in very different ways, for Greenberg, Fried, and Clark). For Fuller, for example, a breakdown in the 'shared symbolic order' had brought the disintegration of 'believable' conventions and meanings in modern western art: a disintegration profoundly persisting *across* any claimed division between epochs of 'modernism' and 'post-modernism'. What I've called Clark's bad complexity thesis implies basically the same judgement, although his account and evaluation of modernist painting bears virtually no comparison with that of Fuller's.[22]

For culture broadly defined, processes of fragmentation in contemporary society have created ghettoized communities intent on excluding threatening groups. The Bonaventure Hotel in Los Angeles, for example, according to Jameson, created a hermetic world of 'postmodern hyper-space', protecting itself from the life outside. The hotel creates a controlled internal ambience and physical environment premised on segregated social existence, or 'zoning', practised widely in US society. In intellectual terms, for Clark, 'fragmentation' is a destructive and debilitating process. While 'pluralism' has become something of an offi-cial and administrative ideology, for Clark the ideology works to segment and deflect attention *away* from the central questions and issues, disintegrating focus and concentrated scrutiny. In contrast, however, Wainwright and others see the disintegration of traditional party poli-tics – and the monopoly of the Left in Britain by the Labour Party – as a positive development, brought about by the rise of a heterogeneity of single-issue groups which, *at least potentially*, might become aligned as part of a new, creative, globalized, and anti-colonial political bloc.

How far have I travelled, then, from the critical complexities of Greenberg, Fried, and Clark?

Two conclusions follow from this discussion. First, that no matter how attractive or convincing an analogy might appear between the identification of a phenomenon like 'fragmentation' in something called postmodernist art and 'fragmentation' understood as a feature of eco-nomic or social relations in the contemporary world, the connection remains merely suggestive and anecdotal. Neither can something called the 'postmodern' world (understood as 'social being', to use a phrase of Marx's) be said to determine in any univalent manner the form or content of art called 'postmodernist' (understood as a kind of 'social consciousness'). In any case, the analogy itself is only possible when one feature is selected from *one* reading of postmodernist art and then mapped onto another selected feature said to be characteristic of post-modern society. Any counter-assertions, identifying analogous features, perhaps, of 'unification' – 'globalization' in contemporary art and social life might be a candidate here – are subject to the same stricture.[23]

Second, that there is nothing to be gained from minimizing differences in judgements made by radical (supportive) and conservative (hostile) critics of artistic postmodernism. It is *always* the case that critics are highly selective in their choice of artists and artworks – as Greenberg, Fried, and Clark are – because such tactical choices allow them to propound their preferred theses about innovation and decay in art (modernism versus: theatricality/vulgarity/kitsch). These patterns of choice can, in most cases, be traced back to much earlier positions developed in relation to *modern*, not postmodern, art and society. Peter Fuller, for example, was quite open in his affiliation to what he thought John Ruskin and William Morris, for instance, stood for at the end of the nineteenth century. The *continuities*, that is, between the modern and the postmodern – in art, culture, and social development; the immanent possibilities and threats of 'annihilation' or 'totality' – remain profoundly more significant than any claimed disjunctions.

Notes

1. I shall usually refer to all writings by Greenberg, Fried, and Clark in the present tense in order to encourage a sense of debate (sometimes an out-and-out argument) between them. Occasionally, as will become clear, these writers literally *were* engaged with each other in such debate and argument. In order to pursue my chosen themes, questions, and problems I have, of course, been partial and selective in establishing the terms of, and constructing the 'moments' in, the broader debate. While my selection undoubtedly exhibits some polemical features, I have attempted overall to remain faithful to the *whole* bodies of work produced by my triumvirate over about a sixty-year period (*c*.1939–1999). Fried chose to open the introduction to his collection of critical essays, *Art and Objecthood: Essays and Reviews* (Chicago and London: University of Chicago Press, 1998; hereafter referred to as *AO*) with this quotation from Heidegger's essay 'The Origin of the Work of Art' (see reference in n. 19): 'Each answer remains in force as an answer only as long as it is rooted in questioning.' This could stand as a fitting additional epigram to my study.

2. Greenberg's most famous essay first appeared as a 'Voice of America' pamphlet printed in December 1960, a few weeks before its author's radio talk for the US government in February 1961. Numerous subsequent versions appeared in print, for instance, in *Arts Yearbook* no. 4, 1961: 101–108, and then in *Art and Literature* no. 4, Spring 1965: 193–201. For detailed discussion of the career of this essay and the historical circumstances of its mutation, see Francis Frascina 'Institutions, Culture, and America's "Cold War Years": the Making of Greenberg's Modernist Painting', *Oxford Art Journal* vol. 26, no. 1; 2003: 69–97. For two contrasting views, see Yves-Alain Bois 'Greenberg's Amendments', *Kunst*

und Museumjournaal 5, no. 1, 1993: 1–9, and Thierry de Duve *Clement Greenberg: Between the Lines* (Paris: Éditions dis Voir, 1996). In this study I shall use the version published in *Arts Yearbook* and reprinted in John O'Brian (ed.) *Clement Greenberg: The Collected Essays and Criticism. Volume 4: Modernism with a Vengeance* (Chicago and London: University of Chicago Press, 1995: 85–94; hereafter referred to as *CGCEC4*).

3. My Ph.D. was eventually published as *Federal Art and National Culture: The Politics of Identity in New Deal America* (New York and Cambridge, Cambridge University Press, 1995), and 4–6 in particular.

4. Interview conducted with Lily Leino ('USIS Feature', United States Information Service, April 1969), *CGCECW4*: 303–314 (310).

5. *The New Art History: A Critical Introduction* (London and New York: Routledge, 2001). See Michael Baxandall *Patterns of Intention: On the Historical Experience of Pictures* (New Haven and London: Yale University Press, 1985). On 'Theory', see *The New Art History*, Chapter 1.

6. *Culture* (Fontana: London, 1981): 119–121.

7. The course was called 'Modern Art: Practices and Debates'. Its four principal books were co-published with Yale University Press in 1993. On 'canon', see *The New Art History*, 40–41 and 50–56.

8. See my 'Modernism and Culture in the USA, 1930–1960', Book 4 of the course, in Francis Frascina, Jonathan Harris, Charles Harrison, and Paul Wood *Modernism in Dispute: Art Since the Forties* (New Haven and London: Yale University Press, 1993: 2–76). The anthology of essays for the course I co-edited with Francis Frascina *Art in Modern Culture: An Anthology of Critical Texts* (London: Phaidon, 1992), also represented, in its selection and section introductions, a considered response to that interrogation. Of course, in one sense I *was* moved by these artworks, but not in the ways conventionally associated with, or ratified by, modernist criticism or traditional art history 'appreciation'.

9. See Tamar Garb 'Gender and Representation', in Nigel Blake, Briony Fer, Francis Frascina, Tamar Garb, and Charles Harrison *Modernity and Modernism: French Painting in the Nineteenth Century* (New Haven and London: Yale University Press, 1993): 219–290; Gill Perry 'Primitivism and the "Modern"', in Francis Frascina, Charles Harrison, and Gill Perry *Primitivism, Cubism, Abstraction: The Early Twentieth Century* (New Haven and London: Yale University Press, 1993: 2–85); and Briony Fer 'The Language of Construction' and 'Surrealism, Myth and Psychoanalysis', in David Batchelor, Briony Fer, and Paul Wood *Realism, Rationalism, Surrealism* (New Haven and London: Yale University Press, 1993: 87–249).

10. Clyfford Still to Betty Parsons, 20 March, 1948, Archives of American Art, N 68/72.

11. See, in particular, *The Long Revolution* (London: Chatto & Windus, 1961); *Marxism and Literature* (Oxford: Oxford University Press, 1977); *Writing in Society* (London and New York: Verso, 1984); and *The Politics of Modernism: Against the New Conformists* (London and New York: Verso, 1989, published posthumously with an introduction by Tony Pinkney).

12. On the dangers of canon formation, see Williams 'When Was Modernism?', in *The Politics of Modernism* (31–35); on culture 'as a whole way of life', see *The Long Revolution* (57–88); and on 'cultural materialism', see *Marxism and Literature* (I, 'Basic Concepts', and II, 'Cultural Theory'), *Problems in Materialism and Culture* (Verso: London, 1980), and *Culture*.

13. *Cambridge Dictionary of Philosophy* (Cambridge and New York: Cambridge University Press, 1999): 885.

14. *Marxism and Literature*: 211.

15. See Louis Althusser's still invaluable discussion of the categories of production and reproduction in 'Ideology and Ideological State Apparatuses', in *Lenin and Philosophy and Other Essays* (New York and London: Monthly Review Press, 1971: 127–186): particularly 127–134 and 148–158.

16. *Farewell to an Idea: Episodes from a History of Modernism* (New Haven and London: Yale University Press, 1999; hereafter referred to as *FTAI*).

17. This is most evident in Williams's – highly qualified – belief in the creative possibilities of popular culture and new technologies. Studies such as *Television: Technology and Cultural Form* (London: Fontana, 1974) seem now, from our present, to be bathed in the idealistic light that the utopian side to the 1960s continued to exude until the mid-1970s oil crisis hit.

18. Michael Podro *The Critical Historians of Art* (New Haven and London: Yale University Press, 1982): see, for instance 209–217.

19. Ibid.: 176 and 205. Heidegger's notion of the ' "worlding" of the world' is pertinent here – he uses this neologism to suggest the making of the human world through human actions, including painting. See 'The Origin of the Work of Art' (a lecture given in 1935 and published in an earlier form as *Der Ursprung des Kunstwerkes*, Universal-Bibliothek Nr. 8446/47 [Stuttgart: Reclam, 1960]), in Heidegger *Poetry, Language, Thought* (translated and introduced by Albert Hofstadter, New York: Harper & Row, 1971: 17–87) 44–45, and R. Raj Singh 'Heidegger and the World in an Artwork', *Journal of Aesthetics and Art Criticism* vol. 48, no. 3; Summer 1990: 215–222.

20. Podro *The Critical Historians of Art*: 216–17. Fried on Wittgenstein, *AO*: 30–33; Clark, *FTAI*: 223.

21. *Manet's Modernism or, the Face of Painting in the 1860s* (Chicago and London: University of Chicago Press, 1998; hereafter referred to as *MM*): 525–526, n. 114. Fried is retrospectively commenting on his own essay

'Manet's Sources, Aspects of His Art, 1859–1869', originally published in *Artforum* 7, March 1969: 28–82. On Manet's ambition, see *MM*: 23–27.

22. On representations of women in Manet's painting, see Fried 'Manet in His Generation', in *MM*: 262–364, especially nn. 169, 188, 203, and 207; and T.J. Clark *The Painting of Modern Life: Paris in the Art of Manet and His Followers* (Princeton, NJ: Princeton University Press, 1986; hereafter referred to as *PML*), 'Olympia's Choice': 79–146. On Picasso's Cubism, see Clark 'Cubism and Collectivity', in *FTAI*: 169–223. See also Michael Fried 'Art and Objecthood', originally published in *Artforum* 5, June 1967: 12–23, reprinted in *AO*: 148–172 and *Absorption and Theatricality: Painting and Beholder in the Age of Diderot* (Berkeley and London: University of California Press, 1980).

23. Guy Debord *The Society of the Spectacle* (New York: Zone Books, 1994), Ken Knabb (ed. and trans.), *Situationist International Anthology* (Berkeley: Bureau of Public Secrets, 1981), and T.J. Clark and Donald Nicholson-Smith 'Why Art Can't Kill the Situationist International' *October* 79, Winter 1997: 15–31. On Fried's response to Clark's socio-historical reading of Manet's paintings, see, for example *MM*: 14–19 and 567, n. 63.

24. 'Clement Greenberg's Theory of Art', originally published in *Critical Inquiry* September 1982, vol. 9, no. 1: 139–156. This and related subsequent essays by Clark and Fried are reprinted in Francis Frascina (ed.) *Pollock and After: The Critical Debate* (London: Harper & Row, 1984: 47–88). For Clark's critique of art understood as an 'independent source of value', see 55–58.

25. See Maurice Merleau-Ponty 'Cézanne's Doubt', originally published as 'Le Doute de Cézanne', *Fontaine* no. 47, December 1945; reprinted in his *Sense and Non-Sense* (Evanston: Northwestern University Press, 1964: 9–25): 9.

26. See Heidegger 'The Origin of the Work of Art' in Heidegger *Poetry, Language, Thought*: 19.

27. 'Psycho-Analysis and the History of Art', in his *Meditations on a Hobby Horse and Other Essays on the Theory of Art* (London and New York: Phaidon, 1978): 39–40. Later on we shall encounter another even more backward relative of this significant underclass of cleaners and shippers, the 'ignorant Russian peasant' in Greenberg's 'Avant-Garde and Kitsch', originally published in *Partisan Review* vol. vi, no. 5, Fall 1939: 34–49; reprinted in John O'Brian (ed.) *Clement Greenberg: The Collected Essays and Criticism. Volume I: Perceptions and Judgements, 1939–1944* (Chicago and London: University of Chicago Press, 1986: 5–22; referred to hereafter as *CGCEC1*): 14.

28. See Donald Judd 'Specific Objects', *Arts Yearbook* no. 8, 1965: 'A work needs only to be interesting': 78. Fried discusses this remark in 'Shape as

Form: Frank Stella's Irregular Polygons', originally published in *Artforum* 5, November 1966: 18–27 (reprinted in *AO*: 77–99): 98–99, n. 9. Judd later stated: 'I was especially irked by Fried's ignorant misinterpretation of my use of the word "interesting". I obviously use it in a particular way but Fried reduces it to the cliché "merely interesting"', in Judd *Complete Writings 1959–1975* (Halifax: Press of the Nova Scotia College of Art and Design, 1975): 198.

29. Merleau-Ponty, deeply fascinated by the fragmentation of form in Cézanne's paintings, stressed the materiality of subjective perception with an observation curiously analogous to Gombrich's: 'When through the water's thickness I see the tiling at the bottom of a pool, I do not see it *despite* the water and the reflections there, I see it through them and because of them . . .' 'Eye and Mind', in Harold Osborne (ed.) *Aesthetics* (Oxford: Oxford University Press, 1972): 77.

30. See Terry Eagleton *The Ideology of the Aesthetic* (Oxford: Basil Blackwell, 1991): 120–152 and David Roberts *Art and Enlightenment: Aesthetic Theory after Adorno* (Lincoln, NE and London: University of Nebraska Press, 1991): 7–12 and *inter alia*.

31. Interview conducted by Lilly Leino, *CGCECW4*: 314.

32. Ibid. For a socio-historical analysis of the emergence of Enlightenment philosophical aesthetics, see Paul Mattick Jr (ed.) *Eighteenth-Century Aesthetics and the Reconstruction of Art* (New York and Cambridge: Cambridge University Press, 1993).

33. 'Arguments about Modernism: A Reply to Michael Fried', in Frascina (ed.) *Pollock and After: The Critical Debate* (81–88): 85.

34. Podro *The Critical Historians of Art*: 213.

35. Fried and Clark, for different reasons, dispute the usual meanings and efficacy of the term 'tradition'. I come to their arguments later. For a synoptic overview, in the light of postmodernist notions of 'hybridity', see Jonathan Harris 'Hybridity, Hegemony, Historicism' and 'Hybridity versus Tradition: Contemporary Art and Cultural Politics', in Harris (ed.) *Critical Perspectives on Contemporary Painting: Hybridity, Hegemony, Historicism* (Liverpool: Liverpool University Press and Tate Liverpool, 2003): 15–35 and 233–246.

36. Arnold Hauser *The Social History of Art*, vol. III *Rococo, Classicism, and Romanticism*, and vol. IV *Naturalism, Impressionism, the Film Age* (introductions by Jonathan Harris) (London and New York: Routledge, 1999).

37. Ibid., vol. III: 144 and vol. IV: 172. In this judgement Hauser is wrong, or at least seriously misleading. Contemporary art by the late nineteenth century had become, rather, a relatively *marginal* facet of culture and social life, though it maintained its own support structures, both in terms of economic relations of production and a range of existing and new institutions, including both state- and privately owned museums and galleries,

in which it could be sold, curated, taught, and exhibited. Its emergent public is a set of identifiable specific groups with different interests and values – professional critics, historians, scholars, teachers, as well as 'lay' art appreciators, collectors, and gallery visitors.

38. See, for example, ibid., vol. IV: on Picasso and Surrealism, 221–223.

39. Alois Riegl *Late Roman Art Industry* (Rome: G. Bretscheider, 1985) and Karl Schnaase *Geschichte der bildenden Künste im 15 Jahrhundert* (Stuttgart, 1879). See Podro's discussion in *The Critical Historians of Art*: 81.

40. Meyer Schapiro 'Style', in Morris Philipson (ed.) *Aesthetics Today: Selected Writings* (Cleveland, OH: World Publishing Co., 1961: 81–85): 81. See Alan Wallach's revaluation 'Falling into the Void', *Journal of Aesthetics and Art Criticism* vol. 55, no. 1, Winter 1997: 11–15.

41. 'Three American Painters: Kenneth Noland, Jules Olitski, Frank Stella', originally published Cambridge, MA: Fogg Art Museum, 1965; in *AO* (213–265): 263, no. 15; Greenberg 'Modernist Painting', *CGCECW4*: 85, 91.

42. '. . . the relation of the traditional concept of style to modernist painting . . . is far from simple, and . . . the task of redefining [not *replacing*] that relation will not be easy', ibid.: *AO*: 263, n. 15.

43. Ibid.: 214. I will deal later with some of the ideas developed in Fried's own long note to this statement (*AO*: 260–262, n. 4).

44. Ibid.: 260–261.

45. Ibid.: 261–262. Fried's claim that Manet's painting is, indeed, a kind of 'realism' will be addressed in Chapter 6.

46. 'How Modernism Works: A Response to T.J. Clark', in Frascina (ed.) *Pollock and After: The Critical Debate* (65–79): 70.

47. Review in John O'Brian (ed.) *Clement Greenberg: The Collected Essays and Criticism. Volume 3: Affirmations and Refusals, 1950–1956* (Chicago and London: University of Chicago Press, 1995: 94–98; hereafter referred to as *CGCEC3*): 94. On the reception of Hauser's *The Social History of Art*, see Michael Orwicz 'Critical Discourse in the Formation of a Social History of Art: Anglo-American Responses to Arnold Hauser', *Oxford Art Journal* vol. 8, no. 2, 1985: 52–62 and Jonathan Harris 'General Introduction', printed in each volume of *The Social History of Art*.

48. 'Three American Painters', *AO*: 219.

49. See Michel Foucault 'Nietzsche, Genealogy, History', in *Language, Counter-Memory, Practice* (edited by Donald F. Bouchard, Ithaca: Cornell University Press, 1977) and Stephen Bann *The Inventions of History: Essays on the Representation of the Past* (Manchester and New York: Manchester University Press, 1990).

50. By historicity here I mean the whole gamut of ways in which human arte-facts, including paintings, are claimed to accrue meanings and values 'over' or 'through', and 'in', time. See Anthony Giddens *The Constitution*

of Society: Outline of the Theory of Structuration (Cambridge: Polity Press, 1984): 203.

51. See Karl Popper 'Situational Logic in History. Historical Interpretation', in *The Poverty of Historicism* (London: Routledge & Kegan Paul, 1961) and Clark 'Cubism and Collectivity', *FTAI*: 175.

52. 'The Unhappy Consciousness', *FTAI* (299–369): 361.

53. 'The Origin of the Work of Art', in Heidegger *Poetry, Language, Thought*: 80. Heidegger is quoting from Hegel's *The Philosophy of Fine Art* (4 vols, trans. by F. Osmaston: New York: Hacker Fine Art, 1975), vol. I: 125–144.

54. 'The Origin of the Work of Art', in Heidegger *Poetry, Language, Thought*: 80.

55. 'An Introduction to My Art Criticism', *AO*: 18 and 55–56, n. 10.

56. See Fried *Absorption and Theatricality*, *Courbet's Realism* (Chicago and London: University of Chicago Press, 1992), and *MM*.

57. *MM*: 512, n. 26. Foucault's 1967 essay is reprinted in *Language, Counter-Memory, Practice*: 91–93.

58. See Fried's 'Manet's Sources, 1859–1869' and 'Manet's Sources Reconsidered', in *MM*: 23–184.

59. *The Critical Historians of Art*: 68–70.

60. 'Three American Painters', *AO*: 218.

61. 'The Unhappy Consciousness', *FTAI*: 351. Clark uses this phrase in discussing the role of critics in acclaiming the value of Pollock's *Untitled* (*Cut-Out*).

62. 'We Field-Women', *FTAI* (55–137): 55–56.

63. Ibid.: 55.

64. 'How Modernism Works: A Response to T.J. Clark', in Frascina (ed.) *Pollock and After: The Critical Debate*: 72.

65. 'Morris Louis', originally published as 'The Achievement of Morris Louis' *Artforum* 5, February 1967: 34–40, *AO* (100–131): 129.

66. Albert Gleizes and Jean Metzinger *Du Cubisme*, trans. as *Cubism* (London: T. Fisher Unwin, 1913): 16.

67. 'New York Painting Only Yesterday', originally published in *Art News* summer 1957, reprinted in *CGCEW4* (19–26): 21.

68. 'Modernist Painting', in *CGCEW4*: 91.

69. *AO*: xvii and, for instance, 'An Introduction to My Art Criticism', pp. 3, 9, 11, and 19.

70. For some of their comments on each other's work see, for instance, *MM*: 400, 466–467, n. 61; *Courbet's Realism*: xviii; *FTAI*: 68; 176.

71. See, along with 'Clement Greenberg's Theory of Art', in Frascina (ed.) *Pollock and After: The Critical Debate*, 'More on the Differences Between Comrade Greenberg and Ourselves', in Benjamin H.D. Buchloh, Serge Guilbaut, and David Solkin (eds) *Modernism and Modernity: The Vancouver Conference Papers* (Halifax, Nova Scotia: The Press of the

Nova Scotia College of Art and Design, 1983: 169–187), and *FTAI*: 107 and 127–128.

72. 'Édouard Manet', originally published as 'Une nouvelle manière en peinture: Édouard Manet', *Revue du XIX Siècle*, 1 January 1867, reprinted in translation in Charles Harrison and Francis Frascina (eds) *Modern Art and Modernism: A Critical Anthology* (London: Harper & Row, 1982: 29–38): 38.

73. 'The Critic as Artist', Parts I and II, in *Plays, Prose Writings, and Poems* (London: Dent, 1978: 3–65): 24 and 63.

74. 'The Impressionists and Édouard Manet', first published in English (original French version is lost) in *Art Monthly Review* vol. 1, no. 9, 1876, reprinted in Harrison and Frascina (eds) *Modern Art and Modernism: A Critical Anthology* (39–44): 39.

75. Ibid.: 44.

76. 'Interview with Emile de Antonio' [1970] in John O'Neill (ed.) *Barnett Newman: Selected Writings and Interviews* (Berkeley: University of California Press, 1992): 307–308.

77. 'How Modernism Works: A Response to T.J. Clark', in Frascina (ed.) *Pollock and After: The Critical Debate*: 78.

78. 'Manet's Sources, 1859–1869', *MM*: 73.

79. 'Three American Painters', *AO*: 219.

80. Ibid.: 219–220.

81. 'Complaints of an Art Critic', originally published in *Artforum* vol. 6, no. 2; October 1967: 38–39, reprinted in Charles Harrison and Fred Orton (eds) *Modernism, Criticism, Realism: Alternative Contexts for Art* (London: Harper & Row, 1984: 3–8): 4.

82. Book Review, originally published in *Partisan Review* March–April 1942; reprinted in John O'Brian (ed.) *Clement Greenberg: The Collected Essays and Criticism. Volume 1: Perceptions and Judgments, 1939–1944* (Chicago and London: University of Chicago Press, 1988: 93–95; referred to hereafter as *CGCEC1*): 93.

83. 'Abstract Art', originally published in *The Nation* 15 April 1944; reprinted in *CGCEC1* (199–204): 204.

84. Autobiographical Statement, originally published in *Twentieth Century Authors* (New York: The H.W. Wilson Company, 1955); reprinted in *CGCEC3* (194–196): 196.

85. 'Avant-Garde and Kitsch', originally published in *Partisan Review* Fall 1939; reprinted in *CGCECW1* (5–22): 7.

86. Susan Bucks-Morss *The Origin of Negative Dialectics: Adorno, Benjamin, and the Frankfurt School* (New York: Free Press, 1977): 131, 188; Theodor Adorno *Aesthetic Theory* (trans. C. Lenhardt, London: Routledge & Kegan Paul, 1984).

87. 'The Identity of Art', originally published in *Country Beautiful* November 1961; reprinted in *CGCEC4* (117–120): 118.

88. 'Complaints of an Art Critic', in Harrison and Orton (eds) *Modernism, Criticism, Realism: Alternative Contexts for Art*: 4.

89. 'How Modernism Works: A Response to T.J. Clark', in Frascina (ed.) *Pollock and After: Then Critical Debate*: 75.

90. See *FTAI*: (on Kasimir Malevich) 263; (on Pollock) 337; (on Abstract Expressionism) 388–389.

91. 'An Introduction to My Art Criticism', *AO*: 18. Fried is reviewing claims in his 1965 'Three American Painters' essay.

92. See Fried *MM*: 568, n. 71: and Greenberg 'The Case for Abstract Art', originally published in *Saturday Evening Post*, August 1959, reprinted in *CGCEC4* (75–84): 80–81.

93. 'The Identity of Art', *CGCEC4*: 119–120.

94. *Cambridge Dictionary of Philosophy*: 885.

95. 'Arguments about Modernism: A Reply to Michael Fried', in Frascina (ed.) *Pollock and After: The Critical Debate*: 85.

96. *Arguments in English Marxism* (London: Verso, 1980): 28.

97. 'Arguments about Modernism: A Reply to Michael Fried', in Frascina (ed.) *Pollock and After: The Critical Debate*: 85.

98. See Clive Bell 'The Aesthetic Hypothesis' and 'The Debt to Cézanne', in *Art* (London: Chatto & Windus, 1931) and Raymond Williams 'The Bloomsbury Fraction', in *Problems in Materialism and Culture* (London, Verso, 1997: 148–169).

99. *FTAI*: 7.

100. 'The Origin of the Work of Art' in Heidegger *Poetry, Language, Thought*: 18.

101. Adolphe Retté, *La Plume* (30 May 1896), quoted in Mathieu Robert, 'Varia', *Le Réveil* June 1896: 415. Clark discusses the anarchist Retté's diatribe on Mallarmé in 'We Field-Women', in *FTAI*: 128.

102. See Podro *The Critical Historians of Art*: 26.

103. 'Towards a Newer Laocoon', originally published in *Partisan Review* July–August 1940, reprinted in *CGCEC1* (23–38): 33.

104. 1. Edward Said, *The London Review of Books* 19 July 2001: 11; 2. Jonathan Jones, *The Guardian* 22 April 2003: (G2) 12–13; 3. Adrian Searle, *The Guardian* 17 June 2003: (G2) 10–13; 4. H. Wölfflin, *Principles of Art History* 1909, quoted in *The Critical Historians of Art* 58; 5. Greenberg, 'Towards a Newer Laocoon', in *CGCEC1* 32–33; 6. Podro, *The Critical Historians of Art*: 19.

105. 'Clement Greenberg's Theory of Art', in Frascina (ed.) *Pollock and After: The Critical Debate*: 60.

106. *The Critical Historians of Art*: 213.

107. 'Cubism and Collectivity', in *FTAI*: 215. See Clark *Image of the People: Gustave Courbet and the 1848 Revolution* (London: Thames & Hudson, 1973).

108. See Nancy Jachec 'Modernism, Enlightenment Values, and Clement Greenberg', *Oxford Art Journal* vol. 21, no. 2; 1998 (121–132).

109. *FTAI*: 8.

110. *PML*: 12.

111. Raymond Williams *Politics and Letters: Interviews with the New Left Review* (London: New Left Books, 1979), especially 'Britain 1956–78': 361–383 and 'Two Roads to Change': 406–437. On culture as 'a whole way of life', see *The Long Revolution*: 62–63.

112. See Ernst Cassirer *Kants Leben und Lehre* (Berlin, 1918), discussed by Podro in *The Critical Historians of Art*: 181–182.

113. 'Eye and Mind', in Harold Osborne (ed.) *Aesthetics*: 85.

114. *Cambridge Dictionary of Philosophy*: 163.

115. I would speculatively claim that Clark's 1973 study of Courbet is 'good complexity'-oriented, still rooted in its author's socialist idealism. His 1984 book on Manet is a work 'of the break' – to allude to Althusser's distinction between phases in Marx's writings – not towards 'science', as Althusser had it as far as Marx was concerned, but towards the more thorough-going critical pessimism of *Farewell to an Idea* (1999). See Jonathan Harris ' "Stuck in the Post"? Abstract Expressionism, T.J. Clark and modernist history painting', in David Green and Peter Seddon (eds) *History Painting Reassessed* (Manchester and New York: Manchester University Press, 2000): 18–30.

116. Robert Morris 'Notes on Sculpture', originally published in two parts in *Artforum* February and October 1966; in 'Art and Objecthood', *AO*: 153 and see 168, n. 2.

117. Ibid.: 168.

118. *Absorption and Theatricality: Painting and Beholder in the Age of Diderot*: 104.

1 Modernism's modern art

1. On the retrospection of modern critics *and* artists, see Thierry de Duve 'The Monochrome and the Blank Canvas', in Serge Guilbaut (ed.) *Reconstructing Modernism: Art in New York, Paris, and Montreal 1945–1964* (Cambridge, MA: MIT Press, 1990: 244–310).

2. 'After Abstract Expressionism', originally published in *Art International* 25, October 1962, *CGCEC4* (121–134): 132.

3. *FTAI*: 7.

4. Ibid.: 134.

5. See Podro's discussion of this in *The Critical Historians of Art*: 6–7.

6. See *FTAI*: (on Cubism) 176–180 and 223; (on Pollock) 338–343. On Pollock as 'nature', see Fred Orton and Griselda Pollock 'Jackson Pollock, Painting, and the Myth of Photography', *Art History* vol. 6, no. 1; March 1983: 114–121 and Michael Leja 'Jackson Pollock: Representing the Unconscious', *Art History* vol. 13, no. 4; December 1990: 542–565.

7. See Lucien Goldman *Towards a Sociology of the Novel* (trans. Alan Sheridan, London: Tavistock Publications, 1964) and Fredric Jameson *The Political Unconscious: Narrative as a Socially Symbolic Art* (London: Methuen, 1981).

8. 1: 'Clement Greenberg's Theory of Art', in Frascina (ed.) *Pollock and After: The Critical Debate*: 60; 2: 'Three American Painters', *AO*: 235–236; 3: 'Modernist Painting', *CGCEC4*: 86.

9. *FTAI*: 10.

10. *FTAI*: 401. Compare with Fried: '. . . the paintings themselves manifest a high degree of formal self-awareness, and this may come about as the result of decisions the painter himself insists on calling intuitive . . . [the] . . . analogy at work here, between modernist painting and a verbal language, is drastically inexact and deeply problematic. But it is also potentially highly instructive . . .' ibid., *AO*: 236–237. For Mallarmé's much earlier use of the term 'lyric', see n. 34 below.

11. According to Fried, what lies *between* such specific media, consisting in the visual arts of painting and sculpture, 'is theatre'. Concepts of aesthetic quality and value, and that of art itself, he notes, are 'meaningful, or wholly meaningful', only within the 'individual arts'. Fried acknowledges the ineffable nature of these claims – that is, they cannot be empirically verified, see 'Art and Objecthood', *AO*: 163–164. I return to these stipulations in my Conclusion.

12. 'Eye and Mind', in Osborne (ed.) *Aesthetics*: 61.

13. Ibid.: 58. On Merleau-Ponty's carnal phenomenology, subjectivity, and art, see Brendan Prendeville 'Merleau-Ponty, Realism, and Painting: Psychological Space and the Space of Exchange', *Art History* vol. 22, no. 3; September 1999: 364–388.

14. See Alison Rowley and Griselda Pollock 'Painting in a Hybrid Moment', in Harris (ed.) *Critical Perspectives on Contemporary Painting: Hybridity, Hegemony, Historicism* (37–79): especially 55, 64–66, 77, n. 32; Susan Hiller (ed.) *The Myth of Primitivism: Perspectives on Art* (London and New York: Routledge, 1991); and Sally Price *Primitive Art in Civilized Places* (Chicago and London: University of Chicago Press, 1991).

15. For an overview of the art-historical debate on Van Gogh's painting of shoes, see Craig Owens 'Representation, Appropriation, and Power', in Owens *Beyond Recognition: Representation, Power, and Culture* (Berkeley: University of California Press, 1992: 88–113): 93–99.

16. *FTAI*: 9.

17. Robert Coates, 'The Art Galleries: Abroad and at Home', *New Yorker* no. 22, 30 March 1946; Harold Rosenberg 'The American Action Painters' *Art News* vol. 51, no. 8; December 1952: 22–23, 48–50; Greenberg '"American-Type" Painting', originally published in *Partisan Review* Spring 1955, in *CGCEC3*: 217–236.

18. See Donald Kuspit's intellectual biography *Clement Greenberg: Art Critic* (Madison: University of Wisconsin Press, 1979).

19. On the academicization of art history and art theory after 1950, see Jonathan Harris *The New Art History: A Critical Introduction*: Introduction, Chapter 1, and *inter alia*.

20. Several essays had also been published previously in different versions. See *FTAI*: vi–viii. See the review by Robert Herbert 'Goodbye to All That', *New York Review of Books* 4 November 1999: 28–31.

21. *FTAI*: 9–10.

22. Ibid.: 8.

23. 'Eye and Mind', in Osborne (ed.) *Aesthetics*: 64–65.

24. Quoted by John O'Brian, in the Introduction, *CGCEC1*: xxiv.

25. 'Eye and Mind', in Osborne (ed.) *Aesthetics*: 61.

26. See Clark 'Olympia's Choice', in *PML*: 79–146. The literature on this painting is massive. I include reference to some of it in Chapter 6.

27. John Berger *The Success and Failure of Picasso* (London: Writers and Readers, 1980 [1965]): 70–71.

28. 'We Field-Women', *FTAI*: 8 and 130.

29. 'The Origin of the Work of Art', in Heidegger *Poetry, Language, Thought*: 40.

30. For a review of the basic issues, see Michael Podro 'Derrida on Kant and Heidegger', *Art History* vol. 11, no. 3; September 1988: 433–439. I consider these questions further in Chapter 5.

31. *FTAI*: 12. Unfortunately there was no space here to include substantive discussion of Clark's essay 'God is Not Cast Down': 225–297.

32. Ibid.: 12 and 369.

33. 'Jules Olitski', originally published as a catalogue essay for the exhibition *Jules Olitski: Paintings 1963–1967*, Corcoran Gallery of Art, Washington, DC, 28 April–11 June, 1967, *AO* (132–147): 146, n. 12.

34. Quoted in translation by Arthur Symons in *The Symbolist Movement in Literature* (London: Dutton, 1958).The passage is from Mallarmé's essay 'Crise de vers'. Fried discusses it in 'Morris Louis', *AO*: 126–127.

35. See 'Shape as Form: Frank Stella's Irregular Polygons', originally published in *Artforum* 5, November 1966: 18–27, *AO* (77–99): 78–79. Greenberg noted, for instance, that he first saw Newman's artwork in 1950 and 'liked it. I certainly didn't need the help of anybody's words, and I haven't since . . . there was nothing said or written about Mondrian that I'd heard or read that helped me, and certainly Mondrian's own words were no help. You looked first. Now it's a widespread notion . . . that modernist art depends on titles and what's said about it, otherwise its opaque. Of course that's preposterous. It's a vulgar notion.' Interview with James Faure Walker (1978), in Robert C. Morgan (ed.) *Clement Greenberg: Late Writings* (Minneapolis, MN: University of Minnesota Press, 2003: 149–168): 160.

36. 'Morris Louis', *AO*: 126.

37. Ibid.

38. 'Three American Painters', *AO*: 251.
39. See Fredric Jameson 'The Deconstruction of Expression', *New Left Review* 146 July/August 1984: 53–92.
40. 'Jules Olitski', *AO*: 145.
41. Fried here is quoting the critic Walter Darby Bannard, *Jules Olitski at the New Gallery*, exhibition catalogue, University of Miami, 25 February– 25 March 1994 (unpaginated), see *MM*: 618, n. 20.
42. *MM*: 416.
43. Ibid.: 317.
44. 'The Impressionists and Édouard Manet', in Frascina and Harrison (eds) *Modern Art and Modernism*: 40.
45. I examine Greenberg's use of the term opticality, and Fried's and Clark's commentaries, later in this study. See Rosalind Krauss *The Optical Unconscious* (Cambridge, MA: MIT Press, 1994): especially 'Six': 243– 320. This study constitutes, among other things, an oblique feminist reading and critique of Greenberg's and Fried's accounts of modernism.
46. See note 26 above and, for example, Bradford Collins (ed.) *Twelve Views of Manet's Bar* (Princeton, NJ: Princeton University Press, 1996) and Ruth E. Iskin 'Selling, Seduction, and Soliciting the Eye: Manet's *Bar at the Folies Bergère*', *Art Bulletin* vol. lxxvii, no. 1; March 1995: 25–44.
47. Robert L. Herbert *Impressionism: Art, Leisure and Parisian Society* (New Haven and London: Yale University Press, 1988): 7.
48. *The Social History of Art* vol. III: 25.
49. Ibid.: 177. See also my Introduction to the volume: xl.
50. Ibid. See Albert Boime *The Academy and French Painting in the Nineteenth Century* (London and New York: Phaidon, 1971).
51. 'Complaints of an Art Critic', in Harrison and Orton (eds) *Modernism, Criticism, Realism: Alternative Contexts for Art*: 4.
52. See, for example, Rozsika Parker and Griselda Pollock *Old Mistresses: Women, Art, and Ideology* (London: Pandora Press, 1981); Linda Nochlin *Women, Art and Power and Other Essays* (London: Thames & Hudson, 1988); and Marcia Pointon (ed.) *Art Apart: Artifacts, Institutions, and Ideology in England and North America from 1800 to the Present* (Manchester: Manchester University Press, 1994).
53. See Barbara Reise 'Greenberg and the Group: A Retrospective View', originally published in *Studio International* vol. 175, no. 901; May 1968: 354–357 (Part 1) and vol. 175, no. 902; June 1968: 314–316 (Part II), reprinted in Francis Frascina and Jonathan Harris (eds) *Art in Modern Culture: An Anthology of Critical Texts* (London: Phaidon, 1992: 252–263).
54. *The Social History of Art* vol. III: 177.
55. 'Avant-Garde and Kitsch', *CGCEC1*: 11 and 20–22. See Paul Hart 'The Essential Legacy of Clement Greenberg from the Era of Stalin and Hitler', *Oxford Art Journal* vol. 11, no. 1; 1988 (76–87).

56. 'Modernist Painting', *CGCEC4*: 93. See Frascina 'Institutions, Culture, and America's "Cold War Years": the Making of Greenberg's Modernist Painting': especially 69–76.

57. See Greenberg 'Where is the Avant-Garde?', originally published in *Vogue* June 1967; *CGCEC4*: 259–265; 'Avant-Garde Attitudes: New Art in the Sixties', originally published in *Studio International* April 1970; *CGCEC4*: 292–303; and 'Counter-Avant-Garde', originally published in *Art International* 15, May 1971: 16–19; in Robert C. Morgan (ed.) *Clement Greenberg: Late Writings*: 5–18.

58. See Peter Bürger *Theory of the Avant-Garde* (trans. Michael Shaw: Minneapolis: University of Minnesota Press, 1984).

59. See Serge Guilbaut *How New York Stole the Idea of Modern Art: Abstract Expressionism, Freedom, and the Cold War* (Chicago and London: University of Chicago Press, 1983) and Michael Leja *Reframing Abstract Expressionism: Subjectivity and Painting in the 1940s* (New Haven and London: Yale University Press, 1993).

60. Reprinted in *CGCEC3*: 122–152. Greenberg had thought this essay significant enough to include it, modified, in his own collection *Art & Culture: Critical Essays* (New York: Beacon, 1961).

61. See, for example, Barnett Newman 'The First Man Was An Artist' *Tiger's Eye* October 1947: 57–60 and 'The Sublime is Now' *Tiger's Eye* December 1948: 51–53; both reprinted in John P. O'Neil (ed.) *Barnett Newman: Selected Writings and Interviews*: 60–61 and 170–173.

62. 'The Unhappy Consciousness', *FTAI*: 369.

63. 'Towards a Newer Laocoon', *CGCEC1*: 28.

64. 'Three American Painters', *AO*: 217.

2 Pure formality: 1960s abstract painting

1. See Introduction, *AO*: 17–19 and 56, n. 14. Fried discusses the role of the 'formal critic' in 'Three American Painters', ibid., 219–220 and see 262, n. 8. 'Formalism' as a critical and theoretical perspective in literary studies has its roots in the early twentieth century in Eastern Europe. There it had developed in close and argumentative relation to Marxist accounts of art and language. See, for instance, Fredric Jameson *Marxism and Form* (Princeton, NJ: Princeton University Press, 1971) and *The Prison-House of Language: A Critical Account of Structuralism and Russian Formalism* (Princeton, NJ: Princeton University Press 1972).

2. For Fried's account of his relations with artists in the early 1960s, see ibid.: 4, 7–9, 11–13.

3. *Post Painterly Abstraction*, originally an exhibition catalogue essay published by Los Angeles County Museum of Art, April–June 1964; reprinted in *CGCEC4*: 192–197. Griselda Pollock's dictum that modern artists, in establishing themselves, have to refer and defer to, and then

differ from, their established peers is also true of art critics and historians. See Griselda Pollock *Avant-Garde Gambits: Gender and the Colour of Art History* (London: Thames & Hudson, 1992): 14.

4. See Fried's 'Shape as Form: Frank Stella's Irregular Polygons', *AO*: 78–79, 95, and 99, n. 11. The descriptive adequacy of the terms 'painter' and 'sculptor' begins radically to weaken, however, when Minimalism's *producers* – to adopt a more neutral term – for instance, Carl Andre, began to make works out of pre-existing industrial materials such as house bricks, which Andre then arranged and exhibited in 1966, as part of a set, under the title *Equivalents I–VIII*. On Andre's *Equivalent I–VIII*, see Martha Buskirk *The Contingent Object of Contemporary Art* (Cambridge, MA and London: MIT Press, 2003): 30–31.

5. 'Modernist Painting', *CGCEC4*: 86.

6. Ibid.: 91. The finality of this judgement seems particularly striking given that Greenberg attaches the term 'self-criticism', which surely implies self-consciousness, to modernist art! Fried also finds it odd. 'Greenberg writes in "Modernist Painting"', he notes, '"No one artist was, or is yet, consciously aware of [the self-critical tendency of modernist painting], *nor could any artist work successfully in conscious awareness of it*" ... a surprising claim in view of Greenberg having just elucidated that tendency with all the clarity at his command. What did he think would become of modernist painting now that he had laid bare its inner workings?' (Fried's italic), *AO*: 65 n. 48.

7. 'Modernist Painting', *CGCEC4*: 87.

8. 'After Abstract Expressionism', originally published in *Art International*, 25 October 1962; reprinted in *CGCEC4* (121–134): 131.

9. Introduction: 17–19 and 'Three American Painters', *AO*: 214–215.

10. 'How Modernism Works: A Response to T.J. Clark', in Frascina (ed.) *Pollock and After: The Critical Debate*: 69. Fried is quoting his own words, with minor amendment, from his 1967 essay 'Art and Objecthood'.

11. Ibid.: 71–72.

12. 'Art and Objecthood', *AO*: 168–9, n. 6. See also Fried's Introduction, 37–38.

13. Ibid.: 38. Wittgenstein (from his *Remarks on the Foundation of Mathematics*, 1956) quoted in 'Jules Olitski', *AO*: 132 and 145, n. 1.

14. 'After Abstract Expressionism', *CGCEC4*: 131–132.

15. Ibid.: 132.

16. 'Art and Objecthood', *AO*: 153. Fried is discussing Morris's two-part article 'Notes on Sculpture', reference in my Introduction, n. 116.

17. *AO*: 159. For a different perspective on the meaning of 'situation', see Kenneth Baker *Minimalism: Art of Circumstance* (New York: Abbeyville Press, 1989).

18. 'Shape as Form: Frank Stella's Irregular Polygons', *AO*: 88. Minimalism has, however, been subject to numerous critiques since the 1970s

attacking and defending its perceived *metaphoric* meanings. See, for instance, Anna Chave's feminist attack 'Minimalism and the Rhetoric of Power', *Arts Magazine* vol. 64, no. 5, 5 January 1990: 44–63 and Hal Foster's defence of its 'everyday' qualities 'The Crux of Minimalism', in Howard Singerman (ed.) *Individuals: A Selected History of Contemporary Art* (New York: Abrams, 1986: 162–183). Fried's own discussion of Minimalism as 'literalism' is itself, of course, also a reading that awards its object certain metaphoric properties.

19. 'Shape as Form: Frank Stella's Irregular Polygons', *AO*: 95.
20. Ibid.: 94.
21. 'Jules Olitski': 138 and 'Modernist Painting', *AO*: 89.
22. 'Jules Olitski', *AO*: 146, n. 12.
23. 'The Unhappy Consciousness', *FTAI*: 330.
24. Ibid.: 330. This passage is in 'Three American Painters', *AO*: 224–225.
25. 'The Unhappy Consciousness', *FTAI*: 330–331.
26. Ibid.: 336. See Fried's 'Three American Painters', *AO*: 222–223.
27. 'Clement Greenberg's Theory of Art', in Frascina (ed.) *Pollock and After: The Critical Debate*: 55. Clark's reference to 'becoming' here may or may not be an intentional reference to the claim Fried makes in 'Three American Painters' that the most recent modernist art has 'become' to be specifically about aesthetic value. This is discussed on p. 80 and note 55 below.
28. See 'Clement Greenberg's Theory of Art', in Frascina (ed.) *Pollock and After: The Critical Debate*: 57–60 and, in addition to his chapters on *Olympia* and *A Bar at the Folies Bergère*, Clark's Introduction to *PML*: 12–14. Fried applauds this discussion, though, in a mostly implicit criticism of Clark aimed at closing down again the range of meanings for 'flatness', claims that Manet's later paintings, including *A Bar at The Folies Bergère*, represent his engagement specifically with the 'conception of painting and of pictorial unity' in Impressionist art, *MM*: 17 and 642, n. 48. Why should that, though, foreclose on the broader meanings the term 'flatness' attracts?
29. 'How Modernism Works: A Response to T.J. Clark', in Frascina (ed.) *Pollock and After: The Critical Debate*: 70.
30. Ibid.: 66–67.
31. 'Jules Olitski', *AO*: 138–189.
32. Introduction, *AO*: 46–47. 'Grace', whatever its spiritual or mystical overtones, is also a key term in Leon Battista Alberti's treatise on pictorial composition *Della Pittura* (1435). It refers to the quality achieved when there is precise conformity in an 'istoria' (narrative composition) between the depiction of human physiognomy and the action narrated.
33. 'Modernist Painting', *CGCEC4*: 86. See Greenberg's comment on 'pure' and 'purity', note 67 below.
34. Ibid.: 90.

35. Introduction, *MM*: 18–19. Fried believes, in retrospect, that Greenberg attempted to reduce the 'pictorial' to the 'optical' – to what he himself, in 'Three American Painters', of course, in discussing Pollock's paintings, had called 'eyesight alone'. See Clark's discussion of this, reference in note 24 above.

36. 'Modernist Painting', *CGCEC4*: 89.

37. 'Shape as Form: Frank Stella's Irregular Polygons': 78 and 'Three American Painters', *AO*: 232.

38. Ibid.: *AO*: 234.

39. I examine Fried's discussion of Impressionism in relation to Manet in Chapter 6. For Fried's response to Krauss's book, see *MM*: 465, n. 61. For another reading, see Brian Grosskurth 'Drawing on Lacan', *The Oxford Art Journal* vol. 17, no. 2; 1994: 138–142.

40. 'Louis and Noland', originally published in *Art International* May 1960; reprinted in *CGCEC4* (94–100): 97.

41. Ibid.: 97–98.

42. In contrast, see Clark's quite extensive discussion of titles to Pollock's paintings, 'The Unhappy Consciousness', *FTAI*: 317, 333–334, 336–337.

43. See 'Review of Exhibitions of Marc Chagall, Lyonel Feininger, and Jackson Pollock, originally published in *The Nation* 27 November 1943; reprinted in *CGCEC1* (164–166): 165 and 'The Present Prospects of American Painting and Sculpture', originally published in *Horizon* October 1947; reprinted in John O'Brian (ed.) *Clement Greenberg: The Collected Essays and Criticism. Volume 2: Arrogant Purpose, 1945–1949* (Chicago and London: University of Chicago Press, 1988: 160–170, hereafter referred to as *CGCEC2*): 166.

44. 'Clement Greenberg's Theory of Art', in Frascina (ed.) *Pollock and After: The Critical Debate*: 58.

45. 'Aesthetic' is one of the most promiscuously metaphoric terms. As its Greek form *aesthesis* indicates the term refers, Terry Eagleton notes, to 'the whole region of human perception and sensation, in contrast to the more rarified domain of conceptual thought'. See *The Ideology of the Aesthetic* (Oxford: Blackwell, 1990): 13. For discussions of Greenberg's use of Kant's ideas, see Paul Crowther 'Kant and Greenberg's Varieties of Aesthetic Formalism' *Journal of Aesthetics and Art Criticism* vol. xlii, no. 4; 1983 (442–445) and Mark A. Cheetham *Kant, Art, and Art History* (New York and Cambridge: Cambridge University Press, 2001): 87–100.

46. 'Arguments about Modernism: A Reply to Michael Fried', in Frascina (ed.) *Pollock and After: The Critical Debate*: 82–83.

47. 'How Modernism Works: A Response to T.J. Clark, in Frascina (ed.) *Pollock and After: The Critical Debate*: 74.

48. 'Clement Greenberg's Theory of Art', in Frascina (ed.) *Pollock and After: The Critical Debate*: 52. See Greenberg's 'Avant-Garde and Kitsch', *CGCEC1*: 8.

49 'Clement Greenberg's Theory of Art', in Frascina (ed.) *Pollock and After: The Critical Debate*: 59.

50. Ibid.

51. Ibid.: 58.

52. 'The Case for Abstract Art', originally published in *Saturday Evening Post* August 1959; reprinted in *CGCEC4* (75–84): 81. 'Those who have grown capable of experiencing this know what I mean', he adds, in cryptic terms that suggest that only some, unfortunately, will ever learn to experience art *relevantly*.

53. 'Introduction to an Exhibition of Morris Louis, Kenneth Noland, and Jules Olitski', originally published as *Three New American Painters: Louis, Noland, Olitski*, Norman MacKenzie Art Gallery, Regina, Saskatchewan, January–February 1963; reprinted in *CGCEC4* (149–153): 153.

54. See, for example, 'Shape as Form: Frank Stella's Irregular Polygons': 84–85. 'Morris Louis': 101–102, and 'Art and Objecthood', AO: 165–166.

55. 'Shape as Form: Frank Stella's Irregular Polygons', *AO*: 98–99, n. 9.

56. 'Three American Painters', *AO*: 215.

57. 'Preface and Acknowledgements', *AO*: xvii.

58. Introduction, *AO*: 7.

59. Ibid.

60. 'Shape as Form: Frank Stella's Irregular Polygons', *AO*: 77–78. Note that Fried, here, is not talking about Stella's *Six Mile Bottom* but I believe his verdict on this painting would have been similar.

61. Ibid.: 80.

62. Ibid.: 95.

63. 'Morris Louis', *AO*: 101.

64. 'Shape as Form: Frank Stella's Irregular Polygons', *AO*: 79.

65. 'Morris Louis', *AO*: 128 and 125.

66. 'Shape as Form: Frank Stella's Irregular Polygons', *AO*: 80 and 84. Note that Fried doesn't retract these judgements in his retrospective comments, he merely admits that 'my remarks about the imminent opening up of so large a zone of freedom [in modernist painting] proved to be absurdly utopian', *AO*: 63–64, n. 46.

67. 'Shape as Form: Frank Stella's Irregular Polygons', *AO*: 79–81. Greenberg, however, in 1978 added, to my mind, a rather disingenuous postscript to the reprinting of 'Modernist Painting' in the collection *Esthetics Contemporary*, edited by Richard Kostelananetz (New York: Prometheus, [1978] 1989), in which he claimed that his purpose in that essay had been radically misunderstood: 'Many readers . . . seem to have taken the "rationale" of Modernist art outlined here as representing a position adopted by the writer himself: that is, that what he describes he also advocates. This may be a fault of the writing or the rhetoric . . . The writer is trying to account in part for how most of the very best art of the hundred-odd years came about, but he's not implying that that's how

it *had* to come about, much less that that's how the best art still has to come about. "Pure" art was a useful illusion, but this doesn't make it any less of an illusion', quoted in 'Modernist Painting', *CGCEC4*: 93–94.

68. William Powell Frith's painting of *Paddington Station* (1862), Clive Bell notified his reader, has 'provided thousands with half-hours of curious and fanciful pleasure, it is [however] no less certain that no one has experienced before it one half-second of aesthetic rapture', 'The Aesthetic Hypothesis', *Art* (Chatto & Windus, 1931), reprinted in Frascina and Harrison (eds) *Modern Art and Modernism: A Critical Anthology*: 71. Bell's Bloomsbury contemporary John Maynard Keynes had declared: 'Our apprehension of good was exactly the same as our apprehension of green.' (*Two Memoirs*, cited in S.P. Rosenbaum (ed.) *The Bloomsbury Group*: Toronto: University of Toronto Press, 1975: 52–59).

69. Introduction, *AO*: 15.

70. Ibid.: 51. For an account of US art politics in the late 1960s, see Francis Frascina *Art, Politics and Dissent: Aspects of the Art Left in Sixties America* (Manchester and New York: Manchester University Press, 1999).

71. 'Art and Objecthood', *AO*: 160 and 165. For a different account of 'conviction' in late 1960s US art, one with radical political implications, see David Craven 'Robert Smithson's Liquidating Intellect' *Art History* vol. 6, no. 4; December 1983: 488–496.

72. 'Morris Louis', *AO*: 102.

73. 'The Crisis of Abstract Art', originally published in *Arts Yearbook 7*, 1964; reprinted in *CGCEC4* (176–181): 180–181. See Irving Sandler *The New York School: The Painters and Sculptors of the Fifties* (New York: Harper and Row, 1978).

74. Introduction: 46 and 'Art and Objecthood', *AO*: 148.

75. Fried notes that later 'Andre sent me a note gently chiding me for "suggesting that Frank's [*sic*] soul had been put at risk between us" and reminding me, entirely correctly, that "Frank had always been too much his own man to let his soul be swayed too easily" '. 'Introduction', *AO*: 71, n. 67.

76. 'Modernist Painting', *CGCEC4*: 87, quoted in n. 7 above.

77. See my *Critical Perspectives on Contemporary Painting: Hybridity, Hegemony, Historicism* and Fried, 'Art and Objecthood' *AO*: 164–165. Fried acknowledges here an interest in the experimental, and politically radical, 'anti-theatrical' drama of Bertold Brecht (172, n. 23), asserting, however, that such experiments as exposed lighting are fated to become 'mere' conventions in themselves. See John Willett (trans. and ed.) *Brecht on Theatre: The Development of an Aesthetic* (London: Methuen, 2001 [1964]).

78. 'Shape as Form: Frank Stella's Irregular Polygons', *AO*: 88. See Fried's review of this judgement, Introduction: 37.

79. Ibid.: 42 and 'Art and Objecthood', *AO*: 153. What were the limits to this 'theatricality' in contemporary art? Fried claims it 'is theatricality . . . which links all these [Minimalist] artists to other figures as disparate

as Allan Kaprow, Joseph Cornell, Robert Rauschenberg, Claes Oldenburg, Dan Flavin, Robert Smithson, Edward Kienholz, George Segal, Lucas Samaras, Christo . . . the list could go on indefinitely', ibid.: 170, n. 13.

80. Introduction, *AO*: 42. For reviews of this position, see David Clarke 'The Gaze and the Glance: Competing Understandings of Visuality in the Theory and Practice of Late Modernist Art', *Art History* vol. 15, no. 1; March 1992: 80–98 and Anne Wagner 'Performance, Video, and the Rhetoric of Presence', *October* 91, Winter 2000: 59–80.

81. 'Art and Objecthood', *AO*: 153.

82. Ibid.: 161.

83. Ibid.: 151.

84. Ibid.: 167.

85. Ibid.: 166–167.

86. See, for instance, David Harvey *The Condition of Postmodernity: An Enquiry into the Origins of Cultural Change* (Oxford: Blackwell, 1989) and Fredric Jameson *Postmodernism, or the Cultural Logic of Late Capitalism* (London: Verso, 1991).

87. 'Art and Objecthood', *AO*: 168.

88. Ibid.: 155, 160–161, and Introduction, *AO*: 45.

89. 'The Origin of the Work of Art', in Heidegger *Poetry, Language, Thought*: 20 and 71.

90. Ibid.: see translator's note: 71 and Julian Young *Heidegger, Philosophy, Nazism* (Cambridge and New York, Cambridge University Press, 1997): 61–62 and 65–66.

3 Pollock, or 'abstraction'

1. 'The Unhappy Consciousness', *FTAI*: 369.

2. Introduction, *FTAI*: 12. Modern art has a utopianism built into its core, suggests Clark in his preface to the 2003 edition of *The Painting of Modern Life* (London and New York: Thames & Hudson): painting is 'a practice, a set of possibilities, a dream of freedom', xxx.

3. 'The Unhappy Consciousness', *FTAI*: 338–339. On metaphoricity and modernism, see Jonathan Harris 'Alterity, Metaphor and Formation: Around the Edges of a Paradigm', *Oxford Art Journal* vol. 14, no. 2; 1991: 88–95.

4. (1) Application statement for a Guggenheim Fellowship, 1947, quoted in 'The Unhappy Consciousness', *FTAI*: 306; (2) Interview for *Life* magazine, 18 July 1949, quoted ibid.: 324; (3) Phrases from interviews with Pollock, quoted ibid.: 334, sources cited in 439, n. 91.

5. 'Modernist Painting', *CGCEC4*: 91–92.

6. 'The Unhappy Consciousness', *FTAI*: 354 and 356.

7. Ibid.: 347–349, 351. For Fried's discussion, see 'Three American Painters: Noland, Olitski, Stella', *AO*: 237–239.

8. 'The Unhappy Consciousness', *FTAI*: 351.
9. Ibid.: 306–307.
10. Ibid.: 307.
11. Ibid.: 335.
12. Ibid.: 336–337.
13. 'Arguments About Modernism: A Reply to Michael Fried', in Frascina (ed.) *Pollock and After: The Critical Debate*: 82.
14. 'The Unhappy Consciousness', *FTAI*: 366. 'Tradition' always carries more than a mild whiff of teleology for Clark. He is equally sceptical on the granting of special significance to any one artist in the development of modern art. On the pivotal place often allotted to Marcel Duchamp, for instance, see Clark's 'All The Things I Said About Duchamp: A Response to Benjamin Buchloh', *October* no. 71; Winter 1995: 141–143: 'I too would like there to be, at the center of modernism, a figure of negation and nihilism, of endless centrifugal questioning of Art as a category and institution . . . I think it is deeply misguided to think there could be one': 143. Clark's essay is a response to Buchloh's Introduction to the journal's special edition on Duchamp, *October* no. 70; Fall 1994: 3–4.
15. 'The Present Prospects of American Painting and Sculpture', originally published in *Horizon*, October 1947; reprinted in *CGCEC2* (160–170): 166.
16. Ibid. See O'Brian's footnote for details of attacks on Greenberg's judgement.
17. 'Jackson Pollock: "Inspiration, Vision, Intuitive Decision"', originally published in *Vogue* 1 April 1967; reprinted in *CGCEC4* (245–250): 249.
18. 'The Unhappy Consciousness', *FTAI*: 305.
19. Ibid.: 302–306.
20. Ibid.: 340. On the spectacularization of the modern male artist, see Amelia Jones 'Clothes Make the Man: The Artist as a Performative Function', *Oxford Art Journal* vol. 18, no. 2; 1995 (18–32) and Mathew Rampley 'Identity and Difference: Jackson Pollock and the Ideology of the Drip', *Oxford Art Journal* vol. 19, no. 2; 1996: 83–94.
21. 'The Unhappy Consciousness', *FTAI*: 337.
22. Ibid.: 336.
23. Ibid.: 304. See William Empson's entertaining programmatic attempt to identify literary – mostly poetic – kinds of uncertainties in his *Seven Types of Ambiguity* (London: Chatto and Windus, 1953). Though I have to say I found Empson's study disappointingly unilluminating as far as visual modern art is concerned he confirms my basic claim that the identification of ambiguity – synonym for complexity – *is* about saying why a painting, or a poem, is valuable (8). He also acknowledges the debt critics of complexity increasingly come to owe particularly to psychoanalysis as a new science of occluded or mixed meanings. If Rosalind Krauss or Donald Kuspit had not existed, one might playfully paraphrase this

development as far as modern art is concerned, it would have been necessary to invent them.

24. 'The Unhappy Consciousness', *FTAI*: 363.

25. Ibid.: 364. See Clark's account of Courbet's *Burial at Ornans* (1848) in his *Image of the People: Gustave Courbet and the 1848 Revolution*.

26. 'Review of Exhibitions of Mondrian, Kandinsky, and Pollock; of the Annual Exhibition of the American Abstract Artists; and of the Exhibition *European Artists in America*', originally published in *The Nation* 7 April 1945; reprinted in *CGCEC2* (14–18): 17.

27. 'Review of Exhibitions of the American Abstract Artists, Jacques Lipchitz, and Jackson Pollock', originally published in *The Nation* 13 April 1946; reprinted in *CGCEC2* (72–75): 74–75.

28. 'My argument so far has been that the drip paintings are involved in an effort to dismantle or jam metaphor, or, at least, not to have metaphor congeal into totalization; and one aspect of that dismantling, it seems to me, is a gradual questioning or bracketing of the "masculine" theatrics of, say, the handprints in *Number 1, 1948*.' 'The Unhappy Consciousness', *FTAI*: 356. On the broader sexual politics of post-war American abstract art, see Griselda Pollock 'Killing Men and Dying Women: A Woman's Touch in the Cold Zone of American Painting in the 1950s', in Orton and Pollock *Avant-Gardes and Partisans Reviewed*: 219–294.

29. 'Review of Exhibitions of the American Abstract Artists, Jacques Lipchitz, and Jackson Pollock', *CGCEC2*: 75.

30. 'Three American Painters: Noland, Olitski, Stella', *AO*: 222.

31. 'Morris Louis', *AO*: 106.

32. Ibid.

33. Ibid.: 107.

34. 'Three American Painters: Noland, Olitski, Stella', *AO*: 226.

35. Greenberg's notion of 'homeless representation', however, perhaps anticipates something of Fried's radicalized idea of figuration: 'I call "homeless representation" ... a plastic and descriptive painterliness that is applied to abstract ends, but which continues to suggest representational ones. In itself, "homeless representation" is neither good nor bad, and maybe some of the best results of Abstract Expressionism in the past were got by flirting with representation.' Greenberg here, in contrast with Fried, is markedly diffident and 'a-historicist' in tone. 'After Abstract Expressionism', *CGCEC4*: 124.

36. (1) 'Three American Painters: Noland, Olitski, Stella', *AO*: 229; (2) 'The Unhappy Consciousness', *FTAI*: 330.

37. See Fried's own retrospective account of his intellectual career, 'An Introduction to my Art Criticism', *AO*: 47–54 and his 'Introduction: Manet before Impressionism', *MM*: 1–22.

38. 'Arguments about Modernism: A Reply to Michael Fried', in Frascina (ed.) *Pollock and After: The Critical Debate*: 83.

39. Introduction, *FTAI*: 7.
40. 'The Unhappy Consciousness', *FTAI*: 331–332.
41. Ibid.: 332.
42. Ibid.: 333.
43. Ibid.
44. Ibid.: 324 and 362–363.
45. Ibid.: 373. Malevich's painting *Black Square* (1915) is discussed by Clark in 'God is Not Cast Down', *FTAI*: 254–255.
46. 'The Unhappy Consciousness', *FTAI*: 385.
47. Ibid.: 335.
48. 'The Situation at the Moment', originally published in *Partisan Review*, January 1948; reprinted in *CGCEC2* (192–196): 193.
49. Ibid.: 194.
50. 'The Jackson Pollock Market Soars', originally published in *The New York Times Magazine*, 16 April 1961; reprinted in *CGCEC4* (107–114): 114. O'Brian points out that Greenberg objected strongly to the title given to his article by its publishers.
51. Gustave Flaubert to Louise Colet, 16 January 1852, quoted in 'The Unhappy Consciousness', *FTAI*: 299.
52. Ibid.: 300.
53. Ibid.: 302.
54. Ibid.: 309.
55. Ibid.: 310 and 382.
56. See Serge Guilbaut's discussion of Greenberg's views in 'The Creation of an American Avant-Garde, 1945–1947', Chapter 3, in his *How New York Stole the Idea of Modern Art: Abstract Expressionism, Freedom, and the Cold War*: 101–163.
57. See Frascina (ed.) *Pollock and After: The Critical Debate* for a collection of some early key contributions to this historiography. Eva Cockcroft's essay 'Abstract Expressionism: Weapon of the Cold War', was first published in *Artforum* vol. xii, no. 10; June 1974: 39–41. See also, for example, Jonathan Harris 'Mark Rothko and the Development of American Modernism: 1938–1948', *Oxford Art Journal* vol. 11, no. 1; 1988: 40–50; Michael Leja *Reframing Abstract Expressionism: Subjectivity and Painting in the 1940s* (New Haven and London: Yale University Press, 1993); Fred Orton 'Footnote One: The Idea of the Cold War', in Orton and Pollock *Avant-Gardes and Partisans Reviewed*: 205–218; David Craven *Abstract Expressionism as Cultural Critique: Dissent During the McCarthy Period* (New York and Cambridge: Cambridge University Press, 1999); and Nancy Jachec *The Philosophy and Politics of Abstract Expressionism* (New York and Cambridge: Cambridge University Press, 2000).
58. 'In Defense of Abstract Expressionism', *FTAI* (371–403): 371.
59. See Harold Rosenberg 'The American Action Painters', *Art News* vol. 51, no. 8; December 1952: 22–23, 48–50; reprinted in Harold Rosenberg *The*

Tradition of the New (Chicago: University of Chicago Press, 1982) and Fred Orton 'Action, Revolution, and Painting' in Orton and Pollock *Avant-Gardes and Partisans Reviewed*: 177–203.

60. 'In Defense of Abstract Expressionism', *FTAI*: 403.
61. 'The Unhappy Consciousness', *FTAI*: 311.
62. Ibid.: 318.
63. Ibid.: 311.
64. Ibid.: 310.
65. Ibid.: 313.
66. For references, see Introduction, n. 76 and n. 10 respectively.
67. 'The Unhappy Consciousness', *FTAI*: 313–314.
68. 'In Defense of Abstract Expressionism', *FTAI*: 400.
69. Ibid.: 374.
70. Ibid.
71. Compare this with, for example, the evidence in C. Wright Mills *The Power Elite* (New York and Oxford: Oxford University Press, 1959) which, in some ways, attempts to deal with the same cultural-political nexus.
72. For a useful overview of these issues, see Fred Orton and Griselda Pollock 'Avant-Gardes and Partisans Reviewed', in Orton and Pollock *Avant-Gardes and Partisans Reviewed*: 141–164.
73. 'In Defense of Abstract Expressionism', *FTAI*: 388. Also see Clark's insightful though purely anecdotal remarks on definitions of social class: 441, n. 10.
74. Ibid.: 401.
75. See Robert Herbert 'Goodbye to All That', *New York Review of Books*: 31. See also, in comparison, the very negative review of Clark's *The Painting of Modern Life: Paris in the Art of Manet and His Followers*, in Adrian Rifkin 'Marx's Clarkism', *Art History* vol. 8, no. 4; December 1985: 488–495. Though now highly anachronistic in its scientistic structuralist pieties – Clark's value judgements, the review asserts, 'have no place in social and semiotic investigations' – Rifkin's would-be pejorative description of Clark's study as 'historical art criticism' seems now quite fair and accurate as an account of Clark's intentions!
76. 'In Defense of Abstract Expressionism', *FTAI*: 376 and 389.
77. Ibid.: 389.
78. Ibid.: 376–377 and 387.
79. See my discussion of this in 'Ideologies of the Aesthetic: Hans Hofmann's "Abstract Expressionism" and the New York School', in David Thistlewood (ed.) *American Abstract Expressionism* (Liverpool: Liverpool University Press, 1993): 77–96.
80. 'In Defense of Abstract Expressionism', *FTAI*: 397.
81. Ibid.: 378, 396, 387, and 392.
82. Ibid.: 390.

83. Stéphane Mallarmé 'The Impressionists and Édouard Manet', reprinted in Frascina and Harrison (eds) *Modern Art and Modernism: A Critical Anthology*: 41.

84. 'The Present Prospects of American Painting and Sculpture', *CGCEC2*: 166.

85. 'The Unhappy Consciousness': 355 and 'In Defense of Abstract Expressionism', *FTAI*: 379.

4 Cubism's complexities

1. 'Avant-Garde and Kitsch', in *CGCEC1*: 15. Greenberg is responding here to an article on cinema in Soviet Russia by Dwight Macdonald published in the Winter 1939 edition of *Partisan Review*. MacDonald initially proposed the hypothetical situation which Greenberg explores in his essay. Greenberg signals some doubts about the scenario but nevertheless thought it was worth pursuing. Note, however, that he does not discuss any particular paintings by either Picasso or Repin.

2. Ibid.: 16–17. Kant had also indicated the need to 'train' those who wished to exercise their capacities for autonomous aesthetic judgement, thereby acknowledging that 'disinterestedness' was not a naturally occurring phenomenon but rather something that required selection and cultivation. See Richard Shusterman 'On the Scandal of Taste: Social Privilege as Nature in the Aesthetic Theories of Hume and Kant', in Mattick, Jr (ed.) *Eighteenth Century Aesthetics and the Reconstruction of Art*: 115–118.

3. Ibid. Realism is a notoriously layered term. For a range of accounts, see Harrison and Orton (eds) *Modernism, Criticism, Realism*; especially texts 11, 12, 19–24.

4. Ibid.: 16, and see 'The Case for Abstract Art', *CGCEC4*.

5. 'In Defense of Abstract Expressionism': 401 and Conclusion, *FTAI*: 406. Clark is alluding here to his earlier discussion (388) of Beethoven and Adorno's *Introduction to the Sociology of Music*. 'If we listen to Beethoven,' Adorno stated, 'and do not hear anything of the revolutionary bourgeoisie – not the echo of its slogans, the need to realize them, the cry for that totality in which reason and freedom are to have their warrant – we understand Beethoven no better than does the listener who cannot follow his pieces' purely musical content, the inner history that happens to their themes'.

6. 'Avant-Garde and Kitsch', *CGCEC1*: 20–22.

7. See O'Brien, Introduction, ibid.: xx. Fried and Clark both also write and publish poetry, though the latter appears to have started to do so – at least under the name 'Clark' – only quite recently. See, for example, Fried's collection *To The Center of the Earth* (New York: Farrar, Straus, and Giroux, 1994) and the three poems published by Clark in the *London Review of Books* vol. 26, no. 2; 22 January 2004: 15. See Fried's highly

recalcitrant discussion of his poetry in 'An Interview with Michael Fried' (377–404) and Hans-Jost Frey 'Poetry and Art Theory in Michael Fried' (361–376), in Jill Beaulieu, Mary Roberts, and Toni Ross (eds) *Refracting Vision: Essays on the Writings of Michael Fried* (Sydney: Power Publications, 2000). I suspect the writing of poetry symbolizes, for Fried and Clark, among other things, a meticulous attention to form and detail in composition, and therefore is part of their identification with, and self-image as, critics.

8. 'Clement Greenberg's Theory of Art', in Frascina (ed.) *Pollock and After: The Critical Debate*: 59. Greenberg, speaking in retrospect, was categorical in his rejection of Saul Ostrow's contention – echoing Clark's – that avant-garde art was a 'form of *resistance* to bourgeois cultural dominance' (my italic): 'The avant-garde and so forth is unpolitical for the most part. It's not a resistance to politics or anything else, no. It was, let's say, a dissent from the bourgeois order ... The truth is that modernism and the avant-garde were traditionally a form of dissent.' In 'The Last Interview' (1994), in Morgan (ed.) *Clement Greenberg: Late Writings* (230–243): 237. 'Dissent' is, literally, a form of 'speaking against'; a 'dissenter' someone who disagrees strongly with an established order or belief. 'Resistance' may have smacked too much for Greenberg of organized activity. I examine below the political connotations of other key critical terms.

9. 'The Unhappy Consciousness', *FTAI*: 307. On the primitivism of *Demoiselles d'Avignon* defined in the narrower 'orientalist' sense, see, for example, Patricia Leighton 'The White Pond and "l'Art negre": Picasso, Primitivism, and Anticolonialism' *Art Bulletin* December, vol. lxxii, no. 4; December 1990: 609–630 and Anna C. Chave 'New Encounters with *Les Demoiselles d'Avignon*: Gender, Race and the Origins of Cubism', *Art Bulletin* vol. lxxvi, no. 4; December 1994: 597–612.

10. 'Cubism and Collectivity', *FTAI*: 215.

11. See, however, John Berger's *Art and Revolution: Ernst Neizvestny and the Role of the Artist in the USSR* (London: Writers and Readers, 1969) for a sombrely critical account of the situation of artists in post-revolutionary Russian society.

12. 'Clement Greenberg's Theory of Art', in Frascina (ed.) *Pollock and After: The Critical Debate*: 50, 54, and 60–61, n. 2.

13. Ibid.: 56 and 'Avant-Garde and Kitsch', *CGCEC1*: 11.

14. 'Clement Greenberg's Theory of Art', in Frascina (ed.) *Pollock and After: The Critical Debate*: 54.

15. Ibid.: 56.

16. 'The European View of American Art', originally published in *The Nation* 25 November 1950; reprinted in *CGCEC3* (59–62): 62.

17. Ibid.

18. 'The Situation at the Moment', originally published in *Partisan Review* January 1948; reprinted in *CGCEC2* (192–196): 192.

19. Seven years later Greenberg will write that the artists covered by the label 'Abstract Expressionist', by then, have won their freedom from 'late Cubist abstract art. But they all started from French painting, got their fundamental sense of style from it, and maintain some sort of continuity with it. Not least of all, they got from it their most vivid notion of an ambitious, major art, and of the general direction in which it had to go in their time.' '"American-Type" Painting', originally published in *Partisan Review* Spring 1955; reprinted in *CGCEC3* (217–236): 219. On 'American Scene' parochialism, its inertial effects on emergent abstract art, and the historiography of Abstract Expressionism, see Jonathan Harris 'Art, Histories and Politics: The New Deal Art Projects and American Modernism', *Idea and Production* no. 5; Spring 1986: 104–119.

20. 'Three American Painters', *AO*: 214.

21. Ibid.: 215. The literature on *Guernica* is vast. For a useful review of debates about its political meanings and a bibliography, see Jutta Held 'How do the Political Effects of Pictures Come About? The Case of Picasso's *Guernica*', *Oxford Art Journal* vol. 11, no. 1; 1988: 33–39; for its place in Picasso's oeuvre, see Eunice Lipton *Picasso's Criticism 1901–1939: The Making of an Artist-Hero* (New York and London: Garland, 1976), and G. Schiff (ed.) *Picasso in Perspective* (Englewood Cliffs, NJ: Prentice Hall, 1976).

22. 'Review of an Exhibition of School of Paris Painters', originally published in *The Nation* 29 June 1946; reprinted in *CGCEC2* (87–90): 88–89.

23. 'Review of an Exhibition of Pierre Bonnard', originally published in *The Nation* 12 June 1948; reprinted in *CGCEC2* (246–248): 247.

24. 'Review of Exhibitions of the American Abstract Artists. Jacques Lipchitz, and Jackson Pollock', *CGCEC2* (72–75): 75.

25. 'Coda: Manet's Modernism', *MM*: 616–617, n. 18. Fried is here quoting from Greenberg's 'Necessity of Formalism', *New Literary History* 3: Autumn 1971; reprinted in Morgan (ed.) *Clement Greenberg: Late Writings* (45–49): 46.

26. 'Master Léger', originally published in *Partisan Review* January–February 1954; reprinted in *CGCEC3* (164–173): 167.

27. Picasso in conversation with Christian Zervos (1935), reprinted in H.B. Chipp (ed.) *Theories of Modern Art: A Source Book by Artists and Critics* (Berkeley: University of California Press, 1968: 266–273): 267.

28. 'Master Léger', *CGCEC3*: 166.

29. 'Cubism and Collectivity', *FTAI*: 168.

30. Ibid.: 194.

31. Ibid.: 183. The paradigm of this is Rosalind Krauss 'In the Name of Picasso', in her *The Originality of the Avant-Garde and Other Modernist Myths* (Cambridge, MA and London: MIT Press, 1985). See also Krauss *The Picasso Papers* (London: Thames & Hudson, 1998). I examine Krauss's structuralist reading of Cubism at greater length in *The New Art History: A Critical Introduction*: 47–56.

32. For a robust critique of the structuralist position, see Patricia Leighton 'Cubist Anachronisms: Ahistoricity, Crypto-formalism, and Business-as-Usual in New York', *Oxford Art Journal* vol. 17, no. 2; 1994: 91–102. This is partly a response to, for example, Y.A. Bois 'The Semiology of Cubism', in W. Rubin and L. Zelevansky (eds) *Picasso and Braque: A Symposium* (New York: Museum of Modern Art, 1992). Leighton has made a special social art-historical study of the significance of newspaper cuttings about the Balkan Wars present in Cubist collages; see her *Reordering the Universe: Picasso and Anarchism 1897–1914* (Princeton, NJ.: Princeton University Press, 1989) – and the highly critical review of this by Robert S. Lubar in *Art Bulletin* vol. lxxii, no. 3; September 1990: 505–510.

33. Introduction, *FTAI*: 9–10.

34. 'The Decline of Cubism', originally published in *Partisan Review* March 1948; reprinted in CCEC2 (211–215): 214.

35. Ibid.: 212.

36. 'Cubism and Collectivity', *FTAI*: 170 and 175.

37. See, for example, Maryanne Stevens (ed.) *The Orientalists: Delacroix to Matisse* (London: Royal Academy, 1984); Peter Wollen 'Fashion/Orientalism/The Body', *New Formations* no. 1, Spring 1987: 41–53; James D. Herbert *Fauve Painting: The Making of Cultural Politics* (New Haven and London: Yale University Press, 1992); and John M. MacKenzie *Orientalism: History, Theory and the Arts* (Manchester: Manchester University Press, 1995).

38. 'De Gauguin, de Whistler et de l'Excès des Théories' *L'Ermitage*, 15 November 1905, quoted in *FTAI*: 91–2; original reference 417, n. 61.

39. 'Towards a Newer Laocoon', originally published in *Partisan Review* July–August 1940; reprinted in CGCEC1 (23–38): 35.

40. Cited in 'Cubism and Collectivity', *FTAI*: 176.

41. Ferdinand de Saussure *Course in General Linguistics* (New York: McGraw-Hill, 1966 [1915]).

42. 'Cubism and Collectivity', *FTAI*: 223. Clark generally suppresses the issue of gender in this chapter, though it resurfaces periodically – as in his final paragraphs' discussion of the 'marriage' (power relations) between Picasso and Braque. For an alternative account, see Susan Rubin Suleiman *Subversive Intent: Gender, Politics and the Avant-Garde* (Cambridge, MA and London: Harvard University Press, 1990).

43. 'Cubism and Collectivity', *FTAI*: 223

44. Ibid.: 208.

45. Ibid.: 174.

46. Ibid.: 179.

47. Ibid.: 180 and 186.

48. 'Arguments about Modernism: A Reply to Michael Fried', in Frascina (ed.) *Pollock and After: The Critical Debate*: 82.

49. Ibid.: 82.
50. 'Cubism and Collectivity', *FTAI*: 185.
51. Ibid.
52. Ibid.: 187 and 191.
53. *The Absolute Bourgeois: Artists and Politics in France 1848–1851* (London and New York: Thames & Hudson, 1973).
54. 'Jackson Pollock's Abstraction', in Serge Guilbaut (ed.) *Reconstructing Modernism: Art in New York, Paris, and Montreal 1945–1964*: 172–243. See especially: 222–30.
55. See Michael Baxandall *Patterns of Intention: On the Historical Experience of Pictures* (New Haven and London: Yale University Press, 1985).
56. See Beryl Lake 'A Study of the Irrefutability of two Aesthetic Theories', in Harrison and Orton (ed.) *Modernism, Criticism, Realism: Alternative Contexts for Art*: 25–35.
57. Introduction, *FTAI*: 2–3: '. . . it is just because the "modernity" which modernism prophesied has finally arrived that the forms of representation it originally gave rise to are now unreadable. (Or readable only under some dismissive fantasy rubric – of "purism", "opticality", "formalism", "elitism", etc.) The intervening (and interminable) holocaust was modernization.'
58. Letter to the Editor, originally published in *The Nation* 27 April 1946; reprinted in *CGCEC2*: 67.
59. See also Clark's essay on Pissarro, concerned with the artist's involvement with anarchist politics and philosophy in France in the late nineteenth century: 'We Field-Women', *FTAI*: 55–147.
60. 'Cubism and Collectivity', *FTAI*: 175.
61. Ibid.: 187.
62. Ibid.: 179. Clark himself quotes Fried using this phrase in a passage from 'Three American Painters' [reprinted in *AO*: 224–225], commenting: 'Fried's "wanting to call it" optical, and putting the concept in slightly anxious italic, makes one feel churlish at not wanting to do the same', 'The Unhappy Consciousness', *FTAI*: 330–331.
63. ' "Americanism" Misplaced: Review of *Preface to an American Philosophy of Art* by A. Philip McMahon', originally published in *The Nation* 30 March 1946; reprinted in *CGCEC2* (64–66): 64–65.

5 The materials of seeing: Cézanne and Van Gogh

1. 'Review of Exhibitions of Corot, Cézanne, Eilshemius, and Wilfredo Lam', originally published in *The Nation* 12 December 1942; reprinted in *CGCEC1* (129–131): 129–130.
2. (1) Introduction, *PML*: 12 and 'Freud's Cézanne', *FTAI*: 164; (2) Author's Preface and 'Cézanne's Doubt', *Sense and Non-Sense*: 3, 5, and 9.

3. See Merleau-Ponty's essays 'Concerning Marxism' (1946), 'Marxism and Philosophy' (1946), and 'The War Has Taken Place' (1945), *Sense and Non-Sense*.

4. 'Freud's Cézanne', *FTAI*: 165.

5. Ibid.: 141 and 166.

6. Introduction, *FTAI*: 11.

7. 'Cézanne's Doubt', *Sense and Non-Sense*: 13.

8. See John O'Brian, Introduction, *CGCEC3*: xvi.

9. Introduction, *AO*: 6, 28, and 31. Fried acknowledges the influence of Merleau-Ponty's writings on language and the body in his account of Caro's sculpture, see 61, nn. 36, and 37.

10. 'Arguments about Modernism: A Reply to Michael Fried', in Frascina (ed.) *Pollock and After: The Critical Debate*: 86.

11. 'Between Realisms', *MM*: 607, n. 31. See also Richard Shiff 'Cézanne's Physicality: The Politics of Touch', in Salim Kemal and Ivan Gaskell (eds) *The Languages of Art History* (New York and Cambridge: Cambridge University Press, 1991: 129–180).

12. Interest in 'embodied vision' must extend to the articulation of subjectivities within modern art criticism as well as modern art. I should add, too, that I am sceptical about the political and ideological implications of Merleau-Ponty's emphasis on body. While there certainly is a favourable feminist reading of Merleau-Ponty (see, for instance, Rowley and Pollock 'Painting in a "Hybrid Moment"', in Harris (ed.) *Critical Perspectives on Contemporary Painting: Hybridity, Hegemony, Historicism*) and perhaps even a 'Marxist' one, I think his views contain, as I indicate in this chapter, a strain of idealism bordering sometimes on the metaphysical.

13. 'Modernist Painting', *CGCEC4*: 91.

14. 'Cézanne's Doubt', *Sense and Non-Sense*: 19.

15. Ibid.: 17.

16. Ibid.: 9 and 19.

17. 'Eye and Mind', in Osborne (ed.) *Aesthetics*: 74.

18. Ibid.: 57–58.

19. 'Cézanne's Doubt', *Sense and Non-Sense*: 20.

20. 'Freud's Cézanne', *FTAI*: 146. On time and temporalities in Cézanne's paintings, see Joyce Medina *Cézanne and Modernism: The Poetics of Painting* (Albany: State University of New York Press, 1995).

21. Ibid.: 153.

22. Ibid.: 159.

23. 'Eye & Mind', in Osborne (ed.) *Aesthetics*: 76–77 and 60–61.

24. 'Freud's Cézanne', *FTAI*: 161–162. On the meanings of pre-modern still-life painting, see Norman Bryson *Looking at the Overlooked: Four Essays on Still Life Painting* (London: Reaktion, 1990).

25. 'Cézanne's Doubt', *Sense and Non-Sense*: 20. On the theme of Cézanne's life and artistic persona, see, for instance, Griselda Pollock 'What can

we say about Cézanne these days?', *Oxford Art Journal* vol. 13, no. 1; 1990: 95–101; Michael Doran (ed.) *Conversations with Cézanne* (Berkeley: University of California Press, 2001); and Steven Platzman *Cézanne: The Self-Portraits* (London and New York: Thames & Hudson, 2001).

26. Though Merleau-Ponty adds: 'Zola, Cézanne's friend from childhood, was the first to find genius in him and the first to speak of him as a 'genius gone wrong', ibid.: 9. The 'fall' of the modern artist-god is integral to the paradigm. For Barnett Newman, speaking two years after Merleau-Ponty had published 'Cézanne's Doubt' in France, 'the fall of man was understood by the writer and his audience not as a fall from Utopia to struggle, as the sociologicians would have it, nor, as the religionists would have us believe, as a fall from Grace to Sin, but rather that Adam, by eating from the Tree of Knowledge, sought the creative life to be, like God, "a creator of worlds" . . . and was reduced to the life of toil only as a result of a jealous punishment'. 'The First Man Was An Artist', excerpt from *Tiger's Eye* (New York), no. 1, October 1947: 59–60; reprinted in Chipp (ed.) *Theories of Modern Art*: 552.

27. Freud's 'Project for a Scientific Psychology' (1895) quoted in 'Freud's Cézanne', *FTAI*: 139, and Keynes, quoted in Krauss *The Optical Unconscious*: 127.

28. 'Cézanne's Doubt', Sense and Non-Sense: 11. See Richard Shiff *Cézanne and the End of Impressionism: A Study of Theory, Technique and Critical Evaluation of Modern Art* (Chicago and London: University of Chicago Press, 1984).

29. 'Freud's Cézanne', *FTAI*: 158.

30. 'Cézanne's Doubt', *Sense and Non-Sense*: 11. See Mary Tompkins Lewis *Cézanne's Early Imagery* (Berkeley: University of California Press, 1989).

31. Meyer Schapiro broached the question of a psychoanalytic reading of Cézanne's paintings in his 'The Apples of Cézanne: An Essay on the Meaning of Still Life' (1968), in *Modern Art: Selected Papers* (New York: George Braziller, 1978: 1–38).

32. 'Freud's Cézanne', *FTAI*: 147.

33. Ibid.: 161.

34. 'The Unhappy Consciousness', *FTAI*: 361. The bathos continues: 'Could we even read *Two* and *Male and Female* . . . as Pollock's (predictably slapstick) restaging of the striding figure/dreaming drama in the Barnes [*Large*] *Bathers*? Only now, of course, phallic mother and disconsolate son stand next to one another and exchange blows. Or is it bodily fluids? With Pollock one can never be sure.'

35. 'Freud's Cézanne', *FTAI*: 144. It's not surprising that Greenberg claimed 'I never fooled around with meaning' ('Clement Greenberg: The Last Interview', in Morgan (ed.) *Clement Greenberg: Late Writings*: 239) – though, of course, it fooled around with him. For an alternative psycho-

analytic reading of Cézanne, see Tamar Garb 'Visuality and Sexuality in Cézanne's Late Bathers', *Oxford Art Journal* vol. 19, no. 2; 1996: 46–60.

36. 'Cézanne's Doubt', *Sense and Non-Sense*: 24. This, however, clearly doesn't rule out for Merleau-Ponty its possible value; see: 24–25, and, in more general terms, his essay 'Hegel's Existentialism', ibid.: 63.

37. 'Freud's Cézanne', *FTAI*: 154. Clark is remembering a television sketch by the British comedians Peter Cook and Dudley Moore. For the full text, see 'At the Art Gallery' (1965), in *Tragically I was an Only Twin: The Complete Peter Cook* (London: Arrow, 2003): 116–121.

38. 'We Field-Women', *FTAI*: 71.

39. 'Freud's Cézanne', *FTAI*: 139.

40. 'We Field-Women', *FTAI*: 77.

41. 'Cézanne and the Unity of Modern Art', originally published in *Partisan Review* May–June, 1951; reprinted in *CGCEC3* (82–91).

42. Ibid.: 87 and 91.

43. 'Cézanne's Doubt', *Sense and Non-Sense*: 16.

44. 'The Origin of The Work of Art', in Heidegger *Poetry, Language, Thought*: 26.

45. Meyer Schapiro had initially attacked Heidegger's essay for not stating which painting he was referring to; see Schapiro 'The Still Life of a Personal Object – a Note on Heidegger and Van Gogh', in M.L. Simmer (ed.) *The Reach of Mind: Essays in Honor of Kurt Goldstein* (New York: Springer Publishing Company, 1968: 203–209). Jacques Derrida responded to Schapiro in his 1978 essay 'Restitutions of the Truth in Painting', in *The Truth in Painting* (trans. Geoff Bennington and Ian McLeod, Chicago and London: University of Chicago Press, 1987: 255–382). See reviews of this exchange by John Bruin 'Heidegger and the World of the Work of Art', *Journal of Aesthetics and Art Criticism* vol. 50, no. 1; Winter 1992: 55–56 and Laurent Stern in *Journal of Aesthetics and Art Criticism* vol. 54, no. 1; Winter 1996: 77–79.

46. 'The Origin of The Work of Art', in Heidegger *Poetry, Language, Thought*: 76.

47. 'We Field-Women', *FTAI*: 130.

48. Introduction, *FTAI*: 8.

49. 'The Origin of The Work of Art', in Heidegger *Poetry, Language, Thought*: 33.

50. Ibid.: 34.

51. Ibid.: 35–38.

52. See Louis Althusser, 'Marx and Humanism', in *For Marx* (trans. Ben Brewster, London: New Left Books, 1977: 221–247): especially 229–231.

53. 'The Origin of The Work of Art', in Heidegger *Poetry, Language, Thought*: 18.

54. Stéphane Mallarmé 'The Impressionists and Édouard Manet' (1876), reprinted in Frascina and Harrison (eds) *Modern Art and Modernism: A Critical Anthology*: 44.

55. 'The Origin of The Work of Art', in Heidegger *Poetry, Language, Thought*: 17.
56. Ibid.: 19. What about music? Not all artworks have thinglyness, clearly, in the same ways. See, for instance, Heidegger himself on Beethoven's and Holderlin's music, 'hymns packed in the soldier's knapsack together with cleaning gear ... quartets lie in the storerooms of the publishing house like potatoes in a cellar', ibid. These material items, unlike Van Gogh's pictures, are not identical with the artworks!
57. Ibid.: 19–20 and 40.
58. Ibid.: 19–20.
59. Ibid.: 39.
60. 'Rooted in the Earth: A Van Gogh Primer', in Orton and Pollock *Avant-Gardes and Partisans Reviewed* (1–51): 36.
61. 'We Field-Women', *FTAI*: 130.
62. 'Rooted in the Earth: A Van Gogh Primer', in Orton and Pollock *Avant-Gardes and Partisans Reviewed*: 20–23.
63. 'Review of Exhibitions of Van Gogh and the Remarque Collection', originally published in *The Nation*, 6 November 1943; reprinted in *CGCEC1* (160–162): 161–162.
64. 'Rooted in the Earth: A Van Gogh Primer', in Orton and Pollock *Avant-Gardes and Partisans Reviewed*: 3. On his epileptic condition, see 3 and 43.
65. 'Henri Rousseau and Modern Art', originally published in *The Nation*, 27 July 1946; reprinted in *CGCEC2* (93–95): 93–94.
66. 'The Origin of The Work of Art', in Heidegger *Poetry, Language, Thought*: 40.
67. 'Rooted in the Earth: A Van Gogh Primer', in Orton and Pollock *Avant-Gardes and Partisans Reviewed*: 42. On Van Gogh and representations of the Hague suburbs, see Griselda Pollock 'Stark Encounters' *Art History* vol. 6, no. 3; September 1983: 330–358.
68. See, for instance, Patricia Mathews '[Albert] Aurier and Van Gogh: Criticism and Response' *Art Bulletin* vol. lxviii, no. 1; March 1986: 94–104 and Harrison White and Cynthia White *Canvases and Careers: Institutional Change in the French Painting World* (Chicago and London: University of Chicago Press, 1993). As Paul Smith has pointed out, a dialectic develops between 'real' artists and 'fictional accounts' in late nineteenth century France, each feeding off the other. Marius Roux published his novel *The Prey and the Shadow* (*La Proie et l'Ombre*), a 'vicious satire of Cézanne as the maniacal, money-mad egoist', in 1878, seven years before the appearance of Emile Zola's *L'Oeuvre*. Cézanne, in turn, drew on several literary sources in constructing his own persona. Paul Smith 'Je est un autre' ('I am an other'), unpublished paper, 2003.
69. 'Rooted in the Earth: A Van Gogh Primer', in Orton and Pollock *Avant-Gardes and Partisans Reviewed*: 6 and 4.

70. See Michael Fried *Courbet's Realism*: 100–110 and *MM*: 373–374.

71. Hitler's lecture opened the *Haus der Deutschen Kunst*, a museum which conformed to the rigid Neoclassicism of the official Nazi architectural style. The exhibition of 'degenerate' modern art – part of a collection that numbered about 200,000 items – began in Munich later in the summer of 1937. For the full text of Hitler's speech, see Chipp (ed.) *Theories of Modern Art: A Source Book by Artists and Critics*: 474–483. All further quotations here are from this source.

72. 'Aspects of Two Cultures', ibid. (490–496): 492.

73. See Merleau-Ponty essays on Marxism in *Sense and Non-Sense* and, for example, Sartre's *Search for a Method* (New York: Vintage, 1968).

74. See Walter Benjamin's extraordinary archive of this attempt compiled before the Second World War *The Arcades Project* (trans. Howard Eiland and Kevin McLaughlin, Cambridge, MA and London: Belknap/Harvard University Press, 2002).

75. Introduction, *FTAI*: 8.

76. 'Rooted in the Earth: A Van Gogh Primer', in Orton and Pollock *Avant-Gardes and Partisans Reviewed*: 48.

77. 'Modernist Painting', *CGCEC4*: 86. Mallarmé reference in n. 54 above.

6 Modernism's Manet

1. 'Is this picture true? No. Is it beautiful? No. Is it attractive? No. But what is it, then?', Henri Houssaye (on *A Bar at the Folies Bergère*) 'Le Salon de 1882', in *L'Art francais depuis dix ans*, Paris 1883: 241–242, originally published in *La Revue des Deux Mondes*; quoted in *PML*: 243.

2. Irving Sandler's *The Triumph of American Painting* (New York: Praeger, 1970) is literally a textbook example of this modernist hagiography. For some elliptical commentary on Fried's 'Manet to Stella' trajectory, see T.J. Clark 'Modernism, Postmodernism, and Steam' *October* no. 100; Spring 2002: 154–174. Here Clark, unlike Fried, takes Stella's titles seriously: 164.

3. Clark states 'I will not look again at Manet because I do not want to recognize in him the enormous distance of modern art from its circumstances, and the avant garde's willingness to seize on the side of secularization – the cult of expertise and technicality – that seemed to offer it a consoling myth of its own self-absorption', *FTAI*: 12.

4. Ibid. Clark also cites Fried's *Courbet's Realism*. See Paul Smith's review of *MM* 'Manet's Bits', *Art History* vol. 20, no. 3; September 1997: 477–482 and that of David Carrier in *Art Bulletin* vol. lxxix, no. 2; June 1997: 334–337.

5. Also see Fried's Introduction, *AO*: 47–54.

6. 'Olympia's Choice', *PML*: 138–139. I have transposed two of Clark's sentences here.

7. Ibid.: 140. Fried demurs from some aspects of Clark's reading of Ravenel's comments, see *MM*: 587, n. 188.
8. Ibid.: 401.
9. *PML*: 79.
10. Ibid.: 92.
11. Ibid.: 80. On these multiple meanings, see David Carrier 'Manet and His Interpreters', *Art History* vol. 8, no. 3; September 1985: 320–335 and George Hamilton Heard *Manet and his Critics* (New York: Norton, 1969).
12. See *MM*: 356–360. I discuss this claim below. For further views and reviews of Manet's art, see the special edition of *Art Journal* vol. 44, no. 1; Spring 1985.
13. *PML*: 235.
14. Ibid.: 260.
15. Ibid.
16. Ibid.: 96.
17. Ibid.: 95–96.
18. Ibid.: 110, 111, 133.
19. Ibid.: 134 and 240. Resistance to interpretation has given way to its opposite – seeming endlessness to interpretation ('meaninglessness' and 'meaningfulness' are, to repeat, equivalents): see, for example, Bradford Collins (ed.) *Twelve Views of Manet's Bar*.
20. *PML*: 251.
21. Victor Fournel (pseudonym: Geronte) 'Les Excentriques et les grotesques', *La Gazette de France*, 30 June 1865; quoted in ibid.: 97.
22. Ibid.: 133. On the culture of the 'feminine commodity', see Carol Armstrong 'Facturing Femininity: Manet's *Before the Mirror* [1875–1876]', *October* no. 74, Fall 1995: 75–104.
23. Ibid.: 253.
24. *MM*: 215.
25. Ibid.: 228–229.
26. Ibid.: 406–407.
27. Ibid.: 406.
28. Ibid.: 3.
29. Ibid.: 149.
30. Ibid.: 131.
31. Ibid.: 190.
32. Ibid.: 131. Fried notes that 'Chesneau almost came close when he spotted the dependence of the *Le Déjeuner sur l'herbe* on Raimondi's engraving after Raphael . . . But he regarded Manet's use of Raphael as eccentric, incomprehensible . . .'
33. Ibid.: 272.
34. Emile Zola 'Édouard Manet', originally published as 'Une nouvelle manière en peinture: Édouard Manet', 1 January 1867 *Revue du XIX*

Siècle; reprinted in Frascina and Harrison (eds) *Modern Art and Modernism: A Critical Anthology* (29–38): 35.

35. *MM*: 317.

36. Jules-Antoine Castagnary had concurred 'I have nothing to say about this painter who for ten years seems to have made it his task in each Salon to show us that he possesses part of the qualities necessary to make *tableaux*. I don't deny those qualities; but I'm waiting for the *tableaux*.' 'Salon de 1870' *Salons*, I., quoted in ibid.: 272.

37. Ibid.: 399–401: 'I want to acknowledge that, for all the efforts I have made to come to grips with individual canvases by Manet as well as to trace the parameters of certain of his overarching (though far from unchanging) intentions and preoccupations, my chapters on his art do not culminate in any single, sustained account of his extraordinary achievement . . . I am all too aware that my own accounts of individual works are fragmentary (for want of a better word) and that my attempt to do justice to a broad spectrum of critical and historiographical issues . . . has meant that my chapters . . . can't be said to produce the effect of a unified whole.'

38. Ibid.: 170.

39. Ibid.: 174.

40. Ibid.: 404.

41. Ibid.: 402–403. The Impressionists, Fried notes, also displayed antipathy – for different reasons, however – toward the goal of the tableau, see 565, n. 43.

42. See Introduction, *AO*: 13 and *MM*: 4.

43. *MM*: 27. Fried, rather predictably however, doesn't pursue any of the political or ideological implications of this idea of 'Frenchness as universality'. This theme is central to Carol Duncan's and Alan Wallach's influential essay about the Louvre 'The Universal Survey Museum', *Art History* vol. 3, no. 4; December 1980: 448–469.

44. *MM*: 75.

45. *MM*: 24 n. 8. Fried is referring to Schapiro's review of Joseph C. Sloane's *French Painting between the Past and the Present*, in *Art Bulletin* vol. 36, June 1954: 163–165.

46. *MM*: 68. Fried, unfortunately, doesn't engage in any serious attempt to define or examine the notion of 'realism' here, though he goes on to specify what he regards as different kinds of it, which I discuss below. For an account of Manet's political views and how this affected his painting see, for example, John Hutton 'The Clown at the Ball: Manet's *Masked Ball of the Opera* [a painting rejected by the Salon of 1874] and the Collapse of Monarchism in the early Third Republic', *Oxford Art Journal* vol. 10, no. 2; 1987: 76–94.

47. *MM*: 71.

48. Ibid.: 126. This sidestep avoids, too, the question of the reconcilability of 'realist' and 'modernist' aims and achievements in modern art. It should

be fairly obvious by now that what I've been calling Clark's 'bad complexity' might be restated in the equally ugly neologism 'realist-modernism'.

49. Ibid.: 127.

50. Ibid.: 406.

51. Carle Desnoyers (pseudonym: Le Capitaine Pompilius) 'Lettres particulières sur le Salon', *Le Petit Journal* no. 131; 11 June, 1863; quoted in ibid.: 305.

52. Théodore Duret *Les Peintres francais en 1867*; quoted in ibid.: 304.

53. Théodore Pelloquet *L'Exposition: Journal du Salon de 1863*, no. 22, 23 July 1864; quoted in ibid.: 305.

54. Ibid.: 268 and 276.

55. Ibid.: 267.

56. Ibid.: 268. Fried cites the critic Albert Wolff 'Salon de 1869', *La Figaro* 11 May 1869: 558 n. 7.

57. Théodore Pelloquet *L'Exposition: Journal du Salon de 1863*, no. 22, 23 July 1864; quoted in *MM*: 272. Fried adds in clarification: 'The reference is plainly to the *Déjeuner*, whose population has grown in his memory.' The extraordinary 'Salon des Refusés' of 1863 was organized by the French government after public outcry over the paintings refused a place in that year's usual Salon exhibition.

58. Ibid.: 266.

59. Ibid.: 22.

60. Ibid.: 21.

61. Ibid.: 185.

62. Ibid.: 465–467, n. 62. Fried here is quoting his own remarks on Manet from a footnote to *Three American Painters: Kenneth Noland, Jules Olitski, Frank Stella* (1965) and adds that this confirms he had thought since then of Manet as a 'realist' painter. Needless to say, 'realist' and 'abstract' here take on meanings almost wholly alien to their normative descriptive functions in art-historical scholarship.

63. Ibid.: 404–405.

64. Ibid.: 22.

65. Ibid.: 401.

66. Ibid.: 399.

67. Ibid.: 127.

68. Ibid.: 405.

69. Charles Baudelaire *Correspondance générale* 5: 96–97, 11 May 1865; quoted in *PML*: 82. Jean Clay believes Baudelaire meant to imply by this that Manet aimed to place painting in an 'untenable position': 'Ointments, Makeup, Pollen', *October* no. 27, 1983 (3–44): 9. Hal Foster avers that Baudelaire thought Manet was 'corrupting' what Foster calls the 'memory-structure' of painting, a corruption brought about because Manet's 'citations are too explicit, too various, too photographic': 'Archives of

Modern Art', *October* no. 99, Winter 2002 (81–95): 84. Thierry de Duve claims that Baudelaire's statement carried the judgement that art after Manet could never be 'great' in ways that past art had been, only 'significantly' *of* the times in which is was made: 'The Monochrome and the Blank Canvas', in Guilbaut (ed.) *Reconstructing Modernism: Art in New York, Paris, and Montreal 1945–1964*: 299.

70. *PML*: 250. Clark here is implicitly questioning notions of 'real', 'reality', and 'realism'. See also Gregory Galligan 'The Self Pictured: Manet, the Mirror, and the Occupation of Realist Painting', *Art Bulletin* vol. lxxx, no. 1; March 1998 (140–171).

71. 'Three American Painters', *AO*: 260–261, n. 4.

72. *MM*: 466–467, n. 62. Fried in his 1965 essay added the jibe 'What one takes to be the salient features of his [Manet's] situation is open to argument; an uncharacteristically subtle Marxist could, I think, make a good case for focusing on the economic and political situation in France after 1848', *AO*: 261 n. 4. Clark supplied this focus, of course, in his books on Courbet and Manet.

73. 'Three American Painters', *AO*: 262, n. 4 and *MM*: 466–467, n. 62.

74. Ibid.: 319–320. Fried also discusses the example of Manet's *Self-Portrait with a Palette* (1878–1879), seeing in it a 'commitment to . . . a speed or instantaneousness both of seeing and execution [that] places eye and body, or rather *eye and hand* in exactly the same situation or at least under exactly equivalent pressure ("Hand" rather than "body" . . .)', ibid.: 397. These passages inevitably recall Merleau-Ponty's account of Cézanne's painting.

75. Charles Baudelaire 'The Salon of 1859: The Modern Public and Photography', originally published in four instalments in *Revue Francaise*, 10 June–20 July 1859; reprinted in Frascina and Harrison (eds) *Modern Art and Modernism: A Critical Anthology* (18–21): 21.

76. *MM*: 291.

77. Ibid.

78. Ibid.: 568, n. 71. Fried notes here that this putative 'instantaneousness' has a correlate in what Greenberg had called 'at-onceness'. Fried warns, however, that neither 'instantaneousness' nor 'sheer duration' as 'temporal effects' should be thought to carry any necessary value or to exist in any necessary relation of hierarchy.

79. Ibid.: 294.

80. Ibid.: 296.

81. *PML*: 253.

82. Ibid.: 142.

83. Ibid.: 255.

84. *MM*: 343.

85. Ibid.: 346–364.

86. Charles Baudelaire 'The Salon of 1846: On the Heroism of Modern Life', originally published as a review booklet on 13 May 1846; reprinted in

Frascina and Harrison (eds) *Modern Art and Modernism: A Critical Anthology* (17–18): 17.

87. Ibid.: 372.

88. Ibid.: 372 and 380.

89. Ibid.: 387.

90. Ibid.: 380.

91. All of Greenberg's attempts after about 1970 to theorize modernism as 'formalism' or 'art-for-art's sake' seem to me to end up creating only more problems to do with questions of definition, value, and interests – something which he implicitly recognizes himself in, for example, 'Necessity of "Formalism"': 'Art is, art gets experienced, for its own sake, which is what modernism recognized in identifying aesthetic value as an ultimate value. But this doesn't mean that art or the aesthetic is a *supreme* value or end of life. The neglect of this distinction by the original art-for-art's-sakers – most of whom were not modernists anyhow – compromised a valid perception', in Morgan (ed.) *Clement Greenberg: Late Writings*: 49.

92. *PML*: 11. Clark, of course, is quoting from Greenberg's 'Modernist Painting' (the revised version published in *Art and Literature* Spring 1965).

93. *MM*: 409: '. . . the Impressionist emphasis on visuality and "decoration" led in just a few steps to what became the standard formalist-modernist account of the essence of painting, an account that was then able to return to and claim for modernism Manet's pictures of the 1860s, indeed that recognized in them the first modernist paintings [quoting here Greenberg's 'Modernist Painting'] "by virtue of the frankness with which they declared the surfaces on which they were painted"'.

94. Introduction, *AO*: 40. Fried notes, however, that Emile Zola had remarked of Manet that his 'insistence on the artistic irrelevance of considerations of subject matter and . . . praise of Manet's technique of painting by "colored patches" sketched the terms in which Manet would eventually be assimilated to the history of modern art', *MM*: 2. Matisse, in addition, had stated in 1932 that ' "Manet is the first painter who immediately translated his sensations, thereby liberating his instinct" . . . in general what might be called the formalist-modernist view of Manet followed these lines', ibid.: 5–6.

95. 'Towards a Newer Laocoon', *CGCEC1*: 29–30. I have transposed these two statements.

96. Introduction, *AO*: 21–22. See *CGCEC4*: 90 which includes the sentence revised out of the 1965 version published in *Art and Literature*. For analyses of this, and other changes to the essay, see O'Brian's Introduction to *CGCEC3*: xv–xxxiii; Yves Alain-Bois 'Greenberg's Amendments', *Kunst und Museumjournal* 5, no. 1, 1993: 1–9; *MM*: 462–463 n. 51; and Frascina 'Institutions, Culture, and America's "Cold War Years": the Making of Greenberg's "Modernist Painting"', *Oxford Art Journal* vol. 26, no. 1; 2003 (69–97).

97. See Introduction: 17 and 'Three American Painters', *AO*: 214.
98. 'Modernist Painting', *CGCEC4*: 87.
99. *PML*: 99–100.
100. Ibid.: 253 and also 251. See Fried's remarks on these claims, *MM*: 287–288.
101. Stéphane Mallarmé 'The Impressionists and Édouard Manet', in Frascina and Harrison (eds) *Modern Art and Modernism: A Critical Anthology*: 42. See also *MM*: 408–412 (footnote).
102. Ibid.: 409–410.
103. Ibid.: 410.
104. Ibid.: 407.
105. Ibid.: 394.
106. Ibid.: 397.
107. Ibid.: xxvii. Clark, in his Acknowledgments to *Farewell to an Idea*, states that Fried's 'opposition has been true friendship' (vi). No statement ever has only a single meaning. One reference point for this statement is William Blake's *The Marriage of Heaven and Hell*, which includes a picture-poem or dream of a dialogue between a man and an angel arguing over realms both physical and metaphysical. Of course Blake is in there, and Fried and Clark (and Greenberg). The statement itself is written over Blake's picture of a writhing sea-serpent. Opportunities for 'hermeneutic penetration' are legion! I prefer to see the picture and the superimposed words as a simple reminder that, as this book has shown, Fried's and Clark's own words have come to *be* the pictures in some fundamental way, and, perhaps, without this ever really being their intention. I owe thanks to Colin Trodd for bringing the Blake reference to my attention.
108. See Fried 'Painting Memories: On the Containment of the Past in Baudelaire and Manet', *Critical Inquiry* vol. 10, no. 3; March 1984 (510–542).
109. *MM*: 357–358.

Conclusion: 'post' script

1. 'Art and Objecthood', *AO*: 164 and 171, n. 20. Fried himself demonstrates an indirect interest in Sherman, see 69–70, n. 63. On Sherman, see Rosalind Krauss (with an essay by Norman Bryson) *Cindy Sherman 1975–1993* (New York: Rizzoli, 1993).
2. J.-L. Godard *Introduction à une véritable historie du cinéma* (Paris: Albatross, 1980); Peter Gidal *Materialist Film* (London: Routledge, 1989); J. Orr *Cinema and Modernity* (Cambridge: Polity Press, 1993); and Colin McCabe *Godard: A Portrait of the Artist at 70* (London: Bloomsbury, 2003).
3. 'Interview with James Faure Walker' (1978), in Morgan (ed.) *Clement Greenberg's Late Writings* (149–168): 156–157.

4. Conclusion, *FTAI*: 405, 408.

5. See Fried's discussion of writings by Minimalists in his Introduction and essays reprinted in *AO* and, for instance, Greenberg 'Recentness of Sculpture', originally published in *American Sculpture of the Sixties* Los Angeles County Museum of Art, April–June 1967; reprinted in *CGCEC4*: 250–256.

6. 'Introduction', *AO*: 15.

7. See the clearly but differently 'evaluative' writings on contemporary art by, for example, John Berger, Hal Foster, Douglas Crimp, Benjamin H.D. Buchloh, Charles Harrison, Joseph Kosuth, Michael Baldwin, Rosalind Krauss, Lucy Lippard, Suzi Gablik, Griselda Pollock, bell hooks, and Amelia Jones. This list of US/UK-based authors only scrapes the surface, of course.

8. For a recent review of value issues in contemporary art, see Dave Beech and John Roberts (eds) *The Philistine Controversy* (London: Verso, 2002). Caroline Jones explores Greenberg's writings and life in greater detail than me in her 2004 manuscript, prepared for publication as *Eyesight Alone: Clement Greenberg's Modernism and the Bureaucratization of the Senses* which she kindly allowed me to read as I prepared this conclusion.

9. This radicalization of procedures in the study of visual art – both historical and contemporary – has an instructive parallel in the development of English studies. See Raymond Williams 'Cambridge English, Past and Present', 'Crisis in English Studies', and 'Beyond Cambridge English', in Williams *Writing in Society*: 177–226.

10. 'Drama in a Dramatized Society' (1974), in Williams *Writing in Society* (11–21): 19. Williams, writing twenty years ago, cites as 'public drama' the newly televised 'state opening of parliament' in London. The BBC later began to televise parliamentary debates and 'Prime Minister's question-time': in this manner political ritual-theatre becomes everyday event, and everyday event political ritual-theatre.

11. David Harvey *The Condition of Postmodernity: An Enquiry into the Origins of Cultural Change* (Oxford: Blackwell, 1990): 7.

12. Mike Davis 'Junkyard of Dreams', *City of Quartz: Excavating the Future in Los Angeles* (New York: Vintage, 1992): 417.

13. See, for example, Paul Gilroy *The Black Atlantic: Modernity and National Consciousness* (London and New York: Verso, 1993).

14. Fredric Jameson *Postmodernism, or the Logic of Late Capitalism* (London: Verso, 1991): 39–44.

15. Ibid.: 44.

16. Marx wrote: 'On the one hand, there have started into life industrial and scientific forces which no epoch of human history has ever suspected. On the other hand, there exists symptoms of decay, far surpassing the horrors of the latter times of the Roman Empire. In our day everything seems pregnant with its contrary … All our invention and progress seems

pregnant with its contrary ... All our invention and progress seems to result in endowing forces with intellectual life, and stultifying human life into a material force', 'Speech at the Anniversary of the *People's Paper*', in R.C. Tucker (ed.) *The Marx-Engels Reader* (New York: Norton, 1978): 577–578.

17. See, for example, Hal Foster (ed.) *Postmodern Culture* (London: Pluto, 1985); Jean-François Lyotard *The Postmodern Condition: A Report on Knowledge* (Manchester: University of Manchester Press, 1984); and Ihab Hassan 'Pluralism in Postmodern Perspective' in Charles Jencks (ed.) *The Postmodern Reader* (London: St. Martin's Press, 1992).

18. Rosalind Krauss 'Sculpture in the Expanded Field', original published in *October* no. 8, Spring 1979; reprinted in Hal Foster (ed.) *Postmodern Culture*: 31–43. For Krauss's relationship to Greenberg and Fried, see Barbara Reise 'Greenberg and the Group: A Retrospective View', in Frascina and Harris (eds) *Art in Modern Culture: An Anthology of Critical Texts*. Krauss has her own say about this relationship in *The Optical Unconscious*: 'One': 6–8 and 'Six': 243–329. Greenberg, for that matter, had tired of both Fried and Krauss, see his acid comments in 'The Last Interview' (1994), in Morgan (ed.) *Clement Greenberg: Late Writings*: 240 and 242–243.

19. Peter Fuller 'Plus ça Change' and 'Auerbach versus Clemente' in *Images of God: The Consolations of Lost Illusions* (London: Hogarth Press, 1985).

20. Clark 'The Conditions of Artistic Creation', *Times Literary Supplement* 24 May 1974: 561–562.

21. Hilary Wainwright, in Sheila Rowbotham, Lynn Segal, and Hilary Wainwright *Beyond the Fragments: Feminism and the Making of Socialism* (London: Merlin Press, 1980): 9 and 11.

22. Fuller, in his earlier writings, however, associated himself with Marxism and socialism. His dismissive account of Abstract Expressionist painting might now be interestingly re-read alongside Clark's 'In Defense of Abstract Expressionism'. See Fuller 'American Painting since the Last War' and 'Jackson Pollock' in *Beyond the Crisis in Art* (London: Writers and Readers, 1979).

23. See, for example, the two sets of essays on the 'internationalization' of art collected in Harris (ed.) *Critical Perspectives on Contemporary Painting: Hybridity, Hegemony, Historicism* and Harris (ed.) *Art, Money, Parties: New Institutions in the Political-Economy of Contemporary Art* (Liverpool: Liverpool University Press and Tate Liverpool, 2004).

Index

Key Writers on Art: From Antiquity to the Nineteenth Century

Chris Murray

Key Writers on Art: From Antiquity to the Nineteenth Century offers a unique and authoritative guide to theories of art from Ancient Greece to the end of the Victorian era, written by an international panel of expert contributors. Arranged chronologically to provide an historical framework, the 43 entries analyse the ideas of key philosophers, historians, art historians, art critics, artists and social scientists, including Plato, Aquinas, Alberti, Michelangelo, de Piles, Burke, Schiller, Winckelmann, Kant, Hegel, Burckhardt, Marx, Tolstoy, aine, Baudelaire, Nietzsche, Ruskin, Pater, Wölfflin and Riegl.

Each entry includes:

- a critical essay
- a short biography
- a bibliography listing both primary and secondary texts.

Unique in its range and accessibly written, this book, together with its companion volume *Key Writers on Art: The Twentieth Century*, provides an invaluable guide for students as well as general readers with an interest in art history, aesthetics and visual culture.

Hb: 0–415–24301–7
Pb: 0–415–24302–5

Available at all good bookshops
For ordering and further information please visit:
www.routledge.com